Worship

THEMES IN RELIGIOUS STUDIES SERIES

Series Editors: Jean Holm, with John Bowker

Other titles:

Making Moral Decisions
Attitudes to Nature
Human Nature and Destiny
Picturing God
Myth and History
Women in Religion
Sacred Writings
Sacred Place
Rites of Passage

Worship

Edited by

Jean Holm

with John Bowker

PINTER
PUBLISHERS
LONDON, NEW YORK

Distributed exclusively in the United States and Canada by St. Martin's Press

Pinter Publishers Ltd.
25 Floral Street, London WC2E 9DS, United Kingdom

First published in 1994

Distributed exclusively in the USA and Canada by St. Martin's Press, Inc.
Room 400, 175 Fifth Avenue, New York, NY 10010, USA

British Library Cataloguing in Publication Data

A CIP catalogue record for this book is available from the British Library

ISBN 1 85567 110 7 (hb)
ISBN 1 85567 111 5 (pb)

Library of Congress Cataloging in Publication Data

A CIP catalog record for this book is available from the Library of Congress

Typeset by Mayhew Typesetting, Rhayader, Powys
Printed and bound in Great Britain by Biddles Ltd., Guildford and King's Lynn

Contents

Series Preface

The person who knows only one religion does not know any religion. This rather startling claim was made in 1873, by Friedrich Max Müller, in his book, *Introduction to the Science of Religion*. He was applying to religion a saying of the poet Goethe: 'He who knows one language, knows none.'

In many ways this series illustrates Max Müller's claim. The diversity among the religious traditions represented in each of the volumes shows how mistaken are those people who assume that the pattern of belief and practice in their own religion is reflected equally in other religions. It is, of course, possible to do a cross-cultural study of the ways in which religions tackle particular issues, such as those which form the titles of the ten books in this series, but it soon becomes obvious that something which is central in one religion may be much less important in another. To take just three examples: the contrast between Islam's and Sikhism's attitudes to pilgrimage, in *Sacred Place*; the whole spectrum of positions on the authority of scriptures illustrated in *Sacred Writings*; and the problem which the titles, *Picturing God* and *Worship*, created for the contributor on Buddhism.

The series offers an introduction to the ways in which the themes are approached within eight religious traditions. Some of the themes relate particularly to the faith and practice of individuals and religious communities (*Picturing God, Worship, Rites of Passage, Sacred Writings, Myth and History, Sacred Place*); others have much wider implications, for society in general as well as for the religious communities themselves (*Attitudes to Nature, Making Moral Decisions, Human Nature and Destiny, Women in Religion*). This distinction, however, is not clear-cut. For instance, the 'sacred places' of Ayodhya and Jerusalem have figured in situations of national and international conflict, and some countries have passed laws regulating, or even banning, religious worship.

Stereotypes of the beliefs and practices of religions are so widespread that a real effort, of both study and imagination, is needed in order to discover what a religion looks – and feels – like to its adherents. We have to bracket out, temporarily, our own beliefs and presuppositions, and 'listen in' to a religion's account of what *it* regards as significant. This is not a straightforward task, and readers of the books in this series will encounter a number of the issues that characterise the study of religions, and that have to be taken into account in any serious attempt to get behind a factual description of a religion to an understanding of the real meaning of the words and actions for its adherents.

First, the problem of language. Islam's insistence that the Arabic of the Qur'ān cannot be 'translated' reflects the impossibility of finding in another language an exact equivalent of many of the most important terms in a religion. The very word, Islam, means something much more positive to a Muslim than is suggested in English by 'submission'. Similarly, it can be misleading to use 'incarnation' for *avatāra* in Hinduism, or 'suffering' for *dukkha* in Buddhism, or 'law' for Torah in Judaism, or 'gods' for *kami* in Shinto, or 'heaven' for *T'ien* in Taoism, or 'name' for *Nām* in Sikhism.

Next, the problem of defining – drawing a line round – a religion. Religions don't exist in a vacuum; they are influenced by the social and cultural context in which they are set. This can affect what they strenuously reject as well as what they may absorb into their pattern of belief and practice. And such influence is continuous, from a religion's origins (even though we may have no records from that period), through significant historical developments (which sometimes lead to the rise of new movements or sects), to its contemporary situation, especially when a religion is transplanted into a different region. For example, anyone who has studied Hinduism in India will be quite unprepared for the form of Hinduism they will meet in the island of Bali.

Even speaking of a 'religion' may be problematic. The term, 'Hinduism', for example, was invented by western scholars, and would not be recognised or understood by most 'Hindus'. A different example is provided by the religious situation in Japan, and the consequent debate among scholars as to whether they should speak of Japanese 'religion' or Japanese 'religions'.

Finally, it can be misleading to encounter only one aspect of a religion's teaching. The themes in this series are part of a whole interrelated network of beliefs and practices within each religious tradition, and need to be seen in this wider context. The reading lists at the end of each chapter point readers to general studies of the religions as well as to books which are helpful for further reading on the themes themselves.

Jean Holm
November 1993

List of Contributors

Jean Holm (EDITOR) was formerly Principal Lecturer in Religious Studies at Homerton College, Cambridge, teaching mainly Judaism and Hinduism. Her interests include relationships between religions; the relationship of culture to religion; and the way in which children are nurtured within a different cultural context. Her publications include *Teaching Religion in School* (OUP, 1975), *The Study of Religions* (Sheldon, 1977), *Growing up in Judaism* (Longman, 1990), *Growing up in Christianity*, with Romie Ridley (Longman, 1990) and *A Keyguide to Sources of Information on World Religions* (Mansell, 1991). She has edited three previous series: *Issues in Religious Studies*, with Peter Baelz (Sheldon), *Anselm Books*, with Peter Baelz (Lutterworth) and *Growing up in a Religion* (Longman).

John Bowker (EDITOR) was Professor of Religious Studies in Lancaster University, before returning to Cambridge to become Dean and Fellow of Trinity College. He is at present Professor of Divinity at Gresham College in London, and Adjunct Professor at the University of Pennsylvania and at the State University of North Carolina. He is particularly interested in anthropological and sociological approaches to the study of religions. He has done a number of programmes for the BBC, including the *Worlds of Faith* series, and a series on Islam and Hinduism for the World Service. He is the author of many books in the field of Religious Studies, including *The Meanings of Death* (Cambridge University Press, 1991), which was awarded the biennial Harper Collins religious book prize in 1993, in the academic section.

Peter Harvey is Reader in Buddhist Studies at the University of Sunderland. His research is in the fields of early Buddhist thought, and the ethical, devotional and meditational dimensions of Buddhism. He has published articles on consciousness and *nirvāṇa*, the between-lives state, the nature of the *Tathāgata*, the *stūpa*, *paritta* chanting, the signless meditations, self-development and not-Self, and respect for persons. Dr Harvey is author of *An Introduction to Buddhism: Teachings, History and Practices* (Cambridge University Press, 1990) and is currently working on *The Selfless Mind: Selflessness and Consciousness in Early Buddhism* (for Curzon Press), and a work on *Themes in Buddhist Ethics* (for Cambridge University Press). He is a Theravāda Buddhist and a teacher of Samatha meditation; he was a member of the CNAA Working Party on Theology and Religious Studies.

Douglas Davies is Professor of Religious Studies in the Department of Theology at the University of Nottingham, where he specialises in teaching the social anthropology of religion. He trained both in theology and social anthropology and his research continues to relate to both disciplines. His interest in theoretical and historical aspects of religious studies is represented in a major study of the sociology of knowledge and religion, published as *Meaning and Salvation in Religious Studies* (Brill, 1984), and in a historical volume *Frank Byron Jevons 1858–1936, An Evolutionary Realist* (Edwin Mellen Press, 1991). Professor Davies is also very much concerned with practical aspects of religious behaviour and is a leading British scholar of Mormonism and, in addition to various articles, is author of *Mormon Spirituality* (Nottingham and Utah University Press, 1987). He was joint Director of the Rural Church Project, involving one of the largest sociological studies of religion in Britain, published as *Church and Religion in Rural Britain* (with C. Watkins and M. Winter, T. & T. Clark, 1991). As Director of the Cremation Research Project he is conducting basic work on cremation in Britain and Europe and has already produced some results in *Cremation Today and Tomorrow* (Grove Books, 1990).

Anuradha Roma Choudhury is a Librarian working with the South Glamorgan County Library Service and is responsible for its Asian language section. She is also a part-time tutor with the Department of Continuing Education of University of Wales, Cardiff. She studied Sanskrit Literature at the University of Calcutta, India, and taught in schools for a number of years. She holds Gitabharati diploma in

Indian music from Calcutta and is an accomplished singer. She lectures extensively on topics related to Indian music, customs, family life and Hinduism. She is the author of a book on Indian music called *Bilati-gan-blanga Rabindra-sangeet* (Influence of British music on Rabindranath Tagore's songs) written in Bengali and published in Calcutta, 1987. She is also one of the contributors to *The Essential Teachings of Hinduism* (ed. Kerry Brown, Rider, 1988). She is actively involved with multi-cultural arts and inter-faith groups.

Martin Forward is Secretary of the Methodist Church's Committee for Relations with People of Other Faiths, and a Consultant to the Council of Churches for Britain and Ireland's Commission for Inter-Faith relations. He used to work in the Henry Martyn Institute for Islamic Studies, Hyderabad, India. Martin Forward has taught an introductory course on Islam at Leicester University, and now teaches courses on Islam at Leicester University.

Dan Cohn-Sherbok was ordained a Reform rabbi at the Hebrew Union College and has served congregations in the United States, Australia, England and South Africa. Since 1975 he has taught Jewish theology at the University of Kent, and is a Visiting Professor at the University of Essex. He has been a Visiting Fellow at Wolfson College, Cambridge, and a Visiting Scholar at the Oxford Centre for Postgraduate Hebrew Studies. Rabbi Dr Cohn-Sherbok is a Fellow of the Hebrew Union College, and a Corresponding Fellow of the Academy of Jewish Philosophy. He is the author and editor of over thirty books, including *The Jewish Heritage; On Earth as it is in Heaven: Jews, Christians and Liberation Theology; Jewish Petitionary Prayer: A Theological Exploration; Issues in Contemporary Judaism; The Crucified Jew: Twenty Centuries of Christian Anti-Semitism; Israel: The History of an Idea; Exodus: An Agenda for Jewish-Christian Dialogue; The Jewish Faith; Judaism and Other Faiths*; and *An Atlas of Jewish History*.

Beryl Dhanjal is a Lecturer at Ealing Tertiary College. She works on the programme for teaching ESOL (English to Speakers of Other Languages) and has special responsibility for developing community links, working mainly with people from the new commonwealth and with refugees. She studied Panjabi at the School of African and

Oriental Studies, University of London. She has lectured at St Mary's College, Strawberry Hill, and the West London Institute of Higher Education, and has worked in adult education. She has written and translated many books, and particularly enjoys writing books for children and young people – she has written bi-lingual English/ Panjabi books for children.

Xinzhong Yao is Lecturer of Chinese Religion and Ethics, University of Wales, Lampeter. His research interests include classical and modern philosophy, practical ethics, and philosophy of religion and of language; he is currently focusing on comparative philosophy and comparative religion. Dr Yao is author of *On Moral Activity* (People's University Press, Beijing, 1990), *Ethics and Social Problems* (City Economic Press, Beijing, 1989), co-author of *Comparative Studies on Human Nature* (Tienjin People's Press, Tienjin, 1988), *Ethics* (People's Press, Beijing, 1989), co-editor of *Applying Ethics* (Jilin People's Press, Changchun, 1994), and translator of Charles Stevenson's *Ethics and Language* (Social Sciences of China Press, Beijing, 1991). He is a member of the Association of Ethical Studies of China, and Deputy Director of the Institute of Ethics, People's University of China, Beijing.

Ian Reader is Senior Lecturer in Japanese Studies at the University of Stirling, Scotland. He has spent several years in Japan travelling, teaching at Japanese universities and researching into contemporary Japanese religion. His major research interest is in the study of pilgrimage, and he is currently working on a volume on pilgrimage in Japan. Dr Reader is author of *Religion in Contemporary Japan* (Macmillan, 1991), and editor (with Tony Walter) of *Pilgrimage in Popular Culture* (Macmillan, 1993). He has also published numerous articles in journals and collected editions on Buddhism, Japanese religion, pilgrimage and Japanese popular culture, and is a member of the Editorial Advisory Board of the *Japanese Journal of Religious Studies*.

Introduction: Raising the Issues

Douglas Davies

Though *worship* is the title of this book, it is not always the best word to use when describing the actions of devotees in some religions. Most of the following chapters show that theological and philosophical differences between religions mean that *worship* may give a false impression of the goal of some religious life.

The chapters on Hinduism, Chinese Religions, and Buddhism talk explicitly about the problem of applying *worship* to the ritual practices of their people, while the Islam, Sikhism and Christianity sections also raise similar problems in terms of people's attitudes.

There are perhaps two key issues in the history of worship within religions. One concerns the stress a religion places on particular aspects of its activity, and the other the distinction between external action and the internal motivation of devotees. Throughout this Introduction both these features will be treated alongside each other.

Every religion engages in a wide variety of endeavours, including serious study of philosophy and theology, ritual activity in sacred places at special times and charitable acts of service and kindness. Each religion varies in the emphasis it places on these endeavours. For some Buddhists, for example, the idea of a god existing separate from all human thought is philosophically untenable. This means that the idea of worshipping something or someone beyond one's own consciousness makes no sense. Islam, by contrast, places the greatest emphasis on a god who definitely exists and to whom believers must submit their lives as in the communal acts of prayer.

Many subtle differences of belief, and strong social differences, help shape people's religious activities, and these may not always be clear to the outsider. Japanese religion provides a good example, where the subtle sense of proximity to the ancestors combines with the strong social fact of the clan group to give 'ancestor worship' its distinctive nature. In the *bhakti*, or devotional, currents of Hinduism the subtle sense of love along with membership in a group of fellow devotees – not, by definition, members of one's own family – gives another basis for worship, one that resembles two lovers rather than an ancestor and descendant. Hinduism is such an immensely broad world of religion that it embraces not only this form of intense devotionalism but also philosophical schools which seem practically atheist and yet maintain meditative practices which, to the observer, might seem to be a form of worship.

Within Christianity there are similar variations. One extreme of formal liturgy and doctrine, especially the idea of the sacrifice of Christ as a substitutionary atonement, approaches worship as a kind of homage paid to God viewed as a feudal lord. By contrast, the informal fellowship of some Charismatic meetings places great emphasis on the immediacy of God through the Holy Spirit, and evokes quite different emotional attitudes.

While it is important to be aware of these differences, they should not be magnified out of all proportion because that would make religious studies an impossible task. One way of summarising this spectrum of worship is to construct a loose network of terms which bear some relationship, or some sort of family resemblance, as philosophers sometimes describe such similarities, to each other while retaining certain differences. As examples we may speak not only of *bhakti* (devotionalism) but also of one's duty or *dharma* in Hinduism; for Sikhs both *nām simaraṇ*, or meditating on the name of God, and *seva* or service to others, are important. Buddhist devotion, and not worship, is depicted as important for Theravāda Buddhists, while Mahāyāna devotees of the far eastern Pure Land schools can be said to worship heavenly *buddha*s. Judaism, Christianity and Islam also combine emphases on the devotional worship of God with practical action in the social world in such a way that, for example, some Christians might speak of work as a form of prayer.

What then are the basic features underlying the myriad acts which make up the realm of worship in religions? In terms of religious studies, worship helps identify the central concern of a religion, pinpointing its meaning and focusing the significance of people's religious life. So, for example, while it is difficult to know whether or not to speak of Buddhists engaging in worship or in devotion, it is obvious that their acts focus on the Buddha, the one whose teaching and power lie at the heart of his followers' way of life. In the explicitly monotheistic religions of Judaism, Christianity and Islam, worship clearly identifies God as the basis of all things. But each of them possesses an additional perspective, one that underlies the whole structure of each religion.

This is where believers speak of revelation as giving a knowledge of God and providing the foundation for particular forms of worship. This mode of revelation deeply influences the path taken in worship. So, in Judaism the Torah is central to the contemporary worship of the synagogue just as it also plays an important part in the life of faith, involving daily study of the sacred scriptures and tradition. In Islam, prayerfulness is singled out as the foundation of the religious life, prayer moulded by the teaching of the Qur'ān given through the Prophet Muhammad. Christianity, as its very name shows, has Jesus Christ as its determining foundation, as is clear through the forms of prayer and the whole sacramental life of Christian churches.

Figures like the Buddha, Jesus, Muhammad and Guru Nanak, all set the tone for worship and show the direction in which it flows. Judaism, Hinduism, Chinese and Japanese religions are not quite the same. Emerging, as they did, over thousands of years within a mixture of social contexts, their origin is not dependent upon any single founder, even though particular individuals and reformers have permanently significant places in those religions.

From the perspective of the history of religions, worship describes patterns of human behaviour, expressing what people believe to be the most important aspects of life. In worship the meaning of life, death and the universe crystallises out in prayers and other devotional activity.

Worship-behaviour takes place at the point where, in the terms of Wilfred Cantwell Smith, 'cumulative tradition' meets 'faith' (1963). Smith defines cumulative tradition as including doctrine, custom, ritual acts and contexts which grow throughout the history of a religion. Faith, by contrast, refers to the individual and personal awareness of the truths of that religious tradition.

The cumulative traditions of different religions, though often complex within themselves, tend to display broadly similar features across religions, and include repetitive and repeated actions located within specific places at recognised times, employing special use of language, music and silence.

Repeated and repetitive actions are clearly visible in formal postures in prayer, as in the case of prostration before the symbolic expression either of an ultimate deity or of an abstract ideal. Though the acts of prostration, bowing, or genuflexion may be interpreted with various shades of difference to mean submission, self-surrender or adoration, they nevertheless involve a physical action through which something is believed to have been achieved. The use of the sign of the cross is as well known in the Eastern Orthodox and Catholic Christian traditions as it is absent in Protestant traditions.

The rosary, a set of beads which recalls religious beliefs as an aid to prayer, is well known within Christianity but is also present throughout Buddhist traditions and in Islam. This is a good example of a physical act triggering memory and bringing to mind central ideas of the religion.

Special places for worship express one of the oldest patterns of human cultural activity as fully studied in another volume, *Sacred Place*, in this series. Purpose-built temples furnish the environment for worship, both for collective and private prayer. But sacred places may also be found in homes, as in Hindu families where they may have a special shelf, or even a room, devoted to images of the deities.

One theme which recurs in some religious traditions as, for example, in the great prophets of Judaism, in the Christian Reformation and in early Sikhism, is an opposition to formal rites at sacred places. Reforming and prophetic figures often stress the inner dimension of faith with its clarity of purpose and sincerity of worship as opposed to institutionalised and formal religiosity devoid of personal devotion. This is a similar strain to that of the Buddhist goal of individuals applying themselves to a genuine quest for enlightenment and not simply following conventional religion. Sometimes the idea of religious conversion or of a deepening grasp of religious truth is associated with a shift from what devotees might call a merely external form of prayer to an internal sincerity of purpose.

Sacred times are also important for worship, whether it is the Friday prayers of Islam, the Sabbath worship of Judaism, the Christian Sunday, or the many other festivals of these religions spread throughout the year, as is also true for the innumerable festivals of Hinduism, Sikhism and Buddhism. Basic to all these sacred times is the fact that the duration of human life is thrown into context as men and women are reminded of their mortality and brought into relationship with the transcendent, or eternal dimension, either of their god or else of the ultimate nature of their own true being.

Music is one of the most important aspects of worship in practically every religious tradition. In Hinduism the very idea of the sound of a *mantra* or sacred verse is of fundamental importance, in the belief that it reflects something of the sound which lies at the centre of all reality. The *mantra* is, in a sense, a meaning in sound. To repeat it is to engage in an activity that brings benefit to the devotee. In a similar way the use of chanting in Buddhism, as a means of meditating on sacred scriptures, achieves a similar end. It is through chanting or rhythmic recitation that many sacred scriptures are learned, and become an immeasurably important resource for the worship both of communities and individuals. This is also true in Judaism, in Islam and in Sikhism. Within the Christian tradition, worship very largely takes place through the medium of music. Liturgies are usually sung or chanted and the hymns of Christendom have become one of its major developments over the last two hundred years.

Music is a complex phenomenon and certainly should not be ignored in the study of worship. Modern psychology has much to say about the relationship between spoken language and music in terms of the integration of rational and symbolic forms of knowledge. It may well be that encasing doctrinal ideas in music is an excellent way of helping to give people a sense of being integrated and whole. Not only this, but song and chant are acts that many people can engage in together, to produce a further sense of unity in worship.

Even so, language is a vitally important part of worship and cannot be fully separated from music. In worship, language is often used in quite different ways from those of everyday life. The repetition of an idea, as in *Rām, Rām,* when Hindus repeat a name of God, or when Christians repeat a phrase such as 'Lord have mercy', brings a strength and emphasis to it. Sometimes worship is thought to benefit from the language used being a sacred language, not used in everyday life. This has been true for example in Islam's Arabic, Hinduism's Sanskrit, Buddhism's Pāli, Sikhism's Gurmukhī, and, until the 1960s, in the Roman Catholic Church's use of Latin for the Mass. Some people have seen a benefit in this, arguing that worship involves a sense of mystery and transcendence over everyday existence. Language is one of the best symbolic expressions of this transcendence, especially if it is not fully understood and is supported by chant or song.

An apparently similar case comes from the Charismatic Movement in Christianity, in which some people speak or sing 'in tongues'. Such *glossolalia* is a form of what might be called shadow-language, a pattern of sounds resembling the ordinary language-sounds of the person but put together in a different way and without any apparent meaning. Some people believe it is a real language or the language of heaven which can be interpreted by other believers under divine guidance.

Because worship is so easily taken for granted as a basic element within religions, it is important to emphasise its radical importance within humanity's history and culture. In particular it needs to be understood in relation to the human imagination and to the meaning and purpose of life.

The human animal is characterised by its large brain, possessing an ability for rational and symbolic thought. This tremendous capacity to engage with the environment seems to be the expression of one of the drives of human nature. The urge to understand and comprehend the world and the universe as our species' environment results not only in science but also in religion. Though science and religion may deal with different aspects of life they are both attempts at explaining the world around us.

Religion has been one of humanity's longest-standing processes of encountering the environment in an attempt to understand it. While this pressure to understand is very likely to have had the purpose of aiding survival and safety in the world, it also seems to reflect a curiosity and wonder basic to human nature. Some psychologists have compared problem-solving activities with the rise of faith, and see religious experience as a kind of process of discovery (Batson and Ventis 1982). Here faith and imagination have much in common.

Human beings not only want to understand the world around them, but also seek a knowledge of their own identity. The sociologist, Hans Mol, has argued (Mol 1976) that once people have a focus for their identity they often tend to invest it with great respect, so much so that it can even be sacralised.

Worship is a complex phenomenon embracing several of these processes, and in different religious traditions it appears with various emphases. In the most general terms, from a non-theological perspective within religious studies, worship may be seen as one way of encountering the mystery of life and the universe. Instead of being dumbfounded by the universe, people worship what they believe to be its source. In this sense worship is a form of sacred bafflement, it is a response to mystery and a means of relating to it. It is positive rather than negative and can lead individuals forward in their quest for understanding. A fundamental aspect of worship is that it engages not only, and often not primarily, the rational mind but also the symbolic and emotional dimensions of existence.

For other people, especially those in religious traditions where absolute certainty is prized, worship is a way of giving thanks for knowing the truth, or for having had the truth revealed to them. In this context, worship expresses something of the process of reciprocity which underlies much social life: worshippers give thanks for what they have been given. In theistic traditions, worship often embraces some such reciprocal relationship between deity and devotee; people make offerings to gain benefits like success in exams, healing from illness or many other things. Some might regard this attitude to worship as ignoble and far too materialistic, preferring to see worship as a kind of self-sacrifice to the deity with no demands involved.

Each of the following chapters reflects these shades of significance implicit in the way religious believers approach their deities and organise their religious life. What is obvious is that in the spectrum of behaviour, respect, piety, devotion and submission all shed their particular light on worship as a fundamental characteristic of humanity.

FURTHER READING

Batson, C.D. and Ventis, W.L. (1982) *The Religious Experience*, New York, Oxford University Press.

Mol, Hans (1976) *Identity and the Sacred*, Oxford, Blackwell.

Smith, W.C. (1963) *The Meaning and End of Religion*, New York, Macmillan.

1. Buddhism

Peter Harvey

For most religions, the key type of practice is usually worship of the divine. This is not the case with Buddhism, for two reasons. First, Theravāda Buddhists hold that the nature of a *buddha* after his death cannot be specified, that he has passed beyond existence as a limited individual being (Harvey 1990: 65–8). This being so, he cannot any longer be thought of as a 'person' who might respond to human actions (though he is seen as having left a store of power for others to draw on). It thus seems inappropriate to say that Theravadins 'worship' the Buddha. A more neutral description is to say that they show devotion to the Buddha and what he represents. Mahayanists, though, can be said to 'worship' the heavenly *buddha*s and *bodhisattva*s[1]. Secondly, and more importantly, most classical Buddhist descriptions of the path to liberation are based on the triad of 'morality, meditation and wisdom', with meditation being the key practice (Harvey 1990: ch. 11). Nevertheless, devotion plays a part here, as it can help purify the mind, and thus aid morality and meditation; in its more refined forms, it may also become a form of meditation.

While the Buddha was critical of *blind* faith, he did not deny a role for soundly based 'trustful confidence' (*saddhā*),[2] for to test out his teachings, a person had to have at least some initial trust in them. The early texts envisage a process of listening, which arouses trustful confidence, leading to practice, and thus to partial confirmation of the teachings, and thus to deeper trustful confidence, and deeper practice, until the heart of the teachings is directly experienced. A person then becomes an *arahant*, a liberated saint who has replaced faith with knowledge. Faith/trustful confidence occurs as one item in the list of the 'five (spiritual) faculties': trustful confidence, energy, mindfulness, meditative concentration, and (reflective and intuitive) wisdom (Conze et al. 1964: 51–65, 185–6). Most Buddhist traditions agree that the faculty of faith should be balanced by, and balance, the faculty of wisdom: trusting, heart-based warmth and commitment must be in equipoise with the cool, analytical, meditative eye of insight. With the faculties strong and in balance, deeper insights can then be developed, which progressively remove the need for faith.

Nevertheless, in some of the schools of Eastern Buddhism[3] faith and worship came to play a completely central role. In China, Korea and Japan, very popular forms of Mahāyāna Buddhism are the Pure Land schools, which focus on faith in the salvific power of the heavenly Buddha Amitābha (Japanese, Amida) (Harvey 1990: 129–30, 152–3, 163–5). One Japanese Pure Land school, the Jodo-shin, is indeed a religion of faith alone, in which one must rely totally on Amida's grace: even one's faith is seen to come from him! This is a religion of pure 'other-power', i.e., reliance on the power of another being. Alongside this school, though, is another Eastern form of Buddhism, Zen (Chinese Ch'an), which is seen as a way of 'self-power': attaining liberation by knowing and manifesting one's innate '*buddha*-nature'. Even here, though, devotional practices play their part, and one even needs faith in one's innate *buddha*-nature (Conze et al. 1964: 295–8)! Most forms of Mahāyāna Buddhism, in fact, are a mix of 'self-power' and 'other-power', combining an emphasis on the cultivation of one's own moral and spiritual qualities, with an emphasis on opening oneself up to the uplifting inspiration and assistance of the heavenly *buddha*s and *bodhisattva*s (Conze et al. 1964: 186–90). In Theravāda Buddhism, 'self-power' is more emphasised, but not exclusively: the Buddha advised his followers to have themselves as 'island' and 'refuge' (i.e., be mindfully self-composed and self-reliant), but also to have the *Dhamma* (path and teachings) as 'island' and 'refuge'. In this, the inspiring and guiding help of those more advanced on the path is also crucial (Brown and O'Brian 1989: 19–21).

Thus, while devotion is not the core of Buddhist practice (except in the Pure Land schools), it plays an important part in the life of most Buddhists. Even in Theravāda Buddhism, which often has a rather rational, unemotional image, a very deep faith in the Buddha, *Dhamma* and *Saṅgha* is common. Ideally, this is based on the fact that some part of the Buddha's path has been found to be uplifting, thus inspiring confidence in the rest. Many people, though, simply have *pasāda*: a calm and joyful faith inspired by the example of those who are well established on the path.

The refuges

The key expression of Buddhist devotion and commitment is 'taking the refuges'. The ancient formula for this, in its Pāli form, begins: *Buddhaṃ saraṇaṃ gacchāmi, Dhammaṃ saraṇaṃ gacchāmi, Saṅghaṃ saraṇaṃ gacchāmi*. This affirms that 'I go to the Buddha as refuge, I go to the *Dhamma* as refuge, I go to the *Saṅgha* as refuge'. Each affirmation is then repeated 'for the second time . . .' (*dutiyam pi* . . .) and 'for the third time . . .' (*tatiyam pi* . . .). The threefold repetition marks off the recitation from ordinary uses of speech, and ensures that the mind dwells on the meaning of each affirmation at least once. The notion of a 'refuge', here, is not that of a place to hide, but of something the thought of which purifies, uplifts and strengthens the heart. Orientation towards these three guides to a better way of living is experienced as a joyful haven of calm, a firm 'island amidst a flood', in contrast to the troubles of life. The 'refuges' remind the Buddhist of calm, wise, spiritual people and states of mind, and so help engender these states. Their value is denoted by the fact that they are also known as the *Ti-ratana*, or 'three jewels': spiritual treasures of supreme worth.

The meaning of each refuge varies somewhat between different traditions. The Theravāda understanding is expressed in a frequently used chant drawn from the Pāli Canon. On the Buddha, it affirms: 'Thus he is the Lord because he is an *arahant*, perfectly and completely enlightened, endowed with knowledge and (good) conduct, Well-gone [to *nirvāṇa*], knower of worlds, an incomparable charioteer for the training of persons, teacher of gods and humans, Buddha, Lord'. The 'Buddha' referred to here is primarily the historical Buddha, Gotama. He is regarded with reverence and gratitude as the rediscoverer and exemplifier of *Dhamma*, and the one who also showed others how to live by and experience it. As the benefits of living by *Dhamma* are experienced, this reverence and gratitude naturally develop greater depth. In Sri Lanka, one recently popularised liturgy states, 'Thus infinite, possessing measureless qualities, unequalled, equal to the unequalled, god to the gods, to me the Lord, my own *Buddha* mother, my own *Buddha* father, the orb of dawn to the darkness of delusion . . .'. The Buddha refuge does not refer only to Gotama, but also to previous and future *buddhas*, and to the principle of enlightenment as supremely worthy of attainment. In this respect, the first refuge can also be taken as a pointer to the faculty of wisdom developing within the practitioner.

The Pāli chant on *Dhamma* is: 'Well-expounded by the Lord is *Dhamma*, visible here and now, timeless, inviting investigation, leading onward [to the stages of sanctity and finally *nirvāṇa*], to be experienced within by the wise'. This emphasises *Dhamma* as immediately accessible to all, and as of progressively greater benefit. As refuge, *Dhamma* is explained as the Holy Eightfold Path. More generally, it refers to: a) *pariyatti*, or the body of teachings, b) *paṭipatti*, or the 'practice' of the way, and c) *paṭivedha*, or 'realisation' of the stages of sanctity – in the highest sense, *nirvāṇa* itself. *Dhamma*, then, is to be heard/read and understood, practised, and realised. It can also mean the 'law-orderliness' inherent in nature, phenomena always occurring according to the principle of Conditioned Arising, from appropriate conditions.

The Pāli chant on the *Saṅgha*, or spiritual Community, is:

> Of good conduct is the Community of the disciples of the Lord; of upright conduct . . .; of wise conduct . . .; of proper conduct . . .; that is to say, the four pairs of persons, the eight kinds of individuals; this Community . . . is worthy of gifts, hospitality, offerings, and reverential salutation, an incomparable field of goodness-power for the world.

Here, the 'four pairs of persons, the eight kinds of individuals' are the *arahant* and three lesser grades of saints (the Non-returner, Once-returner and Stream-enterer), and those established on the paths to these spiritual 'fruits' (Harvey 1990: 64–5, 71–2), that is, all who have attained *nirvāṇa*, glimpsed it, or are on the brink of glimpsing it. This is the precious *ariya-Saṅgha*, the Community of 'Holy' persons, who may be found within the monastic *saṅgha*, its symbolic representative, or among spiritually advanced laypeople or even gods. Being of exemplary conduct, its members are worthy of gifts and respect; the monastic *saṅgha* seeks to emulate them in this. The concept of a 'field of goodness-power' is that, just as a seed planted in better ground yields better fruit, so a gift given to a more virtuous person generates more karmic goodness-power (*puñña* or 'merit'). This idea is partly based on the fact that, if one gives to someone of suspect character, one may regret the act somewhat; whereas in giving to a virtuous or holy person, one puts all one's heart into the act and can rejoice at it. Giving also sets up a bond of association. The Holy *Saṅgha* therefore benefits the world with the opportunity for generating abundant auspicious, purifying, goodness-power.

In the Mahāyāna, the 'Three body' (*Trikāya*) doctrine views buddhahood at three levels: earthly 'Transformation-body' *buddha*s, heavenly Enjoyment-body *buddha*s who manifest these on earth, and the *Dharma*-body, which is the mysterious inner nature of all *buddha*s and, indeed, of all reality (Harvey 1990: 125–8). Thus for a Mahayanist, the Buddha refuge refers not only to Gotama and other Transformation-body *buddha*s, but also, and more importantly, to the Enjoyment-body *buddha*s (Brown and O'Brian 1989: 111–12, 134–7; Conze et al. 1964: 139–40, 190–4). In the Pure Land schools, emphasis is primarily or exclusively on Amitābha. In Ch'an/Zen, the emphasis is on the historical Buddha as a heroic, stirring example, but more particularly on the idea of the *buddha*-nature within: 'take refuge in the three treasures in your own natures. The Buddha is enlightenment, the *Dharma* is truth, the *Saṅgha* is purity . . . take refuge in the Buddha within yourselves . . . . If you do not rely upon your own natures, there is nothing else on which to rely' (Yampolsky 1967: sec. 23). Transformation-body *buddha*s are also figuratively seen as good and wise thoughts within one's mind, and refuge is taken in 'the future perfect Enjoyment-body in my own physical body' (Yampolsky 1967: sec. 20). In the Mahāyāna, the *Dharma* refuge, in its highest sense, refers to the *Dharma*-body, ultimate reality (Brown and O'Brian 1989: 283–4, 137–8). Holy *bodhisattva*s are included in the *Saṅgha* refuge, and taking refuge in them is allied to taking vows, often repeated on a daily basis, to become like them.

In the Mantrayāna[4] of Northern Buddhism, extra refuges are taken. Prior to the three usual ones, a person takes refuge in his *bLama* or Guru (Blofeld 1970: 133–5, 153; Brown and O'Brian 1989: 133–4, 111–17). He or she is seen as the source of the deepening knowledge of the other refuges, and regarded as an embodiment of their virtues. After the usual refuges, individuals may then take refuge in their *yi-dam*, a holy being which is their tutelary deity. An adept preparing for training in meditative visualisations must also complete preliminary practices of a devotional and purificatory nature. Five or six such practices are generally given, each of which must be done a hundred thousand times. One is the 'grand prostration', which is done while holding wooden blocks, to prevent the hands being blistered by repeatedly sliding along the floor (on a special wooden board) to the fully prostrate position. As this is done, the devotee may say: 'I, so-and-so, on behalf of all sentient beings and freely offering my body, speech and mind, bow to the earth in adoration of the Guru and the Three Precious Ones' (Blofeld 1970: 151). Accompanying this affirmation is the visualisation of a 'refuge tree': a concourse of holy beings whose radiant light suffuses the devotee. After a period of struggle and pain, the practice is said to induce great joy. It also conduces to a balance of self-power and other-power: relying on oneself and on the power of holy beings.

Focuses and locations of devotional acts

Devotion to *buddhas* and *bodhisattvas* is focused or channelled by the use of various artefacts such as images. At home, it can be expressed before a home shrine, which may be as simple as a high shelf and a picture in a quiet corner. In temples, there will always be some kind of shrine-room or image-hall, where large images are housed: in Theravāda temples, these are of Gotama Buddha, sometimes flanked by his two chief *arahant* disciples; in Mahāyāna ones, there is often a group of three heavenly *buddhas*, or a *buddha* and two *bodhisattvas*, perhaps with images of sixteen or eighteen chief *arahant* disciples along the walls of the hall. There will always be accommodation for monks and/or nuns, or, as in Japan, married clerics. Thus temples are in fact temple-monasteries, Theravāda ones often being known by the Pāli term for a monastery, *vihāra*. There is frequently a *stūpa* (relic-mound[5]) of some kind, including the multi-roofed form, known in the West as a Pagoda, which evolved in China (Harvey 1990: 78–9). Most *stūpas* are such that one cannot enter them, except for the East Asian multi-roofed form. They can be anything from a metre high, with some large ones being the major feature of a temple. The famous Shwe-dāgon *Stūpa* in Rangoon, capital of Myanmar (Burma) is a hundred and twelve metres tall. It is said to contain some hairs of Gotama, and belongings of three previous *buddhas*. Because of the sanctity of these, it has been encased in gold plates and gold leaf, and topped by an orb studded in diamonds. Temples may also have: a meeting/preaching hall; a separate meditation hall, as in Zen temples; a *bodhi*-tree (the type of tree under which the Buddha attained enlightenment, or *bodhi*), as at many Theravāda temples; a library and administrative buildings, and finally shrines for one or more gods or nature spirits. Most temples are free-standing, but throughout the Buddhist world there are also natural and specially excavated caves, whose cool, calm, rather awesome interiors have been used as temples.

Devotional artefacts may be paid for by a community or an individual. In either case, the community can share in the embellishment: in Southeast Asia, images are often gradually gilded with individual squares of gold-leaf. As giving generates goodness-power, which can be shared, artefacts may be specially donated, perhaps for the benefit of a new-born child, someone who has recently died, success in a business venture, or an end to a war. In 1961 the Burmese government organised the making of 60,000 temporary sand *stūpa*s to avert a world calamity predicted by astrologers throughout Asia. The motive of generating goodness-power means that temples often have more images than are 'needed', and new *stūpa*s may be built beside crumbling old ones. This is because there is generally more joy in starting something new than in repairing it. Greater joy leaves a stronger wholesome 'imprint' on the mind, and so is seen as producing better quality karmic fruits. In Myanmar (Burma), '*Stūpa* Builder' is a title of respect, and 'goodness-power' *stūpa*s are so popular that several can be seen in any landscape.

Attitudes to images

Images always function as reminders of the spiritual qualities of holy beings, if in no other way. When a Theravadin, for example, expresses devotion before an image of Gotama Buddha, he is reminded of his struggle for enlightenment, his virtues, his teachings, and the ideal represented by him. He joyfully recollects the Buddha, developing a warm heart and a pure mind. The spiritual qualities expressed by the form of a good image also help to stimulate the arising of such qualities in one who contemplates it.

In Northern and Eastern Buddhism, except perhaps in Ch'an/Zen, images function as more than reminders. Especially in Mantrayāna schools, they are seen as infused with the spirit and power of the being they represent. Moreover, as image and being 'meet', in both being ultimately 'thought-only' or emptiness (as everything is, in

Mahāyāna philosophy), the image comes to be seen as an actual form of the being. For this, it must have the traditional form and symbolism and be consecrated. This is done by chanting prayers and *mantras* over it; by placing in it scriptures or relics, and even internal organs of clay, and by completing and wetting the eyes. This associates it with holy sounds and objects, giving it a power-for-good, and animates it, the wet eyes suggesting the response of a living gaze.

Even in Southern Buddhism, a temple image seems to act as more than a reminder, for it is generally thought that it must be consecrated before it can function as a focus for devotion (Gombrich 1971: 101, 138–9). Consecration involves the placing of relics in the image, and a monk reciting some Pāli verses over it. In Sri Lanka, these verses are the ones said to have been spoken by the Buddha immediately after his enlightenment. This harmonises with the fact that the eyes are often completed at around 5am, the time at which Gotama became fully enlightened. These two aspects seem to suggest that the consecrated image is seen as a representative of, rather than just a representation of, the Buddha. Other aspects of consecration reinforce this idea. In Sri Lanka, the lay craftsmen completing the eyes act as if this were connecting the image to a source of power which, like electricity, is dangerous if handled carelessly. They ritually prepare themselves for hours, and then only look at the eyes in a mirror while painting them in; till it is completed, their direct gaze is considered harmful. Some westernised monks deny that there is any need to consecrate images.

In Southern Buddhism there is a widely held belief in a kind of '*buddha*-force' which will remain in the world for as long as Buddhism is practised. Indeed, a booklet produced by a Thai temple in London says of the Buddha: 'Although now his physical form no longer exists, his spiritual form, that is his benevolence and great compassion remains in the world'. This attitude is reflected in the way that Southern Buddhists regard relics and *bodhi*-trees as having a protective power-for-good. The '*buddha*-force', which many believe in, is particularly associated with images, especially ones used in devotion for centuries, suggesting that these are seen as having been thus 'charged up' with the Buddha's power. Less educated Southern Buddhists sometimes go so far as to regard the Buddha as still alive as an individual, and as somehow present in consecrated images of himself (Gombrich 1971: 103–43).

Bowing, offerings and chanting

Most Buddhist devotional acts are not congregational in essence, though they are frequently occasions for coming together in a shared activity and experience. In the home, they are often carried out in the morning and/or evening. Temple-visits can be at any time, though they are most common at festivals, or on special 'observance days' (four per lunar month). On visiting a temple, a person performs acts which amount to showing devotion to the 'three refuges'. The Buddha is represented by image, *stūpa* and *bodhi*-tree; the *Dhamma* is represented by a sermon, or informal teachings which the monks may give, and the *Saṅgha* is represented by the monks. Devotion at home or temple is expressed by *pūjā*: 'reverencing' or 'honouring', which involves bowing, making offerings, and chanting.

In Buddhist cultures, people bow on many occasions. Children bow to parents and teachers; adults bow to monks, nuns, *bLamas* and the elderly; and monks bow to those ordained for longer than themselves. Such lowering of the head acknowledges someone else as having more experience of life or of spiritual practice, and develops respect and humility. It is natural, then, to bow before sacred objects which point towards the highest reality, and also to locate a *buddha*-image on the highest 'seat' in a room (Khantipalo 1974: 12–17). Within a shrine-room or the compound surrounding a *stūpa* or *bodhi*-tree, humility is also shown by not wearing shoes, for in ancient times, wearing shoes was a sign of wealth and status.

Bowing before sacred objects is generally done three times, so as to show respect to the 'three refuges'. A person stands or kneels with palms joined in a gesture known as *namaskāra*. They are held at the chest and forehead or, in Northern Buddhism, at the head, lips and chest, symbolising respect offered by mind, speech and body. From a kneeling position, a person then places the elbows, hands and head on the ground. In Northern Buddhism, a fuller form known as a 'grand prostration' involves lying full-length on the ground (Brown and O'Brian 1989: 122–3). Devotion is also shown by circumambulation of *stūpas*, *bodhi*-trees and temples, which in Northern Buddhism may be done by repeated prostrations (Ekvall 1964: ch. 8). Clockwise circumambulation respectfully keeps one's right side facing the revered object, and indicates that the object ideally symbolises what lies at the centre of one's life and aspiration. In Eastern Buddhism, another important practice is repeated, bowing before an image in a spirit of repentance.

Offerings are usually accompanied by appropriate chanted verses. Together, these aim to arouse joyful and devout contemplation of the qualities of a holy being, and aspiration for spiritual progress. Such acts consequently generate goodness-power (Gombrich 1971: 114–27; Khantipalo 1974: 8–12). The most common offerings are flowers. One Theravāda flower-offering verse says, in Pāli:

> This mass of flowers, fresh-hued, odorous and choice,
> I offer at the blessed lotus-like feet of the Lord of sages.
> With diverse flowers, the Buddha/*Dhamma*/*Saṅgha* I revere;
> And through this goodness-power may there be release.
> Just as this flower fades, so my body goes towards destruction.

This combines joyous reverence, aspiration, and reflection on the impermanence of human life. A Zen flower-offering verse aspires that the 'flowers of the mind' should 'bloom in the springtime of enlightenment'.

The pleasant odour of smouldering incense-sticks frequently greets a person entering a Buddhist temple. A Pāli incense-offering verse refers to the Buddha as 'He of fragrant body and fragrant face, fragrant with infinite virtues'. This reflects the idea that the Buddha had an 'odour of sanctity', a certain 'air' about him suggestive of his glorious character and virtues. Incense both reminds a person of this and also creates a sense of delight, which can then be focused on the Buddha. Another common offering is the light of small lamps or candles, a reminder of *buddha*s as 'enlightened' or 'awakened' beings who give light to the world through their teachings. A Theravāda offering verse thus describes the Buddha as 'the lamp of the three worlds, dispeller of darkness'.

In Northern Buddhism (Ekvall 1964: ch. 6), butter-lamps of finely wrought silver often burn perpetually before images. It is also common for seven kinds of offerings to be set before an image. Water 'for the face' and 'for the feet' symbolises hospitality, while flowers, incense, lamps, perfume and food represent the five senses, ideally expressing devotees' dedication of their whole being to spiritual development. The offerings are placed in seven bowls, or water and grain in these are visualised as being the offerings. Devotees also use *mudrās*, ritual gestures representing offerings such as flowers, a lamp, or the whole world, all of this being co-ordinated with complex *mantra*s (Beyer 1978: 143–226). They may additionally offer a white cotton or silk 'scarf of felicity' (Tib. *kha btags*; pron. *kuttha*) to an image. These are normally used as a friendship-offering to put a relationship on a good footing. Here they are used to form a bond of friendship with a holy being.

In all schools of Buddhism, chanting is very common as a vehicle for devotion or other ceremonial acts. Its use derives from early Buddhism, when Indian society made little use of writing, and a learned person was 'much-heard' rather than 'well-read'. Chanting aided accurate memory of the Buddha's teachings, as it has a rhythm which encourages the mind to flow on from word to word, and lacks melody, which might demand that the sound of some words be distorted. It is also a public medium, so that errors of memory could be known and corrected. After the teachings were written down, it was still thought better that they be well memorised, and chanting had also become part of devotional life.

Buddhist chanting is neither singing nor a monotonous dirge. While being deep-toned and slightly solemn, it holds the interest with its small variations of pitch and rhythm. It is particularly impressive when a group of monks chant, for they may use different keys, all blending into a harmonious whole. The chants are usually in ancient languages, such as Pāli or old Tibetan, thus giving them an added air of sanctity. This, plus their sound-quality and accompanying thoughts, generates a mixture of uplifting joy, often felt as a glow of warmth in the chest, and contemplative calm. Such states tend to arise even in those listening to a chant, if they do so with a relaxed but attentive mind. Thus monks and nuns can transmit something of the tranquillity of their way of life when chanting for the laity. Many monks know the full meaning of the chants, as they know the relevant language to some extent, and can explain them to the laity. Vernacular chants also exist.

In all traditions, the most common chants are short verbal formulae, which may be strung together or repeated to form longer continuous chants. A very common Southern Buddhist chant, honouring Gotama Buddha, is: *Namo tassa bhagavato, arahato, sammā-sambuddhassa*, 'Honour to the Lord, *arahant*, perfectly and completely Enlightened One!'. This is repeated three times, and is usually followed by the chanted avowal of commitment to the 'three refuges' and the five moral precepts.

In all traditions, rosaries can be used to count off repeated chants. In Southern Buddhism, a *mantra* may be used such as '*du sa ni ma; sa ni ma du; ni ma du sa; ma du sa ni*'. This is based on the initial letters of the words for the Four Holy Truths: *dukkha* (suffering), *samudaya* (origin of it), *nirodha* (cessation of it), *magga* (path (to cessation)). It concentrates the mind, keeps it alert, and opens it to understanding. A devotional rosary-chant used in Southern Buddhism is 'Buddha, *Dhamma, Saṅgha*'.

Protective chanting

In all schools of Buddhism, chanting, or listening to it, is often used as a form of protection. In Southern Buddhism, chanted passages called *paritta*s, or 'safety-runes' are used (Harvey 1993). Most are excerpts from the Pāli scriptures, the most common one being that on the qualities of the three refuges, as translated above. Other popular ones include: the *Karaṇīya-metta Sutta*, which radiates feelings of lovingkindness to all living beings (Brown and O'Brian 1989: 88–9); the *Maṅgala Sutta*, which describes such 'blessings' as a good education, generosity, hearing the *Dhamma*, and attaining *nirvāṇa* (Brown and O'Brian 1989: 87–8); and the *Ratana Sutta*, which calls down the protection of the gods and praises the 'three jewels' (Nanamoli 1960: 4–6). While most *paritta*s are used as a general protection, some are used against particular dangers, such as one against death from snake-bite, said in the *sutta*s to have been given by the Buddha specifically as a '*paritta*' (*Khandha paritta*). *Paritta*s are used, for example, for warding off wild animals, human attackers or ghosts, exorcising people, curing illnesses, and averting dangers from accidents or natural disasters. They are also used to gain a good harvest, to help pass an examination, to bless a new building, or simply to generate goodness-power. There are limits to their power, though. They are said to work only for a virtuous person with confidence in the 'three refuges', and cannot, for example, cure a person of an illness if it is due to his past *karma* (Horner 1969: I 211–17). Within these limits, the working of *paritta*s is seen as involving a number of factors.

First, to chant or listen to a *paritta* is soothing and leads to self-confidence and a calm, pure mind, due to both its sound-quality and its meaning. As the mind is in a healthier state, this may cure psychosomatic illnesses, or make a person more alert and better at avoiding the dangers of life. Secondly, chanting a *paritta*, especially one which expresses lovingkindness to all beings, is thought to calm down a hostile person, animal or ghost, making them more well-disposed towards the chanter and listeners. Thirdly, as well as making new goodness-power, *paritta*-chanting is thought to stimulate past goodness-power into bringing some of its good results immediately. Fourthly, chanting or listening to a *paritta* is thought to please those gods who are devotees of the Buddha, so that they offer what protection and assistance it is in their power to give. Finally, the spiritual power of the Buddha, the 'greatly compassionate protector' (*Mahā-jayamaṅgala Gāthā paritta*), and of the truth he expressed, seems to be seen as continuing in his words, with its beneficial influence being liberated when these are devoutly chanted. This partly relates to the concept, found in the early texts, of an 'asseveration of truth'. By affirming some genuine virtue of oneself or someone else, or publicly admitting an embarrassing fault, a wonder-working power-for-good is liberated, to the benefit of oneself and others. Accordingly, a *Ratana Sutta* refrain, 'by this truth, may there be well being!', is repeated after various excellences of the 'three jewels' have been enumerated.

While an ordinary layperson or specialist chanter can activate the power of the Buddha's words by chanting, it is more efficacious for monks to do so. This is because they try to live fully the way of life taught by the Buddha. When members of the monastic *saṅgha* chant the *Dhamma*, as taught by the Buddha, there is a powerful combination, of benefit to listening laypeople. To symbolise the protective power passing from the monks, they hold a cord while chanting *paritta*. This is also tied to a *buddha*-image, suggesting that the image is being impregnated with the *paritta*'s power, or, equally, that it is discharging some of its previously accumulated power to add to that of the *paritta*. Afterwards, pieces of the '*paritta*-cord' are tied to the laypeople's wrists as a reminder of, and a 'store' of, the *paritta*'s protective power. When the cord is tied on, a Pāli verse is uttered which means: 'By the majesty of the power attained by all *buddha*s, solitary *buddha*s and *arahant*s, I tie on a complete protection'.

In Eastern and Northern traditions, including Ch'an/Zen, chanted formulae used in a similar way to *paritta*s are *dhāraṇī*s, utterances 'preserving' Buddhism and its followers (Kato et al. 1975: 328–32). These are strings of Sanskrit words and syllables, originating as mnemonic formulae summarising a *sūtra* or teaching, which may be unintelligible without explanation. The Southern '*du, sa, ni, ma* . . .' rosary chant quoted above is akin to these. Likewise, in Northern Buddhism, the use of *mantra*s is common, both in devotion and meditation.

Devotion to Avalokiteśvara

Devotion to Avalokiteśvara pervades Eastern and Northern Buddhism. A text much used in liturgies is the verse section of the *Avalokiteśvara Sūtra*, an extract from the *Lotus Sūtra* (Kato et al. 1975: 319–27; Conze et al. 1964: 194–6). Expressing profound devotion, this speaks of: 'True regard, serene regard, far-reaching wise regard, regard of pity, compassionate regard, ever longed for, ever longed for! Pure and serene in radiance, wisdom's sun destroying darkness. . . . Law of pity, thunder quivering, compassion wondrous as a great cloud, pouring spiritual rain like nectar, quenching the flames of distress!'. Statues and paintings of Avalokiteśvara are found in abundance, depicting him in around a hundred and thirty different ways, each aiming to express some aspect of his nature. In China, as Kuan Yin, 'he' gradually came to be portrayed as female. This may have been because the Chinese saw his compassion as a female quality; it may also have been partly due to the female reference in his *mantra* (see below). Moreover, from the fifth century, some of 'his' popular incarnations were female, and 'he' may also have merged with a pre-Buddhist goddess thought to care for mariners. Kuan Yin thus became an all-compassionate 'mother-goddess', the most popular deity in all of China, being portrayed as a graceful, lotus-holding figure in a white robe. An artistic form common in Tibet and Japan shows Avalokiteśvara with 'a thousand' arms (fewer, for practical reasons, in statues) and eleven heads. Seven hands hold various emblems, while the rest represent his boundless skilful means (ability to help in the most appropriate way). Each makes a *mudrā*, or 'gesture', denoting 'be fearless', and on its palm is an eye, representing his ever-watchful nature, ready to rush to the aid of beings. His eleven heads are explained by a story that, on seeing so many beings suffering in the hells, his horror and tears caused him momentarily to despair of fulfilling his vow to save all beings. His head then split into ten pieces, as he had said it would if he ever abandoned his resolve. Amitābha Buddha then brought him back to life to renew his vow. Making each of the head-fragments into a new head, he assembled them on Avalokiteśvara's shoulders, and surmounted them with a replica of his own head, symbolising that he would continue to inspire the *bodhisattva* in his work. With eleven heads, Avalokiteśvara was now even better equipped to look for beings in need! From Avalokiteśvara's tears, moreover, two forms of Tārā, the 'Saviouress' *Bodhisattva* had been born: themselves the focus of much devotion in Tibet (Conze et al. 1964: 196–202).

The *Avalokiteśvara Sūtra* says that Avalokiteśvara will instantly respond to those who 'with all their mind call upon his name'. 'By virtue of the power of that *bodhisattva*'s majesty', they will be unburnt by a fire; saved at sea in a storm; the hearts of murdering foes will turn to kindness; as prisoners, guilty or innocent, they will be set free from their chains; merchants will be freed from the dangers of robbers; threatening wild beasts will flee; success will be attained in a court of law or battle, and a woman will have a virtuous child, of the sex of her choice. Devotees will also be freed from attachment, hatred and delusion by 'keeping in mind and remembering' Avalokiteśvara. Much of this is comparable to the power attributed to *paritta*-chanting. The wondrous help of Avalokiteśvara is understood both as a literal intervention in the world, perhaps through the aid of a mysterious stranger, or a vision guiding someone through mists on a dangerous mountain, and as coming from the power of a devotee's faith. In the *Śūrangama Sūtra*, it is said that Avalokiteśvara aids beings by awakening them to their compassionate *buddha*-nature, and in accordance with this, any act of great kindness may be seen as the 'help' of Avalokiteśvara.

Ch'an/Zen, for which 'To be compassionate is Kuan Yin' (Yampolsky 1967: sec. 35), generally understands his/her aid in purely internal, spiritual terms: for a 'storm' is anger, 'fire' is desire, 'chains' are simply those of fear, a sense of oppression comes from lack of patience, and animals only threaten one who has ill-will. Accordingly, Ch'an/Zen devotion to Kuan Yin is thought of primarily in terms of 'developing the heart of Kuan Yin': growing the seed of great compassion so that one becomes ever-ready to help others.

In Northern Buddhism, the *mantra* '*Oṃ maṇi padme hūṃ*' is very popular in invoking the help of Avalokiteśvara and in developing compassion (Ekvall 1964: 115–23). *Oṃ* and *hūṃ* are ancient Indian sacred sounds, the first being seen as the basic sound of the universe. *Maṇi padme* literally means 'O jewelled-lotus lady', but in developed exegesis, *maṇi* is seen as referring to the jewel that this *bodhisattva* holds, while *padme* refers to the lotus as his symbol. The jewel symbolises both his willingness to grant righteous wishes, and the pure clarity in the depths of the minds of beings. The lotus symbolises both the pure beauty of Avalokiteśvara's compassion, and the worldly minds of beings which he encourages to 'bloom' into enlightenment. Accompanied by the click of rosaries, the '*Maṇi*' *mantra* is frequently heard on the lips of all who have any degree of devotion to Buddhism. It may be uttered as a person goes about his or her business, either under the breath or as an audible rhythmic murmur called 'purring' by the Tibetans. The Tibetans also activate the power of this *mantra*, and generate goodness-power, by use of the '*Maṇi* religion wheel', known in the West as a 'prayer wheel'. The formula is carved or painted on the outside of a short cylinder, and is written many times on a tightly rolled piece of paper inside. Each revolution of the cylinder is held to be equivalent to the repetition of all the formulae written on and in it, an idea related to that of the Buddha's first sermon as the 'setting in motion of the *Dhamma*-wheel'. '*Maṇi* religion wheels' are of various types. Hand-held ones have cylinders about seven centimetres long, mounted on handles about twelve centimetres long; a small weight attached to the cylinder on a chain enables it to be spun on a spindle fixed in the handle. Wheels around twenty five centimetres high are also fixed in rows along the sides of *stūpa*s or monasteries, so that people can turn them as they circumambulate these. The largest wheels, found at the entrance to temples, may be four metres high and two metres in diameter, and contain thousands of *Maṇi* formulae, along with scriptures and images. There are also wheels driven by streams or chimney smoke. The *Maṇi mantra* is also carved on stones deposited on hill-top cairns, on rock-faces by the side of paths, on long walls specially built at the approaches to towns, and is printed on 'prayer flags'.

Goodness-power accrues to those who pay for any of these or produce them, to all who glance at them, thinking of Avalokiteśvara and his compassion, and even to insects who come into contact with them.

Devotion to Amitābha

Devotion to Amitābha Buddha is found within most schools of the Mahāyāna, but is the essence of the Pure Land schools (Conze et al. 1964: 202–6; Brown and O'Brian 1989: 99–100, 218–19, 251–8). Here, practice centres on the 'Buddha invocation' (Ch. *nien-fo*, Jap. *nembutsu*): repetition of '*Nan-mo A-mi-t'o Fo*' (Ch.) or '*Nama Amida Butsu*' (Jap.), translations of the Sanskrit '*Namo Amitābhāya Buddhāya*', meaning 'Hail to Amitābha Buddha' (Pallis 1980: 84–101). In China, recitation is done in tune with the steady and natural breath, and may be repeated many times a day, as the practitioner never knows when he has done it the minimum necessary 'ten times' with 'unwavering concentration'. A by-product of concentration, focused on Amitābha and the enlightenment attainable in Sukhāvatī, his Pure Land, is that the mind is purified of distracting passions. The *nembutsu* also has a certain *mantra*-like quality, in that it is seen as opening up a channel between a holy being and a devotee: in this case, the channel of grace. Furthermore, when the practice is done wholeheartedly, it becomes spontaneous, and can be seen as reciting itself in a mental space in which the ego has temporarily dissolved. Through association with *nembutsu*-practice, a person's rosary often comes to be a revered object; touching it may immediately start the recitation revolving in the mind, and bring on the associated mental states.

In China, Shan-tao (613–681) came to emphasise the invocation as the 'primary' Pure Land practice. 'Secondary' ones included: chanting the Pure Land *sūtras*; visualisation of Amitābha and his Pure Land; worship of various *buddhas*; singing hymns of praise to Amitābha; resolving to be reborn in his land; and developing generosity and compassion by helping the needy, and through vegetarianism. In Japan, the Jodo-shin school came to put single-minded emphasis on Amitābha Buddha, and on the *nembutsu* as including all other practices, though the secondary practices could be done as expressions of gratitude for salvation. The sole aim of the *nembutsu* is to facilitate the awakening of faith; the moment when this truly occurs is seen as a transcendental, atemporal experience in which the devotee is at one with Amitābha in the form of the numinous *nembutsu*. After faith has arisen, any recitation is done solely as an expression of gratitude, often shown by merely wearing a rosary wrapped around the hand. This is also a reminder that 'sinful humans' are but a bundle of passions compared to Amitābha. Devotees express joyful adoration of Amitābha, and liken him to father and mother, so that he is commonly called *Oyasama*, 'The Parent'.

Amitābha is often depicted seated in meditation with the meeting of his index fingers and thumbs indicating that devotees should give up 'self-power' and rely on 'other-power' for salvation. One famous gilded wooden statue of him is in the Phoenix Hall, near Kyoto, Japan. Made in 1053 CE, it became the model for many later Japanese images of Amitābha. It shows him as a noble, gentle and compassionate being whose light and graceful form seems to float on its lotus-base above a small lake, as if in a vision. In the halo of the image are figures which represent beings newly born in *Sukhāvatī*, the 'Happy Land', which is depicted in paintings and statues on the walls of the image-hall. The aim of the whole is to re-create *Sukhāvatī* on earth, so as to stimulate an uplifting spiritual experience and deepen the aspiration to be reborn, by Amitābha's power, in this Pure Land. Indeed, much Mahāyāna art has been inspired by visionary experiences and has helped to inspire further experiences of a similar kind.

Devotion to Bhaiṣajya-guru

Devotion to the heavenly Buddha Bhaiṣajya-guru, the 'Master of Healing', is important in both Northern and Eastern Buddhism (Birnbaum 1979). In Chinese temples, image-halls most commonly have images of him and Amitābha flanking one of Śākyamuni (the Mahāyāna term for the historical Buddha, and the heavenly *Buddha* who manifested him on earth). He generally holds a bowl said to be made of *lapis lazuli*, an intensely blue gem-stone thought to have healing properties. His body is also said to be like *lapis lazuli*, and to blaze with light. In one Chinese healing rite, a person keeps eight vows for seven days, makes offerings to monks, worships Bhaiṣajya-guru, recites his *sūtra* seventy-nine times, makes seven images of him, and then contemplates his image so that it comes alive with his spiritual force and healing energy. Tuning into this, the devotee then mentally merges with him.

Devotion to the *Lotus Sūtra*

Within the Japanese Nichiren school, the symbolically rich title of the '*Lotus Sūtra* of the True *Dharma*', *Myōhō-renge-kyō*, is a revered focus of devotion. This is known as the *daimoku*, and is seen to represent ultimate reality in its intrinsic purity. Prefaced by *Namu*, 'honour to', it forms the seven-syllable invocatory formula, *Na-mu myō-hō ren-ge-kyō*, whose repetition, accompanied by drums, is the central practice. Chanting this with sincere faith in the power of the truths of the *sūtra* is held to purify the mind, protect and benefit the chanter, lead to the moral uplift of the individual and society, develop the *bodhisattva* perfections, and activate the *buddha*-nature within. The title is also written or carved on a scroll or plaque known as the *gohonzon*, or 'main object of worship'. Down the centre of this is the invocation in bold Japanese characters; above, left and right, are the names of Prabhūtaratna Buddha, a past *buddha* who re-manifests himself in an incident in the *Lotus Sūtra*, and Śākyamuni; at its sides are the names of the 'four great kings', guardian deities who live in the lowest heaven described in ancient Buddhist cosmology; in the remaining space are names of various holy beings mentioned in the *sūtra* – including the *bodhisattva* that Nichiren said he was an incarnation of – and of certain Shinto deities. The *gohonzon* is seen as representing the final truth, as revealed in the *sūtra*, emphasising Śākyamuni Buddha as all-pervading reality and universal power. The *gohonzon* is thus the primary focus of worship and object of contemplation, prominently displayed in Nichiren temples between images of Śākyamuni and Prabhūtaratna. The sub-sect known as the Nichiren Shō-shū, however, has an image of the founder of the Nichiren school, Nichiren (1222–82), in a central position. A secondary Nichiren practice is to chant the sections of the *Lotus Sūtra* on skilful means and the 'eternal' life-span of Śākyamuni. In the twentieth century, a number of 'New Religions' have arisen in Japan, several based on Nichiren Buddhism. The most well known is the Sōka-gakkai, the lay arm of Nichiren Shō-shū, which is a very successful movement which actively seeks converts overseas.

Pilgrimage

Pilgrimage is a fairly common practice in Buddhism, and may be done for a variety of reasons: to bring alive events from the life of holy beings and so strengthen spiritual aspirations; to generate goodness-power; to be suffused by the power-for-good of relics and *bodhi*-trees; to receive protection from deities at the sites; or to fulfil a vow that pilgrimage would be made if aid was received from a certain *bodhisattva*. The most ancient sites are those of the Buddha's birth, first sermon, enlightenment and passing into final *nirvāṇa* at death. The Buddha said these should be visited with thoughts of reverence, such that anyone dying on the journey would be reborn in a heaven. The most important is Bodh-Gayā, whose focus is an ancient *bodhi*-tree directly descended from the one under which Gotama attained enlightenment. Its sagging bows are reverently propped up, prayer flags flutter from its branches, and pilgrims treasure any leaves which fall from it.

As Buddhism spread beyond India, new focuses of pilgrimage developed. For details, see the volume *Sacred Place* in this series.

Festivals

Buddhists enjoy and appreciate festivals as times for re-affirming devotion and commitment, generating goodness-power for the individual and community, strengthening community ties and values, and merry-making (Brown 1986: chs 3, 4 and 8). The Southern, Northern and Eastern traditions each have their major festivals, and there are also national variations on these, as well as local festivals on, for example, the anniversary of the founding of a temple. Some festivals which Buddhists celebrate are not Buddhist as such, but pertain to the agricultural cycle, national deities, or traditions such as Confucianism.

In Southern Buddhism, most major festivals occur at the time of a full moon (Spiro 1971: 219–31; Terweil 1979: 223–37). As in Northern Buddhism, the lunar cycle also marks off the sabbath-like *uposatha*s, or 'observance days', at the full-moon, new-moon and, less importantly, two half-moon days. Except at times of major festivals, observance days are attended only by the more devout, who spend a day and night at their local monastery. The monks are solemnly offered food, commitment to certain ethical precepts is made, the monks chant for the laity, and sometimes a sermon is given; these features also occur at all Southern Buddhist festivals. The rest of the time is spent in expressing devotion, reading, talking to the monks, and perhaps in some meditation.

In the lands of Southern Buddhism, the festival year starts at the traditional New Years, celebrated at various times, for up to four days, in mid-April. On the first day, houses are thoroughly cleaned of the dirt of the old year. Water, sometimes scented, is ceremonially poured over *Buddha*-images and the hands of monks and elderly relatives, as a mark of respect. In Southeast Asia, this is frequently followed by a good-humoured period when the laity throw water at all and sundry. On the second day, in Thailand, Cambodia and Laos, sand *stūpa*s are built in temple-compounds or on river banks. When the new year starts on the next day, the sand is spread out to form a new compound floor, or is washed away by the river. Its dispersal is seen as symbolically 'cleansing' a person of the past year's bad deeds, represented by the grains of sand. Reflecting on past misdeeds, people thus re-dedicate themselves to Buddhist values. Accordingly, the New Year is also a time for aiding living beings by releasing caged birds and rescuing fish from drying-out ponds and streams. Accompanying festivities may include boat races, kite fights, music, traditional dancing and plays.

At the full-moon of the lunar month of Vesākha, usually in May, comes *Vesākha Pūjā*, celebrating the Buddha's birth, enlightenment and final *nirvāṇa* at death. In Sri Lanka, this is the most important festival, when houses are decorated with garlands and paper lanterns, and driveways and temple-courtyards are illuminated. People wander between pavement pantomimes and pavilions displaying paintings of the Buddha's life, with food being given out from roadside alms-stalls. In Myanmar (Burma), *bodhi*-trees are watered with scented water, while in Thailand, Cambodia and Laos, the monks lead the laity in a three-fold circumambulation of a temple, *stūpa* or *buddha*-image. The sermon which follows, on the Buddha's life, sometimes lasts all night.

In Sri Lanka, the next full-moon day marks the *Poson* festival, celebrating the spreading of Buddhism to the island by Mahinda. Paintings of him are paraded through the streets to the sound of drumming, and pilgrimages are made to Anuradhapura and nearby Mihintale, where he met and converted the king.

The next full-moon marks *Āsālha Pūjā*, celebrating the Buddha's renunciation and first sermon, and marking the start of the three-month period of *Vassa* (the 'Rains'). During this, monks stay at their home monasteries, except for short absences, for concentration on study and meditation, and many young men in Southeast Asia take temporary ordination. The laity also deepen their religious commitment. They tend to avoid festivities, especially secular ones such as marriages, and more people than usual observe *uposatha*s at their local monasteries. Most ordinations take place in the time leading up to *Āsālha Pūjā*, with their goodness-power-potential seen as contributing to the timely start of the rains.

At the full-moon marking the end of *Vassa*, the monks hold the ceremony of *Pavāraṇā*. When they chant and meditate, wax drips into a bowl of water from a burning candle, and it is thought that something of the monks' goodness-power, built up during *Vassa*, suffuses and sacralises the water. This is then sprinkled on the laity as a blessing. In Southeast Asia, especially Myanmar (Burma), the following day is the *Tāvatiṃsa* festival, celebrating the time when the Buddha, after spending *Vassa* in the *Tāvatiṃsa* heaven teaching his mother, descended to earth. As the 'light' of the world was then accessible again, this is a festival of lights, which illuminate houses, monasteries and *stūpa*s and may be floated on rivers in small leaf-boats. A special food-offering is also made to a procession of monks, headed by a layman holding a *buddha*-image and alms-bowl, symbolising the returning Buddha.

The following month is the season for *Kaṭhina* celebrations, at which new robes, useful goods and money are given to the monasteries. The focal act is the donation of patches of cloth which the monks dye and make into a special robe, during the same day, commemorating the robes made from sown-together rags in early Buddhism. These highly auspicious ceremonies, held at most local *vihāra*s complete the annual round of the more important festivals in Southern Buddhism.

Other than in Nepal, several festivals in Northern Buddhism more or less coincide with corresponding Southern ones: the celebration of the enlightenment and final *nirvāṇa* of the Buddha (his birth being celebrated eight days earlier), the first sermon and the descent from a heaven (here seen as the *Tuṣita* heaven). The different schools also have festivals relating to their founders, with the death of Tsong-kha-pa (in November) being of general importance; monasteries also have festivals relating to their specific tutelary deity. An important and characteristic festival centres on the Tibetan New Year, in February. In the preceding two weeks, monks dressed in masks and brightly coloured robes perform impressive ritual dances before a large lay audience. Accompanied by booming alpine horns, drums, shrilling oboes and clashing cymbals, they act out a series of solemn but impressive movements, lasting several hours. These are seen as driving away evil powers, while other rituals seek to help beings to progress towards enlightenment. From the fourth to the twenty-fifth day of the first month, monks perform the ceremonies of *sMon lam* (Tib., pron. *Monlam*), the 'Great Vow', centred on a five-day celebration of the Buddha's 'marvel of the pairs' at Śrāvasti (which is said to have involved the Buddha levitating and issuing fire and water from his body). As an event in which rival teachers were confounded, this became an appropriate symbol for the overcoming of evil forces, and of Buddhism's past victory over Bon, the pre-Buddhist religion of Tibet. On the thirteenth day, dances portray Tibetan Buddhism's fierce protector-deities in their struggle against demons and spiritual ignorance. These are represented by a small human effigy which is ritually killed, symbolising victory over evil and the securing of a safe and prosperous new year. To raise people's energy levels for the new year, horse races and archery competitions are held around this period.

In the lands of Eastern Buddhism, the annual round of festivals has fewer Buddhist elements, and more from Confucianism, Shinto and folk traditions. In Communist China, festivals are now largely secularised and politicised, though they continue much as before in Taiwan and Hong Kong and among expatriate Chinese. Among the Chinese, who determine festivals by a lunar calendar, the birth of the Buddha is celebrated in May, as in Korea, while in Japan it is celebrated on 8 April. The principal rite recalls the story that the new-born Śākyamuni stood and was bathed by water sent down by gods: small standing images of the child are placed in bowls, and scented water or tea is ladled over them. For Chinese Buddhists, the festival is also a popular time for the release of living beings into the water or air. In Korea, it is a time for illuminating temples with paper lanterns. In Japan the festival is known as *Hana matsuri*, the 'Flower Festival', and retains elements of a pre-Buddhist festival involving the gathering of wild mountain flowers so as to bring home deities to protect the rice-fields. The Buddhist connection is that Śākyamuni was born in a flower-laden grove, so that the infant-Buddha images are housed in floral shrines.

The other important Chinese Buddhist festivals are those of the 'birth', 'enlightenment' and 'death' of Kuan Yin, and especially *Ullambana*, which is also celebrated by non-Buddhists. This 'Festival of Hungry Ghosts', in August/September, is when ancestors reborn as ghosts are said to wander in the human world, as a potential source of danger. At the full-moon, which ends the three-months 'Summer Retreat', monks transfer goodness-power, put out food and chant *sūtra*s for them, so as to help them to a better rebirth. The laity sponsor the rites and participate by burning large paper boats which will help 'ferry across' hungry ghosts to a better world, thus showing filial regard for ancestors. A favourite story told at this time is that of Mu-lien (Pali Moggallāna), a key *arahant* disciple of the Buddha, who discovered that his mother was reborn as a hungry ghost or in a hell (there are two versions of the story). On the advice of the Buddha, he then helped her attain a better rebirth by transferring goodness-power to her. In Japan, *Ullambana* became *O-bon*, the 'Feast for the Dead', celebrated from 13 to 15 July. Graves are washed and tended, and an altar is set up in or near the home for offerings of fresh herbs and flowers. A fire and candles are lit to welcome ancestral spirits to partake of the offerings and a Buddhist priest is invited to chant a *sūtra* in each home in his parish.

It can thus be seen that Buddhism has a full and rich spectrum of devotional life. It may have a greater range of objects of devotion than some religions, and may contain traditions which warn against an excess of devotion, yet devotion runs deep within its blood, in ways paralleling many other religions. Devotion is a good way to open the heart to calm and the development of liberating wisdom. For the Pure Land tradition, complete faith and devotion are *themselves* the gateway to liberation.

NOTES

1. Beings-for-enlightenment, dedicated to attaining buddhahood.
2. The language of foreign terms, except where indicated, is Pāli, the scriptural and liturgical language of Theravāda Buddhism, or Sanskrit, an early scriptural language of Mahāyāna Buddhism. Terms are given in

their Pāli or Sanskrit forms according to context. Exceptions to this are: *nirvāṇa* (Pāli *nibbāna*), *bodhisattva* (Pāli *bodhisatta*) and *stūpa* (Pāli *thūpa*), which are always given in their more well-known, Sanskrit, forms; and *arahant* (Sanskrit *arhat*), the more well-known, Pāli, form. *Dhamma/dharma* (Pāli/Sanskrit) occurs as is appropriate to context. The terms *saddhā, pasāda, paritta, Tiratana, puñña, uposatha* and *sutta* are Pāli, and *mantra, sūtra, Trikāya* and *dhāraṇī* are Sanskrit. *Bodhi, pūjā* and *vihāra* are the same in Pāli and Sanskrit. A pronunciation guide for Pāli and Sanskrit words is found in Harvey (1990: xxi). As an initial guide, note that a, i and u are pronounced short unless they have a bar over them (ā, ī, ū), in which case they are pronounced long (as are e and o). C is pronounced ch, th as an aspirated t, ph as an aspirated p, ṣ and ś as sh, ñ as ny, and ṃ as a nasal ng.

3. 'Eastern' Buddhism refers to the Buddhism of China, Korea, Japan and Vietnam. 'Northern' Buddhism refers to the Buddhism of Tibet, Mongolia, parts of NW China, Bhutan, parts of Nepal and of Ladakh and Sikkim in India. 'Southern' Buddhism refers to the Buddhism of Sri Lanka, Thailand, Myanmar (Burma), Laos and Cambodia. Southern Buddhism is of the Theravāda variety (though incorporating some past Mahāyāna influence), while Northern and Eastern are Mahāyāna (though the ordination-lines are close cousins of the Theravadin one). For Northern Buddhism, Tibet has been the dominant cultural influence, while for Eastern Buddhism, China has.
4. 'Mantrayāna' refers to those forms of Buddhism in which *mantras* or sacred words of power play an important part: Northern Buddhism, the Japanese Shingon school and the Korean Milgyo school. *Mantras* are mostly meaningless syllables or strings of syllables, which give an arrangement of sound of great potency. When pronounced in the right way, with the right attitude of mind, the sound-arrangement of the *mantra* is seen as 'tuning-in' the practitioner's mind to the being he wishes devoutly to invoke or meditatively to visualise (Conze et al. 1964: 246–55).
5. The 'relics' contained in these are reputed remains from the funeral pyres of the Buddha or any Buddhist saint. Having been part of the body of such a pure being, they are seen as having been infused with an uplifting power-for-good which can benefit those who show devotion in their vicinity.

FURTHER READING

Beyer, S. (1978) *The Cult of Tārā – Magic and Ritual in Tibet*, London, University of California Press, pp. 1–226.

Birnbaum, R. (1979) *The Healing Buddha*, London, Rider, and Boulder, Colorado, Shambhala [Chinese texts and rituals].
Blofeld, J. (1970) *The Tantric Mysticism of Tibet*, New York, Dutton.
Brown, A. (ed.) (1986) *Festivals in World Religions*, London, Longman.
Brown, K. and O'Brian, J. (eds) (1989) *The Essential Teachings of Buddhism*, London, Rider [translations and comments from all schools].
Conze, E., Horner, I.B., Snellgrove, D., Waley, A. (eds), (1964) *Buddhist Texts Through the Ages*, New York, Harper & Row [translations from all schools].
Ekvall, R.B. (1964) *Religious Observances in Tibet*, London, University of Chicago Press.
Gombrich, R. (1971) *Precept and Practice: Traditional Buddhism in the Rural Highlands of Ceylon*, Oxford, Clarendon Press.
Harvey, P. (1990) *An Introduction to Buddhism – Teachings, History and Practices*, Cambridge, Cambridge University Press.
Harvey, P. (1993) 'The Dynamics of Paritta Chanting in Southern Buddhism', in Werner, K. (ed.) *Love Divine – Studies in Bhakti and Devotional Mysticism*, London, Curzon Press.
Horner, I.B. (1969) *Milinda's Questions*, London, Luyac and Co. [a Theravadin text].
Kato, B., Tamura, Y., Miyasaka, K. (trs) (1975) *The Threefold Lotus Sutra*, New York, Weatherhill [a Mahāyāna text].
Khantipalo, Bhikkhu (1974) *Lay Buddhist Practice (Wheel* no. 206/207), Kandy, Sri Lanka, Buddhist Publication Society.
Nanamoli, Bhikkhu (1960) *Minor Readings and Illustrator*, London, Pali Text Society [a Theravadin text and commentary].
Pallis, M. (1980) *A Buddhist Spectrum*, London, George Allen & Unwin.
Spiro, M.E. (1971) *Buddhism and Society – A Great Tradition and its Burmese Vicissitudes*, London, George Allen & Unwin.
Tay, N. (1976–7) 'Kuan-yin: The Cult of Half Asia', in *History of Religions*, 16: 147–77.
Terweil, B.J. (1979) *Monks and Magic – An Analysis of Religious Ceremonies in Thailand*, London, Curzon Press.
Yampolsky, P.B. (1967) *The Platform Sutra of the Sixth Patriarch*, New York, Columbia University Press [a Ch'an/Zen text].

2. Christianity

Douglas Davies

In Christianity worship is the human response to God's greatness, both in creating the universe and in providing salvation for humanity. In worship, men and women become aware of themselves as finite creatures on the one hand and as morally limited beings on the other. In the Christian tradition, growing as it did out of Jewish backgrounds, this moral element is as vitally important as the sense of wonder before the Creator. Creation and salvation stand side by side as the Jewish–Christian foundation for worship, so that worship integrates and echoes a dual framework – of the moral perfection of God and imperfection of humanity as one perspective, and of the greatness of God in creating the universe as the other perspective. This is the major reason why confession followed by absolution from sin is central to Christian worship, and often precedes expressions of God's glory revealed in the created order.

But the distinctive feature of Christian worship is the focus on Jesus Christ, as shown in so many prayers which end with the formula 'through Jesus Christ our Lord, Amen'. Christians believe that through Jesus, God became part and parcel of humanity. The Christmas carol, 'Behold the great Creator makes himself a house of clay', expresses this fundamental Christian conviction that the creator has become part of the creation to bring salvation to humanity. When Christians say 'Amen', they use a Hebrew word meaning 'truly', to emphasise that it is through Jesus as the Jewish Messiah or anointed one – 'Christ' being derived from the Greek word for 'anointed' – that their worship takes place.

In theological terms, worship is based on the idea of God as a Holy Trinity, comprising Father, Son and Holy Spirit. With this pattern in mind, it is often said that worship is offered to the Father, through the Son, by the power of the Holy Spirit. Even so, in different churches and at different times the emphasis placed upon the Father, the Son, and the Spirit, can differ to quite a degree.

From its first days as a new religion, Christianity has been a community of worshipping people. In very many respects worship came before theology, prayer before doctrine. An old Latin phrase, *lex orandi lex credendi*, refers directly to this fact of Christian history that the law of prayer establishes the law of belief, or, in other words, that what is to be believed emerges from prayerful worship.

The priority of worship is perfectly understandable, given the fact that the earliest followers of Jesus were Jews whose established religious practice was grounded in local synagogues and also, to a more limited extent, the Temple at Jerusalem. For centuries Jews had regularly come together to worship God and to hear the words of their sacred scriptures. Jesus was, himself, thoroughly grounded in this practice, and it is perfectly natural to read in the Bible of him being taken to the Temple as a boy (Luke 2: 41–50), of reading the scriptures at the synagogue (Luke 4: 16), and of teaching in synagogues (Mark 1: 21).

Early in the Acts of the Apostles we read of Peter and John going to the Temple to pray, and of Paul, arguing his Christian cause in the synagogue at Corinth during one of his visits there lasting some eighteen months (Acts 18: 4–17). One of the profound issues that arose in the development of Christianity during the century after the death of Jesus was the break-away of Jewish Christians from their Jewish synagogue base as they established their own gatherings for worship, where they were joined by Greeks or others who had become Christians.

Temple and Jesus

There are several points in the New Testament where the status and significance of Jewish places of worship, especially the Temple at Jerusalem, are called into question. There is a well-known story in the gospels where Jesus visits the Temple at Jerusalem and drives from it merchants and stall-holders (Mark 11: 15–17). In the version written in John's Gospel (and it comes very early in that Gospel as though to emphasise the significance of the point being made) Jesus is asked on what authority he drives out these sales-people, or what sign he can give to justify doing it? The text then runs:

> Jesus answered them, 'Destroy this temple and in three days I will raise it up'. The Jews then said, 'It has taken forty-six years to build this temple, and will you raise it up in three days?' But he spoke of the temple of his body. When, therefore he was raised from the dead, his disciples remembered that he had said this; and they believed the scripture and the word which Jesus had spoken.
>
> (John 2: 19–22)

These words hint at one strand of early Christian belief, in which Jesus was believed to be so important in the relationship between God and humanity that his resurrection provided a more significant focus of faith than any sacred building ever could, even the Temple which was initially the resting place of the Ark of the Covenant. A person had replaced a building, just as a new covenant had replaced the old. There is a full-scale discussion of this replacement of the Temple by Christ in the Epistle to the Hebrews, a discussion made all the keener by the fact that Jerusalem's temple was destroyed in 70 CE (a devastating blow as far as Jews were concerned).

Jesus is interpreted as both the high priest (Heb. 9: 11) and the sacrificial victim (Heb. 9: 26) who, through his resurrection, has entered into heaven, which is the true sacred place (Heb. 9: 11–12), to serve as both priest and victim. Earthly things are reckoned, in this epistle, to be but shadows of the heavenly reality. The Christians addressed in this letter are called to the kind of life of faith which sets its mind on the ultimate realities of heaven and not upon transient aspects of earthly life.

> Therefore let us be grateful for receiving a kingdom that cannot be shaken, and thus let us offer to God acceptable worship, with reverence and awe.
>
> (Heb. 12: 28)

Body as Temple

This emphasis on worship is repeated later in the Epistle to the Hebrews to stress the fact that Christians exist not to participate in the sacrifice of animals in earthly temples, but to 'continually offer up a sacrifice of praise to God', a sacrifice which is the 'fruit of lips that acknowledge his name' (Heb. 13: 15). Such sacrifices to God are also said to include doing good and sharing what they had (Heb. 13: 16), so that worship embraces the wider meaning of ethical aspects of life as well as narrower practices such as singing or the like. A very similar picture emerges in the Epistle to the Romans where Paul appeals to believers to present their bodies as a living sacrifice to God, for this very thing is their 'spiritual worship' (Rom. 12: 1). Here worship is seen as a way of describing the Christian life as a whole and not simply as one part of it restricted to the congregational activity within a particular building. This is expressed in a slightly different way when Paul writes that Christians should see their own bodies as a 'temple of the Holy Spirit' (I Cor. 6: 19). This brings worship down to a very personal level as the individual believer is seen as the true focus of worship of God since, through the Spirit, God indwells each person. This view of the relation between the Spirit and the individual transforms the idea of sacred space and sacred architecture.

In fact, the history of worship within Christianity involves a constant relationship between the inwardness and the outwardness of worship, between those who say true worship of God is an inward attitude of the individual believer, and others who do not deny that inwardness but who also stress the outward acts and context of worship.

The period of Jewish history into which Jesus was born involved, in Palestine, strict obedience to the commandment against making 'any graven image, or any likeness of anything that is in heaven above, or that is in the earth beneath, or that is in the water' (Exod. 20: 4). Early followers of Jesus were likely to have held a similar outlook, but with time, and as many non-Jews also became Christians, ideas changed. From the second century on, pictures emerged in Christian contexts, as in the catacombs, and grew in religious significance. One important aspect of this development lay in the Christian belief that God had become part and parcel of humanity in Jesus of Nazareth. This belief came to be enshrined in the doctrine of the Incarnation and changed the way Christian believers looked at the world.

Icons

The doctrine of the Incarnation meant that, instead of God being beyond the material realm, there was now a sense in which God had entered into material reality. Through the process of salvation in Jesus, the stamp of divine approval had been placed upon created things in a new way. This led to Christ, his disciples and martyred followers, along with many aspects of human life, being portrayed in art forms. In Eastern Orthodox religion this ultimately led to the growth of icons. Icons are paintings of Jesus, of the Virgin Mary, and of various saints. They may be simple paintings or highly decorated with precious metals, but whether simple or elaborate they are believed to be a special medium through which spiritual benefits may be derived. In the most fundamental sense, icons are symbols – they participate in that which they represent, they are a vehicle for the power of the person depicted upon them to come through to the pious worshipper. In Greek and Russian Orthodox churches icons play a very significant part in the piety of ordinary believers who often pray before their icons. The *iconostasis* is a screen found in Orthodox churches which separates the sanctuary, with its altar, from the nave where the people stand. It gets its name from the fact that it is covered with icons.

Religious interest in icons grew increasingly in the eastern Mediterranean world until, in the eighth and ninth centuries, there was a flare-up of feeling both for and against their use in the Greek Church. This has been called the Iconoclastic Controversy, from a Greek word for image-breaker. Icons had become increasingly widespread, and some felt that they had become far too significant within popular church life, and it was when some of the Byzantine Emperors adopted this view that the issue reached epidemic proportion. Despite the strength of opposition, the right to use icons was won in 842 CE so that, in practice, icons would continue to be a significant part of eastern Christianity.

Western Christianity had its own problems over the use of images at a later date. It was during the period of the Reformation in the sixteenth century that western Christians argued over images in churches and took different views. Roman Catholics retained the use of images in the form of crucifixes, statues and paintings, as did, to a certain extent, the Lutheran Churches. But the increased emphasis, both upon the personal inwardness of religious experience and, perhaps even more importantly, on the Bible and preaching as the source of knowledge of God, led to the more Calvinist streams of the Reformation making their places of worship increasingly bare in an artistic sense. The Puritans in England in the early seventeenth century objected to any form of church decoration, ritual and the symbolic vestments worn by clergy in church. Several church denominations, including the Presbyterians, Baptists and Independents, were influenced by this outlook and continued to be simple in their church life as far as artistic representations were concerned. But, though the walls of these churches would be bare of all images, these denominations developed a rich tapestry of images within hymns. The tremendous growth of hymns following on from the Reformation generated a form of pictorial poetry which fed the pious through their congregational singing in a way that pictorial images had done for earlier generations.

Eucharist as worship

One major focus of worship in the Christian tradition which has long occupied a central place in Christian life is the Eucharist, the ritual in which the faithful gather together to bless, share, eat and drink bread and wine. It is sometimes called the Liturgy, especially in Greek Orthodoxy, where it stands as the uniquely central vehicle for expressing the doctrine and theology of that tradition. In the Roman Catholic Church it is called the Mass, while in Protestant and Reformed Churches it is called by a variety of names including the Lord's Supper and the Holy Communion.

The Eucharist is traced back to the Last Supper, held by Jesus for his disciples before his death, as recorded in different ways several times in the Bible (eg., Matt. 26: 17ff; Mark 14: 13ff; Luke 22: 8ff; John 13: 1ff; I Cor. 11: 23ff). At first it seems to have been a meal shared by all the faithful, then the action changed in the middle of the second century to focus on the bread and wine over which special prayers were said. The gathering has also switched from an evening to an early morning rite. The great increase in church membership following the Roman Empire becoming nominally Christian led to the Eucharist being increasingly associated with the clergy, as fewer of the total Christian population were involved in it. Its ritual and symbolic meaning were greatly elaborated in different parts of the Christian world.

WORSHIP AND SACRIFICE

One unifying feature in the theology and language of the Eucharist in both the eastern and western Christian traditions lay in the free use of ideas of sacrifice and offering. In the medieval period the western church developed the doctrine of *transubstantiation* to explain the belief that Christ's body and blood were somehow realised in the sacramental bread and wine. As such, they could be offered to God as a re-presentation of Christ, or as a re-offering of the sacrifice Christ had once made of himself. The technical arguments used to define just how the divine presence came to be in, or associated with, the bread and wine were often quite complex and tied up with the way philosophy at that period explained matter. The important point is that the Eucharist was seen as a kind of sacrifice, and that the worship of God was inextricably bound up with the life and death of Jesus as a sacrifice.

DEVOTION TO THE BLESSED SACRAMENT

In the Roman Catholic tradition this belief led to an important form of faith focusing on devotion to Christ as present in the consecrated bread or host. The 'blessed sacrament' was kept after the Mass and placed in a special receptacle called a tabernacle. This was and is a central feature of any Catholic church, representing the constant presence of Christ as a focus for worship and prayer. Often it would be near the high altar as the key focus in a church, or else placed in the Lady Chapel where private prayer and worship could be conducted at any time. From about the thirteenth century on, it became customary at some services to display the reserved sacrament to the people in a container called a monstrance. As time went on, monstrances became increasingly decorated and consisted of a little circular window through which the consecrated host or wafer could be seen, and with precious metal used, for example, to depict radiating rays of the sun coming from the host. Over the centuries a separate service emerged called Benediction, in which the host was displayed in its monstrance, and incense was used along with prayers, hymns and silent adoration. This was especially the case in the nineteenth century as Benediction was used as a special evening service. From the mid-twentieth century Catholics have increasingly held major Masses as evening services which has led to a decline in the service of Benediction. This whole process is a good example of how the rise of a doctrine, that of transubstantiation, fostered a rite which later declined as the rite on which it depended, namely the Mass, changed its own place in the weekly flow of worship celebrating Christ's sacrifice.

In Eastern Orthodoxy this practice never emerged, partly perhaps because of the emphasis on Christ's resurrection rather than on his death. But the death of Jesus as a sacrifice for sin in saving the world was absolutely central to the theology of the Reformation in the West, although it was interpreted in a different way, leading to intense disagreement between Protestants and Catholics over the meaning of the Eucharist and especially over the idea of the Eucharistic Sacrifice. Once more the debate between the inwardness and outwardness of religion in Christian faith came to the surface. For most Protestants the emphasis was placed on the faith of the believer in relation to Christ, and not upon any change in the bread and wine itself. For Catholics, as for the Lutherans to a certain extent, the sacramental bread and wine remained important as a means of interacting with the presence of Christ. The Anglican Church hotly debated the issue and, as a Reformation movement, went theologically for the stress on the faith in the one receiving the elements, and on the ritual as a memorial of the sacrificial offering made by Christ himself. Most Protestant churches retained the Eucharist in some form, often calling it the Lord's Supper, or the Holy Communion, while stressing the aspect of a memorial of Christ's death.

From the later nineteenth century the Eucharist has come increasingly to the centre of worship in Catholic churches on the continent of Europe through the Liturgical Movement, as lay people have been encouraged to use it as a means of fostering their faith. The Second Vatican Council of the mid-1960s further encouraged this by insisting that the Mass should be said in the language of each country and not in Latin. So, too, in the Anglican Church, where the Parish Communion movement from the 1930s strove to establish each parish as a congregation focused on the Eucharist. But other Protestant churches have also increased their emphasis upon the Eucharist in the latter part of the twentieth century.

One interesting feature of the Eucharist is the fact that in the Greek Orthodox Church even very young children are allowed to have the sacred bread and wine once they have been baptised;

Roman Catholics permit them to do so after their first Confession but before the rite of Confirmation, while most Anglicans have resolutely held Confirmation as a necessary qualification for taking Holy Communion. Most Protestant churches also stress the adult, self-conscious awareness of members before they are admitted to Holy Communion. This can be compared with the fact that children, and even the unbaptised, are allowed to sing hymns and otherwise take full part in services in these churches, which shows that even within acts of worship divisions are drawn between who may and may not take full part in them.

Music, Mass and oratorio

To talk of hymns is to come to music as one channel of worship which is practically universal in Christianity. Irrespective of their theology, churches have used musical forms to chant portions of scripture, to sing old and new hymns, and to be the medium for all sorts of services from the earliest days of the faith. The liturgies of eastern and western Christendom as well as the hymns and psalms of Protestantism bear witness to the power of music as a vehicle for worship.

In the medieval period chant was combined with the Latin text of the Mass to give a form of worship that would influence western culture from Bach to Beethoven and on to Andrew Lloyd Webber in the 1980s. In similar ways, the Mass has been set to music under local cultural influences in Africa, South America and other countries. In addition to the Mass, various biblical passages have been set to music in oratorios such as Handel's 'Messiah' or Haydn's 'Creation' and have taken religious themes into the world of more popular culture.

HYMNS AS WORSHIP

But it is in hymns that the greatest number of people encounter music in worship. As general songs for lay people, hymns probably began in about the thirteenth century, though it was from the sixteenth century on, with the birth of the Reformation, that hymn-writing and hymn-singing became a fundamentally more central part of Christian worship and life. The Methodist Revival in Britain in the eighteenth century marked an important change as hymns, alongside sermons, came to be the central means of expressing doctrine and faith, as in the first book, *Hymns and Sacred Poems*, published by John and Charles Wesley in 1739. Developing from metrical psalm-singing, hymns expressed the doctrines of new religious outlooks in language that could be deeply biblical but could also use non-biblical expressions to great effect. The freedom to use ordinary language to mirror and echo biblical turns of phrase was a powerful means of stimulating piety among the faithful, as in Luther's famous hymn, 'A safe stronghold our God is still, a trusty shield and weapon'. Many hymns took biblical ideas and presented them for use in this new form of popular worship. This was especially true in the nineteenth century which was the century when hymns fully entered the life of the great majority of churches in Britain, a shift that was marked by the publication of *Hymns Ancient and Modern* in 1861.

It was in the Protestant tradition that hymn-singing came to be a central and important aspect of worship during the eighteenth and especially the nineteenth century. During this period all the major Protestant churches, including the Church of England, had shifted the centre of gravity of worship away from the Mass or Eucharist to services where the Bible was read, sermons preached, and hymns sung. Because this period was one of astonishing missionary expansion, carried out by members of various European countries establishing Christianity in their numerous empires and dominions, hymns were exported as a fundamental component of Christianity itself.

From the earliest period of the Reformation, Martin Luther's hymn, *A Safe Stronghold*, conveys a clear picture of God as a castle set against the attacking Devil:

A safe stronghold our God is still,
A trusty shield and weapon;
He'll help us clear from all the ill,
That hath us now o'ertaken.
The ancient prince of hell,
Hath risen with purpose fell,
Strong mail of craft and power
He weareth in this hour;
On earth is not his fellow.

But one of the most prolific and influential hymn-writers was Charles Wesley (1708–88), one of the founders of the Methodist movement, who had over two hundred hymns in the *Methodist Hymn Book*, a book which symbolises the importance of hymnody in this Protestant church. The following examples have been chosen to illustrate the theme of Christian worship and to show how diverse strands of human experience and life feed into the central nature of worship.

In 'O for a thousand tongues to sing my Great Redeemer's praise', Wesley takes the theme of salvation as the basis for his praise of God. The triumphs of God's grace have, in Christ, reached into the darkened life of the sinner as into a locked cell:

> He breaks the power of cancelled sin,
> He sets the prisoner free;
> His blood can make the foulest clean,
> His blood availed for me.

The emphasis on Jesus as the atonement for sin, and as the basis for the life of the forgiven sinner, is a dominant chord in Protestant worship, as this hymn stresses in its final verse:

> See all your sins on Jesus laid:
> The Lamb of God was slain,
> His soul was once an offering made,
> For every soul of man.

For Wesley there is a certain wonder and a trigger for worship in the mystery of God's goodness in taking on the problem of human wickedness. The hymn, 'And can it be that I should gain an interest in the Saviour's blood?', involves a profound reflection on the dual theological theme of God's love expressed in the death of Jesus on the one hand, and the human transformation brought about by forgiveness on the other, as these few phrases show: 'Amazing love! How can it be that Thou, my God, shouldst die for me!'; 'Tis mystery all! The immortal dies: Who can explore His strange design?'.

Horatius Bonar (1808–89) explored this same experience of forgiveness in this hymn. As he says,

Not what these hands have done,
Not what I feel or do,
Can give me peace with God;
Not all my prayers, and sighs, and tears,
Can bear the awful load.

This sense of sin as a weight bearing down upon life, or as chains holding people captive, is a powerful one in the spirituality of Protestant religion. It is experienced as part of that total process of conversion or of being 'born again', as someone passes from the oppressive sense of sin to an awareness of forgiveness from God, an awareness often spoken of in terms of light, freedom or peace. Bonar continues his hymn in exactly this way by shifting his attention from himself, first to Christ and then to God:

Thy work alone, O Christ,
Can ease this weight of sin;
Thy blood alone, O Lamb of God,
Can give me peace within.

Thy grace alone, O God,
To me can pardon speak;
Thy power alone, O son of God
Can this sore bondage break.

Wesley's emphasis is thoroughly Christ-focused and rooted in the belief that God's love to humanity is fully revealed in Jesus whose incarnation brings God into the very arena of human life. Human nature itself is perceived as sinful and in need of transforming conversion through God's grace so that men and women may themselves become loving. One of his best known hymns, now widely sung as a Christmas carol, 'Hark the herald-angels sing', uses all these ideas, and uses them as the basis for the worship of Christ.

Christ by highest heaven adored,
Christ the everlasting Lord,
Late in time behold him come,
Offspring of a virgin's womb.
Veiled in flesh the Godhead see,
Hail the incarnate Deity,
Pleased as man with man to dwell
Jesus our Immanuel.

Mild He lays his glory by,
Born that man no more may die,
Born to raise the sons of earth,
Born to give them second birth,
Hail the heaven-born Prince of Peace,
Hail the Sun of Righteousness,
Light and life to all He brings,
Risen with healing in His wings.

Through hymns like this, more than through any formal teaching, millions of people have come to absorb aspects of theology and have been led into worship. It is quite easy to use Wesley's hymns alone as a means of covering the life of Jesus and the nature of God, as these representative titles show:

O Love divine what hast thou done?	(Cross)
Christ the Lord is risen today.	(Resurrection)
Hail the Day that sees him rise.	(Ascension)
Entered the Holy Place above.	(Heavenly Priest)
Rejoice the Lord is King.	(Kingly Rule)
Lo he comes with clouds descending.	(Second Coming)
I want the Spirit of power within.	(Holy Spirit)
Father in whom we live.	(Holy Trinity)
When quiet in my house I sit.	(Bible)
Sinners turn why will ye die?	(Conversion)

Spirituality and worship

Throughout Wesley's hymns there is a sense of inner peace, certainty and assurance which is typical of an important strand of Protestant religion. It is also the hallmark of those described by William James in his important book, *The Varieties of Religious Experience* (1902), as the 'twice-born' type of religious believer – those who undergo a sense of striving with sin and guilt until they feel born-again through God's power that comes to them. James distinguished these people from the 'once-born' type of individual who accept religious ideas and grow in them without any marked stage of conversion or transformation.

ONCE-BORN AND TWICE-BORN WORSHIP

Though it would be quite wrong to distinguish between Protestant and Catholic forms of religion on the basis of the twice-born and once-born categories, it would also be wrong to ignore these different styles of religious outlook and attitudes. It would, of course, be easy to find once-born people in Protestant churches and twice-born individuals in Catholic and Orthodox communities. But, even so, the style of all these churches is influenced by their theology, and Catholic and Orthodox theology emphasises the pattern of sacraments through which a person enters the faith and passes through life by means of that scheme of sacraments. History, too, influences theology and worship, and this is certainly the case in this Protestant example of Methodism.

The early Methodist stress on conversion as the foundation for the life of faith comes out in some of the hymns already mentioned. But hymns, as part of worship, form part of a whole which includes prayers, Bible-reading and sermons. Worship for twice-born individuals offers an opportunity to reflect on God's work as they have experienced it in their own lives. Entry into worship involves a reflection on their own past. This framework for life is an important part of worship because individuals are given a sense of place, an awareness of where they fit into the actual history of the world as understood by their religion. And this is done not simply in a rational and logical way, by some sort of a theory of history, but in a much more personal way through their own experience. Music and songs serve as the vehicles for this process of self-understanding. People sing themselves into Christian history and into the meaning of their own lives. The worship of God and a growth in self-understanding furnish two aspects of the total process of the life of faith and the growth of personal identity. One favourite hymn of nineteenth- and early twentieth-century Protestant church groups has the chorus,

> At the cross, at the cross, where I first saw the light,
> And the burden of my heart rolled away;
> It was there by faith I received my sight,
> And now I am happy all the day.

Many hymns of this sort have been used in worship. When their content is scrutinised it is slightly surprising to find that instead of focusing on God and recounting the wonderful nature of the deity, they dwell very largely on human life and the changes that have come about in it. In hymns we see how closely human identity is linked with the worship of God.

Worship is also intimately linked to the worshipping community because it is in and through the group that individuals gain this sense of their own identity and have a chance to reflect upon it. This is especially true of twice-born people. The identity they once possessed in everyday life is now overtaken by the new sense of themselves as God's specially chosen people. In some Protestant churches there are special occasions when people can talk about their religious experiences and develop their knowledge of how God works in individual lives. Early Methodism held 'Experience Meetings' for this very purpose, and many Evangelical groups allow people to 'give their testimonies'. At such meetings people talk about their former life as unforgiven sinners, and about their new life following their conversion. Their sense of gratitude for this change of outlook motivates and influences their worship to a considerable extent. This provision of a context for life and for understanding existence is also true for those who are once-born Christians, but the way their churches explain reality is different.

Religious life and everyday life

The Catholic and Orthodox traditions of Christianity have strong theological explanations for the history of the world and for the place of the church within it. The use of the sacrament of baptism to make people into members, along with the other sacraments – of confirmation, marriage, absolution and last rites – to accompany them throughout life, provides a pattern through which people can gain a view on the world and grow in their appreciation and knowledge of God. These churches also use music in their worship and have done so from the early centuries of Christianity.

In the case of Orthodoxy, only vocal music in the form of chants is used, the music of organs or other accompaniment being avoided. It was decided at the Council of Laodicea (367 CE) that the congregation in general should take no part in the singing of services in order to keep the purity of the music and ritual. Only the clergy, a special singer or cantor, and a choir are allowed to sing. And all services are sung, an important point since Orthodoxy is quite the opposite of Protestant worship where, apart from hymns which are strongly congregational, no part of worship services would be sung. The Anglican and Lutheran traditions stand out in the sense that parts of their liturgies are sung by priest, choir and people.

The growth of chants and hymn-forms of religious poetry from the fourth century into the middle ages was especially important, fostered as it was through Catholic monastic houses, with their set *canonical hours*, forming a regular pattern of daily worship. Prayers, hymns and readings formed the basis of worship which, in the summer months, started at 1am and proceeded through some five services, interspersed with reading and work until bed at about 8pm. This constant round of prayer was an important phase in the history of Christian worship and marks out the belief in the worthwhileness of particular people giving their lives specifically for the service of God through formal religious services of worship, as well as through prayer, study, and sometimes service to the community at large. For practically a thousand years western Christianity gave special emphasis to this form of religious life of monks and nuns, a life-style which exalted celibacy as the ideal way of life for worship.

As we have already mentioned, from about the thirteenth century hymns were introduced in the ordinary language of people, a change that was in marked contrast to the traditional church use of Latin. This shift into the vernacular was to become dramatically important with the Reformation, as monasteries were increasingly abandoned and as the ideal form of Christian life moved from celibacy to marriage. This change is deeply important as far as worship is concerned because the holy is no longer seen as separate and isolated from everyday life. One need not be a monk or nun in order to give God true and full worship. Worship can take place in the ordinary flow of life with its duties and obligations. Such a 'this-worldly' orientation of faith and worship is enshrined in Wesley's hymn:

> Forth in thy name O Lord I go,
> My daily labour to pursue,
> Thee, only Thee, resolved to know,
> In all I think or speak or do.

An even more famous example is given in the hymn by George Herbert (1593–1632):

Teach me, my God and King,
In all things Thee to see;
And what I do in anything,
To do it as for Thee.

Herbert emphasises the spiritual nature of ordinary existence in this verse, arguing that if a believer does something for God's sake, then even,

A servant with this clause makes drudgery divine;
Who sweeps a room, as for Thy laws, makes that and the action fine.

The belief that drudgery may be divine is closely linked with the idea of the Protestant work ethic which reads religious worth into everyday activity and calls people to be good stewards of their daily work because they work to serve God and not to please others. Their very calling as Christians is worked out through everyday work and duties and not only in formal worship of God.

Worship, sacred languages and society

It is no accident that the prayer book of the Church of England after the English Reformation came to be called *The Book of Common Prayer* (1549), for it was the book to be shared in its use by the whole community, minister and people alike. This book, like the service books of the Roman Catholic and Orthodox churches, along with most mainstream Christian denominations, gives a form and pattern for worship. Such books help provide an established pattern of worship over many centuries and over wide geographical areas. In many respects it is just such books that help reinforce the idea that the religious ritual of worship is extremely conservative and changes very little over time. This can be true, but it is also the case that when change comes, as it did in the Roman Catholic Church from the mid-1960s after the important Vatican 2 conferences on religion and the faith, it comes dramatically and rapidly. Instead of the Mass being said in Latin in the great majority of countries of the world it is now said in local languages. In this the Roman Catholic Church was doing what had been done by the Protestant churches at their birth in the Reformation some four hundred years before, namely putting the worship of the congregation into the everyday language of the people.

In terms of the history of Christian worship, the issue of language had been vital from the earliest days of the church. The first followers of Jesus probably worshipped at their local Jewish synagogue using the Aramaic language, while at Jerusalem's Temple Hebrew would have been used and understood only by those specially educated in it. In other parts of the Mediterranean world where Jews lived and worked, they used Greek in their synagogue life. As far as new Christian congregations were concerned, worship followed the local language. In Rome, for example, the liturgy was initially in Greek because Greek was so widely used as a common language by those of the lower social class groups who constituted the largest group from which converts were drawn. This changed as time went on and, by the third century, most Christians spoke Latin and so the liturgy shifted to its Latin base. Later, in the seventh century, Greek came into use again as more Greek-speaking merchants and others came to be in Rome. As time went on Latin returned to become the dominant language used. Latin went on to become the language of the Roman Empire and many would have had some knowledge of it as a popular tongue. But, with the passage of time and the rise of the more modern European languages, Latin became increasingly a language for literature and scholars, leaving the mass of people ignorant of it, and of the liturgy of the church.

This distance between ordinary believers and the form of worship of their Church was dramatically reversed in the Reformation, as we have already indicated. What is interesting is that the Eastern Orthodox churches had their liturgies in local languages from the outset. But languages are dramatically open to change and what is vernacular in one era can easily come to be less than intelligible in another. Some of the churches that originated in the Reformation have liturgies which are some three to four hundred years old and which are not completely intelligible in the present day. Because most contemporary Christians favour worship that is understandable and direct, some churches have sought to modernise their service books. The Church of England is a good example of this, having published the *Alternative Service Book* (1980) to be used alongside or instead of the 1662 *Book of Common Prayer*.

To compare and contrast some passages from these books is to see not only how language has changed but, even more important than this, how social ideas, conventions, and theological outlooks lying behind the text have changed. The place of social influences upon the texts of worship is easily overlooked but remains radically significant.

The 1662 book assumes a form of society with the monarch as its powerful head, followed by layers of people in authority. In the Prayer for the Queen's Majesty in the service of Morning Prayer, God is said to be 'high and mighty, King of kings, Lord of lords, the only Ruler of Princes', who from his throne beholds all the dwellers upon earth. In the service of Holy Communion, there are prayers for the monarch, 'that under her we may be godly and quietly governed', as well as for the monarch's 'whole Council, and all that are put in authority under her, that they may truly and indifferently minister justice to the punishment of wickedness and vice'. The whole service presumes a strongly hierarchical sense of society moving from God through the monarch and those in power down to the humble believer. The theology of the Holy Communion service follows in this line of thought and sees God as the one whose wayward servants have offended against Him. God is the merciful Father who forgives his humble and penitent servants because of the sacrificial death of his dearly beloved Son, Jesus Christ. True worship follows from a restored relationship with the offended God, and from a life of obedient service.

The 1980 book views the world differently. Its Holy Communion service begins by saying 'The Lord is here. His Spirit is with us'. The scene set is of a democratic community of friends rather than a hierarchy of master, monarch and servants. God as Spirit takes precedence over God as mighty ruling Lord. Even the prayer involving the monarch asks that every nation may be directed in the ways of peace that 'men may honour one another, and seek the common good'. Once more equality replaces hierarchy, and salvation involves a strong sense of community membership, and not only the forgiveness of sins. These subtle differences between the two books show how changes in society influence changes in theological expression and, through that, the way worship takes place.

History does not stand still. There are many modern influences at work and not simply those originating hundreds or thousands of years ago. One major new development in church life and worship belonging to the latter part of the twentieth century that has affected

Catholic as well as Protestant and Anglican churches, is that of the Charismatic Movement. Its importance demands special consideration.

Charismatic worship

A major feature of mainstream Orthodox, Catholic, Anglican, and Protestant church worship is a fixed and written liturgy which is followed through in the service conducted by authorised ministers and priests. The sermon and some of the intercessory prayers offer a degree of freedom for leaders to introduce thoughts of their own but, by and large, there is a fixed expectation of what will take place. Worship is organised.

We have already spoken about once-born and twice-born styles of worship, and these remain important for charismatic worship since charismatic activity often takes place within the overall framework of a traditional religious service. This is especially true in Catholic and Anglican traditions.

The Charismatic Movement gets its name from the *charismata*, or gifts of the Spirit, mentioned in the Acts of the Apostles and in the First Letter to the Corinthians. At the beginning of the twentieth century some revivalist churches emerged in the United States of America which stood in the Protestant and Evangelical tradition, stressing the importance of conversion. These Pentecostal churches, as they were called, went further than this, to talk of the need for individuals to have an additional experience of the Holy Spirit, which brought them to a new level of Christian awareness. As their name suggests, these churches focused on the story of the early Christians in the Acts of the Apostles, of a wind coming from God and inspiring the apostles to preach the gospel, and also giving them the ability to 'speak in tongues'. This form of inspired utterance, or *glossolalia*, was regarded as a special sign of the presence and power of the Holy Spirit, and a sure mark that an individual had received an additional blessing or renewal from God.

In the 1960s a very similar kind of religious enthusiasm emerged in the United States of America and quickly spread to Britain and across the world. It, too, emphasised the gifts of the Spirit, especially *glossolalia* or speaking in tongues, seeing that gift as one of a number of signs that an individual had received a renewal of spiritual life. One important feature of this Charismatic or Renewal

Movement, as it was also called, was that those influenced by it tended to remain within their original denomination or church rather than come out to create new churches. At least this was the case for much of the 1960s and 1970s, with the result that many congregations of the main Christian churches came to have Charismatic members. A relatively small but significant number of clergy, Protestant and Catholic, were also influenced, and experienced a revitalisation of their spiritual lives. This led to some churches having services which included periods of charismatic worship set amidst the traditional liturgy. Some also added new 'Praise' services to their list of ordinary events.

The word 'Praise' came into its own as a description of charismatic worship, when individuals might lift their arms up into the air while singing or as an expression of adoration of God. Some would speak in tongues or even sing in tongues as the whole group stood and swayed to the music. As with many periods of religious enthusiasm and creativity, the Charismatic Movement gave birth to hundreds of new hymns, to much new music, and to a distinctive ethos or mood of spirituality. This is typified by a sense of the immediate nearness and power of God through the Holy Spirit. Anything might happen, and God might decide to say something to a group through someone speaking in tongues or, perhaps, through a revelation. The centre of gravity of worship was in the present. The meaning of life was immediately available. A sense of expectation in worship was connected with gifts of healing that many believed to be given to the church by God.

Many of the new hymns expressed these thoughts. One called, 'For I'm building a people of power', is interesting in that it begins in the first person singular, as though Jesus was giving a direct message through a prophetic utterance:

> For I'm building a people of power,
> And I'm making a people of praise,
> That will move through this land by My Spirit,
> And will glorify My precious Name.

(Dave Richards, 1977)

The second verse then gives the response of believers to this message as they say: 'Build Your Church Lord, Make us strong Lord', and they go on to ask the Lord to join their hearts in one and give them unity in Christ's Kingdom.

Another dimension to this excitement in divine activity was a belief, held by some charismatically inclined Christians, that evil spirits were also active in the world and might even possess people. In some churches, ministers and priests conducted exorcisms to expel spirits from individual lives. Another hymn echoes this aspect of religion:

> For this purpose Christ was revealed,
> To destroy all the works of the Evil One.

The hymn then divides with lines for men and women to sing separately before they reunite to say that in the name of Jesus they stand and claim victory because

> Satan has no authority here,
> Powers of Darkness must flee,
> For Christ has the victory.
>
> (Graham Kendrick, 1985)

A feature of many charismatic hymns, as in the hymns of the Pentecostal Churches of the earlier twentieth century, is a repetitive chorus sung after each main verse. This is characteristic of songs in religious groups where the democratic unity of all members is stressed. So it was that worship of God came to embrace a wide variety of intense experiences and beliefs.

While many Charismatics remained in the mainstream churches, others left to found House Churches, making the House Church Movement a significant point of religious growth in later twentieth-century Britain. These also developed patterns of emotional worship of a charismatic type, and often used buildings of a non-traditional church-style for their meetings. By using, for example, a redundant cinema as a church, such a group expresses its belief that true worship of God does not require architecture or symbolism of a traditional Christian kind. Sincerity of faith is what matters for true worship to be given to God, and not any particular sacred place.

Adaptability of hymns in worship

Hymns are very often taken for granted in most branches of contemporary Christianity, a familiarity which ignores the incredible power hymns have wielded in fostering new and distinctive forms of Christianity. Once hymns became established in eighteenth-century Protestant religion as a means of expressing doctrine and religious experience, they opened up new possibilities for new religious movements. New content could easily be put into the traditional form of a hymn, or new words could be sung to a familiar tune.

The Salvation Army (initially founded in 1865 on the model of an army whose task was actively to convert people to Christianity) established brass bands, rather like military bands, to accompany singing in public places. The founder, 'General' William Booth, encouraged hymn-singing to well-known and popular music on the basis that 'the Devil should not have all the best tunes'. In terms of Christian worship, the Salvation Army is one of the best examples of Christians expanding the meaning of worship to include service to the community. Uniform-wearing members put their faith into action by helping the poor, deprived and distressed in society through active social welfare programmes. In their Citadels, services are held on different occasions for those who are actively committed members of the Army and for members of the general public. Unlike practically all other churches within the Christian tradition, the Salvation Army do not hold services of Holy Communion. Singing, Bible-reading, prayers, sermons and the giving of personal testimony to the work of God in their personal lives, form the basis for services of worship.

If popular tunes helped people think about the Christian message, as with the Salvation Army, so it is very likely that patterns of worship based on hymn-singing, Bible-reading and prayers helped others already familiar with one church to move to others. Familiar patterns of behaviour ease the passage of converts as they leave their former religious base and become members in new churches. Many groups, including Christian Science, Jehovah's Witnesses, Seventh Day Adventists and Mormons, all used hymns as part of their own religious worship.

Sacred places and religious habit

We have already mentioned the tension in Christianity between those who value special places for worship and those who do not. The weight of emphasis has, historically, always fallen on the need for religious buildings, precisely because Christianity is a group-focused and congregationally based religion. Sooner or later a group of Christians requires somewhere to meet. Many new groupings of believers would like to keep their faith free from the impediments of buildings and materialistic concerns. It is often argued that people become too attached to particular places of worship and value the place more than the purpose for which it exists.

In practice, worship is a habit-forming activity. From its earliest days Christianity has been organised for frequent worship, often of groups of people meeting together. Such regularity fosters commitment to a particular place. When people have particular experiences in particular places they associate the one with the other, and over time they can come to be firmly wedded together. Someone may worship in the same church building for many years and may even sit in the same seat. In many traditional societies, where relatively few left their home village or town to live and work elsewhere, many of their memories would be associated with the church building. Moments of joy and moments of sorrow would be connected with that one building. From the theological stand-point of ministers or priests, this situation can easily be interpreted as unfortunate or childish, especially if they have had the wider experience of worshipping in many different places and living in many towns. But the fixed residence of long-term inhabitants gives them their own sense of continuity and habit.

Some sacred places, whether actual buildings like cathedrals, or places of pilgrimage such as Rome or Jerusalem, develop their significance over thousands of years. The habit of many generations is the framework for each new pilgrim or visitor. Some people speak of the 'atmosphere' of some sacred places as positive and beneficial to their own prayers and worship. While it is difficult to describe exactly what is meant by an atmosphere of worship, it marks the readiness of people to pray and worship within a particular church or place. Readiness for worship is probably associated with the traditional triggers for prayer in a culture, not least a certain organisation of space, light, smell and sound.

Cues for worship

Human beings have probably engaged in worship for as long as archaeological evidence is available, and it is certainly the case that all known religions (including folk-Buddhism) contain some aspect of worship directed to their supreme focus. In terms of Christian theology, this is explained as the human awareness of creatureliness. In broader terms, it probably involves the human drive for meaning in the face of a universe and a life that is both beautiful and terrifying. Reason takes us into the world of theology, philosophy and science where arguments help explain the universe and the place of people within it, but such rational explanations often seem to leave the emotional depths of life untouched.

In Christianity these two dimensions of reason and emotion come together in the worshipping life of the church. In worship, Christians do not simply think about the meaning of life, they also respond to the meaning of life. Through theology they learn that God is both the creator of all things and also the one who undertakes to love humankind and to bring meaning to the relationships in which people live. Through worship these ideas are not merely entertained as thoughts but are expressed as worship.

Worship: its nature and dynamics

So, theologically speaking, worship is a response. People worship because they are aware of something. In Christianity this is an awareness of God's self-revelation in creation, in redemption through Jesus, in the life of the Church, and in personal experience. Worship is the grateful response for these loving acts of God, the response of the creature and of the redeemed servant. The important nineteenth-century Danish theologian, Soren Kierkegaard, spoke about the 'first wonder' that humans encountered through nature, a wonder that was lost in despair, and that can come to be replaced by a 'second wonder', or consciousness of God, as the individual is confronted by God in realising the nature of sin and of faith. This is a clear example in the Christian tradition of the double knowledge of God in creation and salvation, and of the two sources of worshipping response.

THE MEANING OF WORSHIP

A further understanding of worship as a human activity can be gained by shifting from a theological to a more sociological outlook, focusing on questions of meaning and identity already hinted at. In terms of meaning, worship is an expression of satisfaction at having discovered truth; it involves commitment to the explanation of life furnished by a particular religion. Knowledge of a religion does not simply involve philosophical, historical and textual study gained in an academic way; there is also a kind of knowing that comes from active participation in the life of a worshipping church community. Such worship can provide a context where other forms of reflection gain a greater significance.

IDENTITY AND WORSHIP

Closely aligned with the meaning gained in worship is the sense of identity that worship helps individuals to gain for themselves. Identity is a complex idea but it refers to those things that give individuals a sense of their past, of who they are and of where they belong in life. It includes the language people speak, the history they share with others, the land where they belong, the kind of music, dance and social occasions that they enjoy. But identity also comes from a particular way of understanding and responding to God. At the community level of particular regions or countries, shared worship can help bind people together into a unified group, but it can also help keep people apart from others whose way of worship, even within the overall world of Christianity, is different from their own. So at the human level of relationships, worship can serve as the focus for wider religious differences that divide people.

One of the sharpest examples of this is the Eucharist itself, since it is a major division between Roman Catholics, Greek Orthodox, Anglicans and other Protestants. This service and its theology, along with those authorised to conduct it, enshrines the history of debate between these churches and ensures that historical differences are perpetuated. Many Christians see this as shameful, since worship should unite believers and not divide them, and since worship is a form of relationship between the human and the divine which belongs to the essential nature of life. This relationship can be perverted if something or someone replaces God as the very centre of adoration, for then worship becomes idolatry. But in the proper ordering of human life, the setting of worship is a powerful context for learning about God, both through acts of worship and also through sermons or other forms of instruction.

Channels of worship

Worship flows through several channels. Traditionally the emphasis is placed upon the church or sacred building, but many Christians engage in private prayer in any setting. When praying, individuals explicitly set themselves in relationship to God in several ways. Very often human language is used as the basic means of addressing God. This can be a formal or a less formal style of language, it may be spoken, intoned, or sung, conducted jointly with others in common prayer or else be private. The substance of prayer may be adoration of God, but may also involve confession of sin, or petition for something that is desired by the worshipper.

In terms of posture, there is great variation both among and within traditions. Some stand to pray, others kneel or sit, while at the Catholic Ordination service the new priests lie full length upon the ground in prostration before God. Eyes may be closed, when there is an inner focus on God's presence, while eyes may be left open if an icon or statue or other form of religious art is part of the total process. Human hands also play a vital part in worship since they may be placed together, making the body symmetrical and balanced, or one hand may be used to make the sign of the cross as believers identify themselves with the cross of Christ, and increasingly, the return of the dance to Christian worship involves the whole body.

The history of western culture is full of sacred music, largely as the vehicle of the Eucharist and its worship, but also in oratorios such as Handel's 'Messiah', where biblical words have been set to music to tell the story of salvation or of some detailed biblical period. At a more general social level, bells have played an important part in making public 'noises', signalling the worship of God.

But worship can take place in silence, and some traditions of Christianity have favoured silence, even for the congregational gathering of believers, as the context in which to wait for God to encounter them. The Society of Friends, started by George Fox (1624–91), believed in the 'Inner Light', which involved a prompting of the Holy Spirit in worship. Their alternative name, the Quakers, indicates another aspect of their religious life in which they trembled or shook as a result of divine influence. Movement as a form of worship was characteristic of the Shakers, who developed in Manchester in the mid-eighteenth century under the influence of some French Protestant refugees called Camisards. After some Shakers emigrated to America, their number grew as they formed and lived in communities. In the nineteenth century they developed complex group dancing as a form of worship. In quite a different religious climate some present day Christians in the mainline denominations have explored liturgical dance as one form of worship. This, along with all the other patterns of worship we have sketched, shows how varied worship can be as different sorts of people at varied times and places respond to the mystery and revelation of God and, in some measure, share in it.

FURTHER READING

Davies, J.G. (ed.) (1986) *A New Dictionary of Liturgy and Worship*, London, SCM Press.

Dix, Gregory (1945) *The Shape of the Liturgy*, London, Dacre Press.

James, William (1902) *The Varieties of Religious Experience*, London, Longman.

LeFevre, Perry D. (1956) *The Prayers of Kierkegaard*, Chicago, University of Chicago Press.

Martin, D. and Mullen, P. (eds) (1984) *Strange Gifts*, Oxford, Blackwell.

Otto, Rudolph (1924) *The Idea of the Holy*, Oxford, Oxford University Press.

Turner, Victor (1982) *From Ritual to Theatre*, New York, PAJ Publications.

3. Hinduism

Anuradha Roma Choudhury

The concept of worship in Hinduism is as varied as the many facets of the religion itself. Hinduism cannot even be called a religion in the formal Western sense. It does not have any one founder and does not have any one Holy Book of instructions. It grew gradually over a period of about five thousand years absorbing and assimilating all the religious, philosophical, ethical and cultural movements of India. Consequently, there is no one ideal of worship. Different schools of philosophical thought prescribe different forms of rituals or no rituals at all. People belonging to different strata of society also interpret worship in different ways. There is no one term for worship in Hinduism. It can be *yajña, homa, upāsanā, sādhanā, bhajanā, archanā, ārādhanā*, etc. The closest general term for worship, as understood in the West, would be *pūjā*. Then again, *pūjā* can mean more than just ritual worship. It means adoration, honour, respect, devotion, obeisance and much more. *Pūjā* actually means honour in expressions like *vidvān sarvatra pūjyate* (a learned man is worshipped everywhere) (*Chānakyanīti* VIII, 20). To a Hindu child, his or her parents are *pūjanīya* (to be respected). It can also mean dedication. Artists or musicians in India often say that pursuing art or music is their life-long *pūjā* to achieve the desired goal.

However, dealing primarily with ritual worship, one has to go back to the earliest period of vedic worship. The world's earliest surviving literature, the Veda[1] (*c.* 1500 BCE), contain hymns praising the all-powerful gods who, more often than not, are the personified elements of nature. The vedic priests around a sacrificial fire chanted hymns with precise intonations. Offerings of milk, clarified butter (*ghṛta*) and *soma-rasa* (an intoxicating drink made from Soma plant) were offered to the friendly god, Agni (fire). Through Agni, the intermediary, gods received the gifts offered by the humans and bestowed blessings on them in return. The objectives of worship in the vedic period were either to appease the wrath of the fearsome gods, the giant forces of nature generating awe and bewilderment in primitive people (e.g., lightning, thunderstorm), or to please the benevolent gods (e.g., rain, fire) for favours of wealth in the form of crops, cattle and children.

The sacrificial worship of the vedic period is known as the *yajña*[2]. Of the four Vedas, the *Yajur-veda* deals specifically with the ritualistic formulae of the *yajñas*. It describes in prose the procedural details of the actual performance of various *yajña*s. Both the words *yajus(r)* and *yajña* are derived from the same root, '*yaj*', which means 'to worship'. The purpose of the *Yajur-veda* is to give the hymns of the preceding *Ṛg-veda* an applied form in ritual worship.

The ideology behind the sacrificial worship probably owes its origin to the *Puruṣa Sūkta* (the Hymn of Man) of the *Ṛg-veda*, describing the great sacrifice of the primal man (*puruṣa*) at the beginning of time. As the universe emerged from an enormous sacrifice, constant repetitions of that original sacrifice seemed necessary to maintain the universe in good working order. The rituals performed by high caste Aryans in the remote Indo-European past are still performed by some orthodox *Brāhmaṇa* families. The purpose of the *yajña*s, however, has changed with time. They began as methods of pleasing gods with offerings of obedience and allegiance to them, but gradually came to be looked upon as ways of practising renunciation and penance.

In the course of time the sacrificial worship of the vedic Aryans was replaced by *pūjā*, worship of the deities or gods with images. The scene of worship changed from the sacrificial ground to the places of pilgrimage and ritual bathing. 'Instead of altars there grew up temples with their special deities' (Sen 1973: 58). It is plausible that in a varied country like India, diverse races and tribes with different ways and objects of worship contributed to the evolution of formalised worship. Some Hindus still worship rivers, specific trees and animals.

The *bhakti* (devotion) cult that grew up with image-worship had its roots in southern India, known as Dravidian country, and points to a non-Aryan origin. As the early vedic sacrificial worship gradually blended in with the non-Aryan ways of worship, each of these cults found a place in Hinduism and influenced it from within. In the transition, even the all-powerful vedic gods were either diminished in stature in competition with the non-Aryan gods or were amalgamated with some of them. For example, the most powerful vedic god Indra lost his importance in later Hinduism and the vedic storm-god Rudra became identified with the non-Aryan Śiva, the god of destruction.

Image-worship

In vedic worship, though many gods were accepted, there was no reference to idols or images. The fact that the Indus Valley civilisation (*c.* 2000 BCE) had many images shows that image-worship may have existed in India before the Aryan invasion and thus may be a non-Aryan contribution to present day Hinduism.

Image-worship (*mūrti-pūjā*) is not idolatry. Hindus do not believe that the image itself is Viṣṇu or Śiva, but accept it merely as a symbol of the deity. They pray not to the image, but to the deity personified by the image. Though Hindus believe in one formless Absolute God (*Brahman*), their prayers are strengthened if there is a tangible object of devotion in front of them. The difficulty of comprehending an abstract Absolute entity as God necessitates a symbolic representation in a concrete form, a *mūrti* (literally, 'crystallisation'), so that the mind can concentrate upon it. A simple stone may serve the purpose just as well as an elaborately sculptured statue with all the specific features prescribed by the Hindu manuals (*śāstras*) on sculpture.

Symbolism

Hindus who worship a simple stone or a particular plant are venerating something greater, beyond that stone or plant. The stone is often kept in a little shrine, washed, smeared with sandal-wood paste and decorated with flowers. Hindus know that the stone itself is not God but is the symbol of God at that moment. It may not be so to others, but to them that does not matter.

The logic of Hindu thinking is as follows. If one really has faith in God being omnipresent, one has to believe that God can be found in anything and everything. Then, all one needs to do is to focus God in *a* thing, be it a stone, a flower or something else. When the scriptures say 'God is omnipresent, omnipotent and omniscient', it sounds so vague and abstract that most people dare not even try to comprehend God. It is too general and too impersonal a statement. But when one focuses, say, on a flower, mentally imposing God on to it, it is possible to meditate on a God who is close at hand, at that instant. Neither the colour of the flower, nor the number of its petals is in focus at that moment, but God is. This simple act makes concentration much easier and meditation more intense. Thus, to a Hindu, anything at all can be an object of meditation once it is chosen as a symbol of God.

However, mention must be made here of a particular symbolic object of worship that is greatly revered by the Hindus. It is the emblem of Śiva in the *liṅga* (phallus) form that symbolises his vast generative energy. A *Śiva-liṅga*, often made of stone, is complete with the phallus standing on a platform representing the *yoni* (vulva) of his consort Śakti. The generative process in nature through the union of male and female, *puruṣa* and *prakṛti*, passive and dynamic, and negative and positive forces, is recognised and worshipped by the Hindus in a *Śiva-liṅga* form. Though it is often described in the West as a primitive fertility symbol and thereby given a sexual connotation, to the majority of the Śiva devotees in India it does not imply any erotic element in his rites. As pointed out by Cavendish (1980: 24), 'the symbol has been a conventional image of the god for so long that most of his devotees do not realise that it has any sexual significance'. In this context one should remember that in Hinduism the conjugal sex-act is venerated as the essential and continuing process of procreation in nature and therefore there is no concept of 'original sin'. Most male deities are balanced by their female counterparts and accordingly worshipped together, and often their offsprings are included as well; for example, Viṣṇu with Lakṣmī, Śiva with Pārvatī/Durgā and their two sons, Kārtikeya and Gaṇeśa.

Another form of symbolism existing in objects of worship is noticed in the physical features of the images of deities. Multiple limbs of the images and a third eye are often added to signify the multifarious as well as super-human attributes of deities. Individual deities have their own characteristic features. For example, Viṣṇu has four arms with hands holding separate implements, each of which represents an activity or aspect of Viṣṇu's identity. Similarly, the ten arms of Durgā, the Mother figure of the Hindu pantheon, and the divine weapons they carry, represent her power of destroying all evils and of protecting the creation. Her third eye represents the all-seeing aspect of the divinity (*divya-dṛṣṭi*).

Apart from the objects of worship there are several other spheres of Hindu meditative activities where symbolism plays an important role.

MANTRA

A *mantra* in Hindu worship may be a short phrase, or a word, or even a sound-syllable, that is uttered repeatedly in meditation to make concentration fixed. It is an aid for the human mind (which is incessantly rushing from one thought to another) to cut out superfluous thoughts and concentrate on one preferred thought. What the symbolic object of worship does for one tangibly, the *mantra* does audibly. *Mantra*s have their specific sound values and sound effects. The correct pronunciation is all-important. In the practice of vedic *mantra*s, it is said, the vibration generated by correct intonation is beneficial not only to the reciter but also to the listeners. Therefore *mantra*s are to be chanted audibly. The pitch, the tonal quality and the length of the sounds are of crucial significance. If a *mantra* were not uttered accurately, it would prove ineffectual and would do more harm than good. That is why it is not considered right to read *mantra*s from the written script (*likhita-pāṭhaka*). A *mantra* should be learnt by ear from the oral chanting of a teacher (*guru*) and then be memorised in the proper manner. To achieve this, one has to have initiation (*dīkṣā*) from a *guru* who is experienced enough to prescribe the appropriate *mantra*, judging the recipient's temperament and spiritual capabilities. Thus, a *mantra* is often considered to be so sacred and personalised a code that it is to be cherished or guarded with secrecy, otherwise it may lose its potency.

Though there are different *mantra*s prescribed by *guru*s for individuals of different mental make-up, there is one *mantra* that all Hindus hold in great reverence. That is 'OM' or 'AUM', known as *Oṁkāra* or *Praṇava*. The *Oṁkāra* is considered to be the seed or essence of the cosmic sound that pervades the whole universe. In the *Upaniṣad*s there are expressions like *Nāda-Brahma* and *Śabdam Brahma*, which show that sound (*nāda/śabda*) is elevated to the level of *Brahman* itself (cf., 'The Word was God' – the Bible, John 1, 1).

'OM', being the symbolic sacred sound, is always uttered at the beginning and at the end of all Hindu religious readings and rituals.

The term *mantra* literally means 'that which liberates oneself by focusing one's mind on it' (*mananāt trāyate iti mantraḥ*). In that sense a particular *mantra* called *Gāyatrī (Ṛg-veda* III 62; 10) is considered by the Hindus as the most liberating of all. It is the most renowned prayer of all the Vedas. The *Gāyatrī* is a *mantra* that glorifies the Sun (*Savitrī*), symbolising the power of light that illumines the earth, the sky and the heaven, and that seeks illumination of the human mind with higher intelligence (*dhī*), i.e., spiritual enlightenment. It is recited daily at sunrise and sunset, usually at the time of the ritual bath. In other scriptures *Gāyatrī* is held in high esteem, as *Manu* declares (*Manu-saṁhitā* II 102) that the chanting of *Gāyatrī* at dawn dispels the guilt of the previous night, and the evening chant destroys the sins committed during the day, thus emphasising the purifying power of the *mantra* itself.

YANTRA

A *yantra* can be described as a symbolic pattern which helps a meditative worshipper to concentrate on the object of worship. *Mantra* and *yantra* complement each other and are used in conjunction in an act of worship. Just as *mantra* is an aid to concentration in sound-form, so is *yantra* an aid in visual form.

'A *yantra* is very often referred to as an energy pattern or a power-diagram' (Mookerjee 1977: 54). It is a pure geometric formation without any iconographic representation. Often these geometric patterns are centred on a single point, upon which meditative concentration is to be fixed. During meditation, by visualising a chosen geometric figure, one can overcome all surfacing superfluous thoughts and be in control of the psyche. Like the sound-element of a *mantra*, the 'patternness' (Rawson 1988: 64) of a *yantra* is vital for its meditative force. The artistic *yantra*s are often made with coloured powders sprinkled on the floor in front of the image of the deity to be worshipped. However, *yantra*s can be made of many different materials such as stone, rock-crystal, etc. The ground plans of most Hindu temples are themselves *yantra*s. The *yantra*s play a very important role in the *Tantra*[3] tradition.

YOGA

As *mantra* channels one's mind by controlling the psyche, *yoga* disciplines the body to be in tune with the mind. Body and mind work together to achieve a unified goal by being complementary to each other. The term *yoga* means 'union', signifying the union of body and mind; and at a higher level it connotes the union of the individual soul with the Universal or Absolute Soul. *Yoga* can have several meanings, depending upon the context. It has the same connotation as 'yoke' in English, meaning togetherness. In mathematical terms *yoga* means the sum of addition.

Concentration is needed to achieve anything, and to master concentration, a Hindu thinks; physical and mental controls have to work together. The yogic exercises, well known in the West now, are not an end in themselves but a means to an end: the achievement of a healthy, responsive body attuned to a steady determined mind. For a Hindu, *yoga* is not important merely as a physical technique for body-building, but for the state of consciousness it generates during the exercises. A true *yogī* is not only a healthier but also a more composed person.

In the context of worship, yogic postures play an important role. The most well-known posture, *padmāsana* (the lotus position), sitting cross-legged on a flat floor with erect spine, helps the worshipper to have a steady supportive body to uphold the meditative mind. Indian sculpture is full of figurines of *yogī*s and of the Buddha in meditative *padmāsana* postures. In tantric worship, yogic postures play a vital role. Specific postures have specific significance and experiences, and one has to follow the steps with the strictest accuracy. According to *Tantra*, the human body has six psychic centres (*chakra*s) along its spine. Through the correct practice (*sādhanā*) of *yoga*, the *chakra*s open one by one, leading to the progressive arousal of dormant energy (called *kuṇḍalinī*) from the lowest physical level to the highest psychic plane.

Various modes of worship

Hindus in general do not distinguish between religion and philosophy. To them the two are overlapping, if not synonymous. That is why worship, which is solely a part of religion in other traditions, is a many-faceted feature in Hinduism, where it changes its modes in accordance with each individual philosophy. The ultimate goal of each mode of worship (*sādhanā*) is to achieve enlightenment or liberation (*mukti/mokṣa*[4]).

Ritual worship is not the only form of worship in Hinduism, and may not suit everybody. As Hinduism does not recognise any single way of reaching God, the concept of religious worship may vary from person to person or sect to sect, and with it vary the details of religious assumptions. 'One may try to reach God through work (*karma*), or meditation and knowledge (*jñāna*), or simply through devotion (*bhakti*). All are equally valid' (Sen 1973: 39). In *Bhagavadgītā* (one of the most well-known Hindu scriptures) Kṛṣṇa, the God incarnate, declares: 'In whatever way men worship Me, in the same way do I fulfil their desires; it is My path men tread, in all ways' (IV, 11). The different ways people view God, some even apparently conflicting, show the infinite aspects of the same Supreme. One individual's level of understanding may be different from that of another, and Hinduism gives every individual the freedom to choose his or her own way of worship. Swami Vivekananda (1963: 76/78) explains:

> A religion, to satisfy the largest proportion of mankind, must be able to supply food for all these various types of minds . . . And this religion is attained by what we, in India, call *Yoga* – union. To the worker, it is union between men and the whole of humanity; to the mystic, between his Lower and Higher Self; to the lover, union between himself and the God of love; and to the philosopher, it is the union of *all* existence.

A person who follows any of these ways of union (*yoga*) is called a *yogī*. A *karma-yogī* worships through his work, a *rāja-yogī* through power of mind, a *bhakti-yogī* through love and devotion, and a *jñāna-yogī* through knowledge and intellect.

KARMA-YOGA: THE PATH OF ENLIGHTENMENT THROUGH WORK

In a society, there are always people whose minds do not dwell on thoughts alone but find a way of consolidating their thoughts with tangible work. *Karma-yoga* explains why such a person should work for work's sake, without attachment or caring for rewards.

Attachment breeds expectation, expectation brings disappointment and disappointment causes pain. If one works because one likes to work and does not care for anything in return, then one can avoid the chain of disappointment and misery. In *Bhagavadgītā* (II, 47) Kṛṣṇa advises an undecided Arjuna to follow the path of action (*karma*): 'Thy right is to work only; but never to the fruits thereof. Be thou not the producer of the fruits of (thy) actions; neither let thy attachment be towards inaction' (Swarupananda 1982: 57).

RĀJA-YOGA: THE PATH OF ENLIGHTENMENT THROUGH CONTROL OF THE MIND

This is the psychological way of enlightenment. Concentration is the keyword in *rāja-yoga*. But proper concentration is very hard to achieve. As soon as one tries to calm oneself and concentrate upon an object of knowledge, thousands of distracting thoughts rush into one's mind. *Rāja-yoga* teaches one how to overcome the limitations of the mind with a firm and steady concentration. As this is the basic requirement of all branches of yoga, *rāja-yoga* is called the king (*rāja*) among the *yoga*s.

BHAKTI-YOGA: THE PATH OF UNION WITH A PERSONAL GOD THROUGH DEVOTION OR LOVE

This path of *yoga* is for people of an emotional nature who find image-worship satisfying. They 'do not care for abstract definitions of the truth. God to them is something tangible, the only thing that is real; . . . *Bhakti-Yoga* teaches them how to love, without any ulterior motives, loving God and loving the good because it is good to do so.' (Swami Vivekananda 1963: 85). Their love of God at times culminates in exuberance of all kinds such as elaborate rituals, decorations, beautiful buildings and so on.

The *bhakti-yogīs* have a very rich tradition of mythology, poetry, songs and ballads. Group singing of devotional songs (*kīrtana*s or *bhajana*s) is an important part of their worship of the loving God. In a singing session, tears of overwhelming emotion are a common sight in a gathering of the *bhakta*s (devotees). The saint poets such as Jayadeva, Mira, Ramaprasada, whose devotional songs win the hearts of millions of Hindus, have been venerated through the ages as great *bhaktas*. Ramakrishna Paramahamsa, the unassuming saint of the last century, was a *bhakta* of Kālī. The Hare-Krishna cult, well known in the West, is an offshoot of the *bhakti* movement, and members of the group are *bhaktas* of Hari and Kṛṣṇa. In a gathering of *bhaktas* it is not uncommon to hear a devotee sing in praise of Śiva while celebrating the birth of Kṛṣṇa or Rāma (both are incarnations of Viṣṇu), and devotees of Kālī join in with the singing. This is because *bhakti* overcomes all barriers, whether intellectual or sectarian.

JÑĀNA-YOGA: THE PATH OF ENLIGHTENMENT THROUGH KNOWLEDGE OR INTELLECTUAL PURSUIT

This is the path for the philosophers and thinkers, who never accept faith or belief as a substitute for their personal realisation of the highest truth. Daily routine of rituals is not for them, nor is devotional singing. Reasoning and logic are their search-lights. Their intellect wants to unravel the mysteries of existence and experience the Truth and eventually become one with the Universal Being (*Brahman*). The quest is for the realisation of the inner self (*ātman*) and for identifying it with the Universal Self (*paramātman*). The ultimate in this form of worship leads to *sannyāsa* (renunciation of the world). The person, a *sannyāsī* or ascetic, is lost to society at large. Certain sects of ascetics aspire to achieve spiritual height by ignoring physical comfort or even torturing the body in different strenuous ways.

None of these four modes of worship (*sādhanā*) is considered less important than the others. Different ways are right for individuals with different propensities and levels of spiritual capability. The variation in spiritual levels in people is taken into consideration when Kṛṣṇa advises Arjuna, his disciple, on how to worship ideally (*Bhagavadgītā* XII, 8–11):

> Fix your mind on Me only, place your intellect in Me, [then] you shall no doubt live in Me hereafter.
>
> If you are unable to fix your mind steadily on Me, then by *abhyāsa-*

yoga [repetitive practice of withdrawing the mind from material objects] do seek to reach Me.

If you are unable to practise *abhyāsa* even, be intent on doing actions for Me. Even by doing actions for My sake, you shall attain perfection.

If you are unable to do even this, then taking refuge in Me, abandon the fruit of all action.

The above quotation shows that there are gradations in the modes of worship. The discipline of the rituals is very important at the beginning to bring one's mind homeward, as it were, from the rushing world's material affairs. One engaged in mere rituals, even without knowing the significance of it all, will gradually calm down through the sheer regularity of performing the rituals. This will set the scene for religious thoughts. One day this person may not need the aid of rituals any more and may become a *jñāna-yogī.* In this way an earlier step lays the foundation for the next step. Each stage or way of worship is valid for the person who finds it worth pursuing. The most important common element in all, however, is sincerity (*śraddhā*). In *Bhagavadgītā* (VII, 21 and XII, 2) Kṛṣṇa states:

> Whatsoever form any devotee seeks to worship with *Śraddhā* – that *Śraddhā* of his do I make unwavering. . . . Those who, fixing their mind on Me, worship Me, ever-steadfast, and endowed with supreme *Śraddhā*, they in My opinion are the best versed in Yoga. (Swarupananda 1982: 174 and 277)

Relationship of the worshipper with the worshipped

The concept of an Absolute Creative Source from which the whole creation materialised is the basis of Hindu theology. This Absolute entity, called *Brahman*, cannot be described, is beyond all attributes (*guṇātīta*), does not have shape or form (*nirākāra*) and does not have a gender (*liṅgātīta*). *Brahman* can be expressed by negation only (i.e., what it is not). The *Upaniṣads*, the *Bhagavadgītā* and other scriptures have tried in various ways to establish a relationship of this unknowable (*ajñeya) Brahman* with the creation at large: it is the Supreme Soul (*paramātmā*) from which the individual souls of all creatures (*jīvātmā*) come, and which they are absorbed into. To achieve spiritual liberation (*mokṣa*) one has to realise the identity of one's individual soul with the Universal *Brahman*, and so on. Yet the concept of *Brahman* is too abstract and too impersonal for ordinary people to comprehend. Only a *jñāna-yogī* (see above p. 72) can endeavour to achieve such a height and declare 'I am He' (*so'ham*) or announce 'You are That' (*tat tvamasi*). For others, a more personal, a more intimate God is needed, a God whom one can pray to and look up to in moments of need or grief, whom one can thank when something good happens, who looks after one's personal well-being. The majority of Hindus are familiar with this concept of a personal God. One's personal God can be male or female: *Īśvara* or *Bhagavān* is prayed to as a father figure, and *Īśvarī* or *Bhagavatī* as the mother.

Though the father-figure portraiture is quite common, to most Hindus the ideal of a protective mother is very close to their heart. The powerful Mother-cult (worshipping of Śakti/Kālī/Durgā as a mother) seems to be a non-Aryan contribution to Hinduism as there is no prominent mother-figure in vedic literature.

God is worshipped not only as a parent but in all sorts of human relationships. The various deities worshipped by individuals represent various relations. Kṛṣṇa (a male deity), the God of love, is never worshipped as a father but as a friend (*sakhā/bandhu*) or a lover (*priya*) or even as a child (*bāla*). Arjuna addresses him (in the *Bhagavadgītā*) as a friend, Mira (a sixteenth-century saint), and most female devotees consider him as a lover, and some even choose to worship him as a child (*bāla-Kṛṣṇa*). Durgā, though primarily worshipped as a protective mother inspiring reverence, is also looked upon as a daughter evoking affection in the minds of the devotees. This is particularly true in Bengal, the eastern region where *Durgā-pūjā* is the most important religious festival. The four-day festival is like the long-awaited annual home-coming of a married daughter. Thus, in Hinduism all human feelings, emotions and relations are established with deities, not just reverence and obeisance.

Choice of deities

Since Hindus believe that the various deities are merely various aspects of the one and only God, individuals have the freedom to choose their own deity to suit their individual need for a personal God. In spite of the fact that there are many distinct deities, at a given moment any of them can be worshipped as though he or she were the supreme deity, encompassing the attributes of all the rest. That is why, in a Hindu family, it is possible to find a mother worshipping child-Kṛṣṇa, a father Śiva, a son Kālī and a daughter Lakṣmī, with the images of all these deities placed in the same family shrine side by side without provoking rivalry. However, more often than not, children follow the family tradition and get used to the discipline of worshipping the deity of their parents' choice.

In some cases unification of deities is conceived, as in *Trimūrti*[5] (i.e., Brahmā, Viṣṇu and Śiva). (Some families keep pictures of the Buddha and of Christ beside those of their family deities, where photographs of the family *guru* or priest and of the departed members of the family are also seen.)

Traditionally, a Hindu worships three types of deities: a personally chosen deity (*iṣṭa-devatā*), the family deity (*kula-devatā*), and the local/village deity (*grāma-devatā*); each may differ from the other. The chosen deity is worshipped in a private, meditative way. The family deity, placed in a niche or on a table, is worshipped daily with simple rituals. The local deity is regularly worshipped by a priest in the local temple. A pious Hindu may visit the temple daily, periodically or occasionally. The local deity is often a regional choice. Considering the vastness of India, one realises why the choice of deities varies not only among families in a region but also between regions. In eastern India Kālī is a popular deity, in the south Śiva and Gaṇeśa/Gaṇapati, in the north Viṣṇu, and so on. In spite of this regionality, sects and sub-sects of Śaivas, Vaiṣṇavas and Śāktas (devotees of Śiva, Viṣṇu and Śakti/Kālī/Durgā respectively) are distributed all over India. Yet, it can honestly be said that, in a Vaiṣṇava ceremony, a devotional song about Śiva can be sung by a Śākta devotee and none of the attendants would find it strange. The Hindus see no contradiction in such complete tolerance because they believe that each group is praying to the same one and only Universal Spirit who is beyond all sectarian claims.

Codes of conduct associated with ritual worship: *Vidhi* (dos) and *Niṣedha* (don'ts)

In popular Hinduism there are a number of observances and avoidances concerning ritual worship. Bathing and fasting before and during worship, breaking fast with only *prasāda* (consecrated food), avoiding shoes (particularly leather ones), are just a few very commonly observed practices.

Some of these regulations are possibly dictated by the climate or by sanitary considerations. Hindu pollution laws of not eating from another's plate or drinking from another's cup are examples of such considerations. Personal hygiene is strictly observed, and water plays an indispensable part in it. Bathing is not just for rituals but is a daily necessity. These daily (*nitya*) and occasional (*naimittika*) observances evolved into a series of treatises, collectively known as *Smṛti*s or *Dharmaśāstra*s, by the early Christian era. The most renowned of these treatises is *Manu-smṛti* attributed to an ancient sage called Manu. It embodies rules and regulations for civic living. 'These civic rules worked within the religious framework and sometimes even had religious sanction' (Sen 1973: 61).

VIDHI (OBSERVANCES)

Snāna (bathing) cleanses the body and pacifies the mind before worship.

Upavāsa (fasting), Hindus believe, helps one to control emotions and passion. It strengthens one's willpower against indulging in greed or pleasure and is thus regarded as a penance. Fasting for ritual worship starts at day-break and continues till the worship is over. It has two advantages: the first is purely physical or physiological and the second is psychological but is very much influenced by the first. The chief objective of fasting is to render the system clean which in turn calms the mind.

Prasāda (literally, kindness/favour), the food that is offered to the deity during worship and thus consecrated, is taken at the end of worship to break the fast. It consists always of simple natural food which is available to all, e.g., various fruits, raisins and lumps of cane sugar. Even the feast that follows the religious ceremonies is almost always purely vegetarian. Vegetarianism became widespread in Hinduism through the influence of the *ahiṃsā* (non-violence) element of Buddhism and Jainism. In the tantric cult, on the other hand, meat of the sacrificial animal offered to the goddess Kālī is consumed by the worshippers as consecrated food.

NIṢEDHA (AVOIDANCES)

There seem to be several reasons for the prohibition of wearing shoes in any religious venue or even near the home-shrine. The most obvious one is general cleanliness; shoes collect dust and dirt on a journey. This is why an Indian, on returning home, takes his or her shoes off outside the threshold and then enters the room barefoot. Secondly, taking shoes off is a sign of humility and respect for the shrine of God (cf. Exodus 3: 5). Thirdly, and most significantly, a non-violence (*ahiṃsā*) factor may be associated with the custom. The conscience of *ahiṃsā* rejects objects made of animal skin, like shoes, in a sacred place. Leather bags or cases are also objectionable. So when they go on pilgrimage, Hindus often choose rubber or canvas shoes for their long arduous journeys.

Prohibition of taking part in rituals during one's 'impure' state is strictly observed in Hinduism. For example, a woman during her menstruating period is not allowed to take part in a ritual. Similarly, in the event of a death, or even a birth, the immediate family is prohibited from taking part in religious rituals for a prescribed period. This period is regarded as impure (*aśaucha*). In the case of a death (*mṛtāśaucha*), it is the period of mourning, and in that of a birth (*janmāśaucha*), it is the period of confinement. The length of such periods depends on one's caste: the lower the caste the longer the period.

Ritual worship

The procedure of a Hindu ritual worship, or *pūjā*, is so elaborate that the majority of Hindus often do not know the significance of the minute details. They are happy to leave it all to the priest who is a *Brāhmaṇa* by caste, knows the scriptures, and is initiated and trained for the practicalities of all rituals.

Despite the multitude of deities, the basic format of Hindu ritual worship is fairly standard, with minor variations for individual deities. The actual ceremony is conducted during the auspicious period prescribed by the Hindu calendar, based on the constellations of stars. As a rule all rituals are governed by precise timings according to Hindu astronomy and astrological calculations.

PREPARATIONS

The fasting priest and the participating devotees bathe before engaging in any preparation.

The floor decorations (*rangoli/ālpanā*) are done in the ceremonial area. *Rangoli*, made by sprinkling powder colours in various formations and diagrams (see *Yantra* above, p. 68), has mystic significance. *Ālpanā* (or *ālimpana*), the floor painting of Bengal, is symbolic of good luck, fortune and fertility because it is made with rice-paste. Strings of fresh flowers (e.g., marigold) and mango leaves are hung to highlight the venue.

The image of the deity is adorned with patterns of sandal-wood paste, dressed in silk of a specified colour (e.g., Viṣṇu – yellow, Sarasvatī – white) and garlanded with fresh flowers. Specific flowers and leaves are used in the worship of particular deities (e.g., red *javā*/hibiscus for Kālī, *tulasī*/ocymum sanctum leaves for Viṣṇu). (Flowers to be used in worship should not be smelt lest they become polluted and are no longer worthy of being offered to God.)

A clay or brass pot (*ghaṭa*) filled with water of the holy river Ganges (*Gangā*), with a bunch of five mango leaves (*āmra-pallava*), is placed at the foreground, often at the centre of the *rangoli/ālpanā* pattern. The full pot denotes the desired completeness of the ceremony. Finally, a green coconut marked with *svastikā*[6] or other auspicious (*māṅgalika*) symbols in red vermilion is placed on top.

The burning of camphor (*karpūra*) and incense (*dhūpa*) purifies the atmosphere and the lighting of lamps (*dīpa*) welcomes the deity.

Offerings (*naivedya*) of fresh fruits, washed rice and grains, coconut and milk sweets are arranged on plates or banana leaves. At the end of worship, this consecrated food (*prasāda*) breaks the fast of the worshippers.

RITUAL

Recitations of appropriate *mantra*s by the priest (*purohita/pūjārī*), invoking the spirit (*prāṇa-pratiṣṭha*) of the deity into the inert image, transforms the image from an object to a person deserving obeisance.

The worship from then on progresses through the stages of welcome (*āvāhana*), chanting of hymns of praise (*stava-stuti*), and offering (*anjali* – literally, 'in cupped hands') of flowers. A sacrificial fire (*homa/havana*) is lit and oblations of clarified butter (*ghṛta*) are made to the deity, Agni (fire). Devotees finally prostrate (*praṇāma*) in complete submission.

The waving of lamps (*ārati*) in front of the image is a special feature of a Hindu *pūjā*. During *ārati* devotees sing hymns together and bells and drums sound. After *ārati* devotees move their hands over the lamp for the warmth of the flame and purify themselves by touching their head. This sacredness of fire can be traced back to vedic worship.

The sounding of conch-shell (*śaṅkha*), hand-held bell (*ghanṭā*) and drum (e.g., *ḍhāk* of Bengal) is incorporated at specific stages of worship.

The sacrifice of animals (often goats) in Śākta worship (of Śakti/Kālī/Durgā) is a rarity now. Ceremonial sacrifice of vegetables (e.g., pumpkins) or fruits is made instead. The practice of animal sacrifice is symbolic of destroying the base qualities within human nature (namely, lust/*kāma*, anger/*krodha*, greed/*lobha*, attachment/*moha*, pride/*mada* and envy/*mātsarya*), and thus of making the devotee a better person.

COMPLETION

The priest sprinkles the devotees with holy water (*śānti-jala*) from the ceremonial pot (*ghaṭa*) and chants the final *mantra* of peace (*śānti-vachana*) to mark the successful completion of the ritual.

At the end of festivals the casting off (*visarjana*) of the spirit of the deity from the image is performed with appropriate *mantra*s. The gesture of *visarjana* demonstrates that Hindus do not practise idolatry in worshipping images. The image is a mere symbol of the deity, and the clay images (*pratimā*s) from temporary public *pūjā*-venues are taken in a procession to a river or lake to be ceremonially immersed.

Forms of worship

Since Hinduism has various modes of worship there is no single, structured, formal way for all to follow and hence no congregational worship. Though there are innumerable Hindu temples all over

India, dedicated to individual deities, they are not places for congregational worship. Terms for a temple, such as *devālaya*, *devagṛha* and *mandira*, literally mean 'a residence/house of God'. Streams of people go there all through the day to have a glimpse (*darśana*) of the deity and offer their respect. They do not gather at a particular time or take their place in the temple in a particular fashion. As the priest goes about doing his own job of decorating the images, preparing for worship, etc., devotees stand or sit or prostrate themselves on the floor, praying as long as they like, irrespective of the priest's presence, and leave when they please. For the majority of Hindus, worship in temples is less important than their worship at home. Some Hindus go to a temple daily, some occasionally, and some seldom. The temples have their own trustees and priests who organise and conduct the daily worship of the deity with prayers and rituals. Devotees are content with the general worship that is done by the priest in the temple but they know that their own particular commitment (worship) to their own personal God has to be met in their own way in their own time and place, usually at home.

Solo worship: Meditative worship is essentially solo. Often a rosary (*japa-mālā*) of a hundred and eight beads is used as a tool in *japa*, the repetitive murmuring of prayers or God's name.

Family worship: The members of a family get together to worship collectively, with the family *guru* or the head of the family conducting the ceremony for the well-being of the whole family. In urban situations it may well be the mother who offers *pūjā* early in the morning on behalf of her family.

***Kīrtana*:** The only form of worship that can be called semi-congregational is the worship of the *bhakti* groups in the form of singing *kīrtana*s (repetitive singing of a sacred phrase or God's name) or *bhajana*s (songs of praise). Even that has no structured format. Devotees get together and sing for hours; people come and join at any point in the continuous singing and leave when they need to.

Time for worship

Although Hindu religious ceremonies are numerous and vary from area to area and from community to community, reflecting the heterogeneity of Hinduism arising from many cultures, yet they may be classified according to their frequency and purpose. Following Sen's (1973: 32) classification:

Daily worship: To be performed twice a day during both the twilight hours: early morning and dusk. *Prātaḥ-kṛtya* (to be performed early in the morning) and *Sandhyā* (at dusk) are performed by the high-caste Hindu daily in his own home where it is usual to have a family shrine with images or symbols of deities (e.g., special *śālagrāma* stone for Viṣṇu or *liṅga* for Śiva). There is also daily worship in most temples conducted by the *Brāhmaṇa* priest. This includes prayers and detailed rituals.

Weekly worship: Some Hindus follow weekly religious observances; for example, fasting on a particular day of the week and ending the fast with a simple ritual worship. Often it is the Thursday (*Bṛhaspati-vāra: Bṛhaspati*/the name of the *guru* of the gods; *vāra*/day), when women fast and worship Lakṣmī for the general well-being of the family. Thursday, known also as *Guru-vāra* (the day of the *guru*), is considered an auspicious day in a Hindu week.

Fortnightly and monthly worship: Some prayers and fastings are observed according to the lunar calendar. The moon is believed to have a direct influence on the human body and mind as it has an influence on nature (e.g., ebb and flow of the tide). Fasting is prescribed at the time of the full-moon and the new-moon to keep one's body fit and one's emotions under control. Fasting usually ends with worship of one's family deity or the deity related to the occasion.

Annual religious festivals: These are mostly connected with the worship (*pūjā*) of various deities of the Hindu pantheon; e.g., *Lakṣmī-pūjā, Sarasvatī-pūjā, Durgā-pūjā, Kālī-pūjā, Śiva-rātri, Gaṇeśa-chaturthī*, and so on. These can be performed at home, in temples or in outdoor temple-like structures temporarily erected for the festival. Some of the annual religious ceremonies even celebrate mythical events like the birth of Rāma (e.g., *Rāma-navamī*) or of Kṛṣṇa (e.g., *Janmāṣṭamī*), and the mythical personalities are worshipped on those occasions.

There are other annual occasions for praying to God for all sorts of reasons. For example, on *Bhrātṛdvitīyā* sisters put sandal-wood marks on the forehead of their brothers and wish them freedom from death. At *Navānna* (the new rice), the harvest festival, God is thanked for the agricultural, thus economic, success of the community. In all these occasions and many others there is ritual worship of God in various forms, depending upon the occasion itself.

Often the same festival may have different names in different regions. For example, what is known as the festival of *Navarātri* (nine nights) in Gujarat and other parts of India is in Bengal known as *Durgā-pūjā*, coinciding with the last three nights of *Navarātri*. The worship of the Mother for nine days and nights finishes with *Dasserā* or *Vijayā* or *Vijayā Daśamī* (the tenth day). Similarly, the harvest festival is called *Navānna* in Bengal, *Pongal* in Tamilnadu and *Onam* in Kerala. During *Dīvālī*, or *Dīpāvalī*, the festival of lights, most regions of India, especially in the north, commemorate the legendary hero Rāma's victory over Rāvaṇa and his home-coming with his wife Sītā, yet in Bengal *Dīpāvalī* is in celebration of *Kālī-pūjā*.

Incidental worship: Occasional worship, such as a *Vrata* (votive worship), is primarily optional. *Vrata*s 'have little scriptural backing, are performed mainly by women, and are intended normally for the welfare of the family or the community. *Sāvitrī Vrata* is for the welfare of the husband, *Shashṭhi Vrata* for the well-being of the children, *Māghamaṇḍala Vrata* for sunshine in the winter months, *Pausha Vrata* for good harvests, and so on' (Sen 1973: 33).

Astronomical occasions: On days of certain auspicious astronomical configurations and eclipses people often gather in temples or at river pilgrimage sites, such as river confluences, for praying and bathing. For example, every twelve years, on the occasion of the auspicious *Kumbha* configuration, people from all over India gather at Allahabad, located at the confluence of the rivers *Gangā* (the Ganges) and *Yamunā*. The gathering (*melā*) lasts for a month. At the height of the *melā*, on a single day about ten million worshippers take a dip in the water and greet the dawn with prayers. In that month a number of non-stop outdoor Hindu ecumenical congresses take place on the mudflats.

Sacraments: Each stage of a Hindu's life is sanctified formally with an act of worship, whether it is a ceremony of *nāmakaraṇa* (naming of a child), *annaprāśana* (a child's first rice-eating) or *vivāha* (marriage). Sixteen such sacraments (*saṃskāras*) are observed throughout life from conception (*garbhādhāna*) to funeral (*antyeṣṭi*). (See the chapter on Hinduism in *Rites of Passage* in this series.)

Places of worship

There is no specified place for worship in Hinduism. There are home-shrines, road-side shrines, temples, places of pilgrimage or the seclusion of the woodlands and the mountains. However, the most common place of worship is one's own family shrine, be it a humble wooden shelf with images of deities on it, an elaborately ornate brass throne with a canopy over it, or a complete room set aside as a *mandir*.

For a *jñāna-yogī* (see p. 72 above) even a shrine with images is unnecessary. A quiet place is all he needs for contemplative meditation. Some prefer to leave the community for seclusion. The caves of the Himalayan foot-hills are renowned secluded spots.

All over India, humble road-side open-air shrines are found, at the base of trees such as *Vaṭas* or *Aśvatthas* (Ficus religiosa), that are considered sacred. A symbolic stone (e.g., *Śālagrāma-śilā* of Viṣṇu) or a *Śiva-liṅga* is often installed there. Flowers or small sums of money are offered by the passers-by as homage to the deity. Thus an abode of a living God for the local communities comes into being.

Temples are the permanent 'residence' of a deity and daily worship is performed by the priest, but the majority of Hindus visit temples only on special occasions. (See the chapter on Hinduism in *Sacred Place* in this series.) Worship in temples is wholly optional for them.

On specific religious festivals, temporary temple-like structures are erected in open fields or parks where statues of the deities are placed and worshipped ceremonially. In Bengal, during festivals such as the grand *Durgā-pūjā, Kālī-pūjā* and *Sarasvatī-pūjā*, the temporary structures become as sacred as the temples.

Places of pilgrimage, associated with the lives of mythical heroes such as Rāma or Kṛṣṇa, or with the birth or enlightenment of a saint, attract pilgrims all the year round. The sites of river pilgrimages do the same on auspicious days (see above, p. 82).

Worship and the arts

Religion and the everyday life of the people are almost inseparable in Hinduism. Consequently, the creative activities of daily life are also inseparable from worship. A musician or an artist, for example, often humbly declares that his whole life is a long act of worship. Whatever he creates is an offering to his God. He considers himself a mere instrument. Through him God is creating beautiful things and no credit is due to him. Often-observed anonymity in Hindu art creation is due to this attitude among artists.

Artists in general are *karma-yogīs* (see p. 70 above) as they achieve enlightenment through their creative work (*karma*). They may join others in celebrating religious festivals without caring much for rituals. To them *pūjā* is dedication and not ritual worship. However, *Sarasvatī-pūjā* is the rare occasion when musicians, artists and artisans place the tools of their trade to be blessed at the feet of Sarasvatī, the goddess of the muses.

MUSIC

Hindu music is rooted in religious worship. It can be traced back to the age of the *Sāmā-veda* (*c.* 1500 BCE) when hymns in praise of individual gods were sung around the sacrificial fire. For the desired result from a sacrifice, the pronunciation of hymns had to be accurate and the singing needed to be precise, with long–short durations of notes (*svaras*) and with prescribed high–low–medium tones. Three musical pitches or tones are mentioned in the Veda for the singing of the hymns: *udātta* (high), *anudātta* (not high, i.e., grave) and *svarita* (sounded, i.e., articulated). Over the ages, from these simple three-pitch plain songs grew a sophisticated system of seven pure (*śuddha*) notes (*svaras*) with their sharp (*tīvra*) and flat (*komala*) variations.

The earliest form of Hindu vocal music, with the complete gamut of musical notes, is known as *dhruvapada* (*dhrupada* for short) which means 'the constant (*dhruva*) syllable (*pada*)'. The themes of *dhrupadas* are always in praise of deities, often of Śiva, as the Lord of cosmic rhythm and dance (*Naṭarāja*).

Communal singing in praise of a deity is a special feature of the act of worship in some sects in Hinduism. The advent of the *bhakti* (devotion) movement in the eleventh and twelfth centuries generated the singing of *kīrtanas/bhajanas* (devotional songs) which became an integral part of a popular form of worship. The simple but passionate songs of great saint-poets like Jayadeva, Chandidasa and Mira won the hearts of millions in their day, and still stir up emotions in present-day Hindus. Music as a powerful medium of spiritual communication is recognised, and *kīrtanas* are sung in groups in temple courtyards or in a procession, though mostly in family gatherings.

The *Bāuls* of Bengal are especially renowned for their simple songs with mystical or metaphysical content. They are the minstrels or bards whose life-style is free and not inhibited by any dogmas or social injunctions. They regard their own body as the temple of God, who resides in it in the disguise of their own soul. They ignore all rituals, and worship their inner-soul (*maner mānuṣ*), the God within, with spontaneous songs. The Nobel laureate poet-musician, Rabindranath Tagore (1861–1941), was greatly influenced by the *Bāuls*' mystic philosophy and their simple moving tunes, and he composed several songs with similar simple tunes and spiritual lyrics.

DANCE

Hindu classical dance-forms, like Hindu music, are associated with worship. References to dance and music are found in the vedic literature, indicating that some form of ritual dancing constituted an integral part of the sacrificial rites. The graceful art is mentioned in the *Ṛg-veda*, and more frequently in the *Atharva-veda* and *Yajur-veda*. But the earliest specific detailed documentation on dancing is found in Bharata's *Nāṭya-śāstra* (*nāṭya*/dramaturgy, *śāstra*/manual – probably compiled between the fourth century BCE and the first century CE) where the arts of music and dancing are dealt with as essential components of the dramaturgy of the day. A divine origin is attributed to dramaturgy itself as a whole. According to the *Nāṭya-śāstra* (I, 11–17), at the request of the gods, Brahmā, the creator, composed *Nāṭya-veda*, taking the text from the *Ṛg-veda*, music from the *Sāmā-veda*, gestures from the *Yajur-veda* and sentiments from the *Atharva-veda*. Śiva and his consort Pārvatī contributed to the dance. Śiva's cosmic dance of destruction constituted the rigorous masculine form – the *tāṇḍava* – and Pārvatī's dance constituted the enchanting feminine style – the *lāsya*. The sage Bharata was authorised to popularise the divine dance-forms to the world through his *Nāṭya-śāstra*.

At the outset of a recital, a classical dancer pays a ritual homage to Śiva as he is the Lord of the dance (*Naṭarāja*). This simple act of *pūjā* shows that dance is considered not merely as an art-form giving expression to physical and emotional exuberance but as an offering to God.

As the cult of Śiva expanded during the period of the seventh to fourteenth centuries, and hundreds of temples were built, dancing developed as one of the principal temple rituals. In south India the *Bharatanāṭyam* dance-form originated as the temple-dance of the *devadāsī*s (handmaidens of God), dedicated for life to God's service. They were ceremonially married to the principal deity of the temple. They offered their dance and song to the deity as oblation. They went through long and rigorous training and were accomplished in dancing and music and other allied arts.

The *Odissi*, the dance-form of Orissa in north-eastern India, also originated as a temple dance. Such dancers were known as the *māhārī*s. During the eleventh and twelfth centuries the cult of Viṣṇu spread through this region. The Vaiṣṇava philosophy of Rāmānuja and Jayadeva's devotional poetry *Gīta-Govinda* influenced the arts tremendously. The worship of Jagannātha (Lord of the world, a form of Viṣṇu/Kṛṣṇa) became widespread. In the temple of Jagannātha in Puri, several *māhārī*s were installed. The synthesis of the Śaiva and the Vaiṣṇava traditions is visible in the *Odissi* dance performance of today. Similarly, the *Kuchipudi* dance of Andhra Pradesh and the *Kathākali* dance of Kerala are also associated with the regional temple dances.

Thus the arts of Hindu dance and music were preserved over the centuries as temple culture, in spite of political upheavals in the country. Manuals (*śāstra*s) of the arts, including sculpture and architecture, were compiled and stored in temples. Temples became centres of learning. Though in northern India temples often fell victim to the Islamic invasion, in the south they survived and so did the great treasure-houses of Hindu culture, providing a remarkable degree of continuity to this day.

THE VISUAL ARTS

Similar to the performing arts, Hindu visual arts also evolved around religion and objects of worship. There is a close relationship between sculpture, painting, architecture and worship. Very often Hindu works of sculpture and painting are devoted to revealing the divine personality in the images, and those of architecture to increasing the dignity of temples. The images of deities are often not anatomically precise, but the aim is to emphasise the emotion or *bhāva* in expression. For expressing specific sentiments or *rasas*,[7] the artists are guided by a number of manuals (*śāstras*) on aesthetic procedure.

Hindu arts, therefore, developed through the ages not just as the execution of an artist's uncontrolled aesthetic inspiration, but also as the expression moulded by the conventions on proportion, pose, gesture and even colour of the images. Because the devotees are also familiar with these conventions, they readily recognise the intended emotion portrayed in the image. The dancing form of Śiva (*Naṭarāja*) or the tri-flexed (*tribhaṅga*) posture of Kṛṣṇa evokes certain emotions in the mind of the worshipper. The colour of Viṣṇu, Kṛṣṇa, Rāma and Kālī is prescribed to be dark, whereas that of Śiva and Sarasvatī is white, and so on. The image installed in the sanctuary of a temple, to be worthy of worship, has to be perfect in proportion, pose and gesture in accordance with the strict scriptural canon. However, the artist has more freedom in making images that are not intended for worship, e.g., the numerous sculpted figures on the outer walls of Hindu temples. Even secular subjects, like a group of musicians or amorous couples, found their way into the temple art of the Hindus. (See the chapter on Hinduism in *Sacred Place* in this series.)

Alongside the classical tradition of prescribed, stylised visual art forms there developed a branch of folk art, especially painting. Like any folk art, it reflects the spontaneity and vivid imagination of the artists at the grassroots. Such paintings are often done on scrolls using the themes of mythological stories of gods and goddesses. The illustrated scrolls are used by wandering bards as an aid to telling stories. In Bengal, religious paintings (*paṭas*) are done on clay plates that are hung on the wall. The colours used are typically vibrant red, blue, yellow, green, black, and so on.

This tradition of folk art, though still continuing today, has taken the new form of printed posters and calendar pictures. People frame these brightly coloured prints of Hindu deities and keep them in their family shrine or hang them on the wall. This mass-produced, easily affordable, religious art-form has made the presence of the deities visible in all Hindu homes worldwide.

Worship as a natural response

The first sound that many Hindus utter when they wake up in the morning is the name of their God, repeated three times, e.g., *Om Rām Rām Rām* or *Om Durgā Durgā Durgā*. They believe that the utterance will see them safely through the day. Going out of the house they do the same, and again at the end of the day before going to sleep. Uttering God's name or praying to God has become so much a part of everyday life that a Hindu does not often stop and think what he or she has been doing. Worship has become second nature.

NOTES

1. The Vedas are the most revered scriptures of the Hindus, believed not to have been composed by humans (*apauruṣeya*) but revealed to the seers (*ṛṣis*). The word *veda* (from the root *vid* meaning 'to know') means knowledge. The four Vedas: The *Ṛg-veda*, the earliest Veda, consists of hymns (*ṛks*), metrical in form, in praise of deities. The *Sāmā-veda*, the Veda of songs (*sāman*), consists mainly of Ṛg-vedic hymns selected to be sung aloud during sacred rites (cf., the Book of Psalms in the Bible). The *Yajur-veda* (*yajus* means 'worship') deals, mostly in prose, with the formulae of actual performance of rituals. The *Atharva-veda* deals with magical formulae for destruction of evils and sins, herbal cure of ailments and other fields of knowledge which may not relate to sacred rituals directly.
2. In a vedic *yajña* the priests of the four Vedas have their respective roles to play. *Hotā*, the Ṛg-vedic priest, recites the hymns from the *Ṛg-veda*; *Udgātā*, the Sama-vedic priest, sings the hymns aloud from the *Sāmā-veda; Adhvaryu*, the officiating priest of *Yajur-veda*, performs the actual detailed ritual and *Brahmā*, the priest of the *Atharva-veda*, supervises the conduct of the *yajña* as a whole.
3. The cult of *Tantra* stresses action rather than renunciation. It believes in overcoming desires and fears by thoroughly experiencing them because

ultimate mastery is achieved by recognising and accepting human limitations.

The central theme of *Tantra* is dualism in which two factors together create a single whole. Each creation is the result of interplay between two equally important principles: the passive experiencing consciousness is the masculine (*Śiva/puruṣa*) and the creative acting force, the feminine (*Śakti/prakṛti*). Sexual *yoga* and rituals in tantric tradition are the result of acceptance of sexuality as the basis of all creation.

4. Spiritual liberation, or *mokṣa*, is the eternal freedom from the cycle of rebirths, by losing one's identity in *Brahman*. The theory of *karma* (action/deed) is based on the law of cause and effect. Every action (*karma*) has a reaction (*phala*). As one does good deeds, one progresses towards liberation through several births. Bad deeds can equally reverse the process. Liberation is not granted by God but is earned through continuous search.
5. *Trimūrti* (three manifestations) is a symbolic unification of three essential attributes of the divine: Brahmā as the creator, Viṣṇu as the preserver and Śiva as the destroyer who paves the way for a new creation.
6. *Svastika/kā* is an ancient symbol of good luck (*svasti* signifying well-being) found all over India on the walls, doorways and arches of Hindu temples. It can be traced back to the Indus Valley Civilisation (*c.* 2000 BCE) where bricks have been found stamped with the sign. It derives from the cross. From a central point the arms extend outwards in four directions signifying that diverse worlds, activities, faiths share a basic unity of spirit. It also implies the continual cyclical movement of time.

   Svastika can face either way, showing two ways to the spirit: (clockwise) right-hand path (*dakṣiṇāchāra*) of rituals and worship, and (anti-clockwise) left-hand path (*vāmāchāra*) of esoteric techniques, e.g., *Tantra*.
7. Hindu aesthetics is based on the realisation of *rasa*. Any art-form, whether performing, visual or literary, has to pass the test of *rasa*, a kind of emotional involvement or relish felt by its recipients. Eight main *rasa*s described in Bharata's *Nāṭya-śāstra* (VI 15) are based on pre-experienced human feelings (*bhāva*s). Thus *bhāva* is the root-cause (*janaka*) of *rasa*, the effect (*janya*). The experience of *rasa* is always pleasant. Even an unpleasant natural human feeling, like grief or fear, can give rise to a pleasurable feeling of pathos or suspense, when *rasa* is achieved through art-forms.

FURTHER READING

Cavendish, R. (1980) *The Great Religions*, London, Weidenfeld & Nicolson [for WHSmith].

Chaudhuri, N.C. (1979) *Hinduism: A Religion to Live By*, London, Chatto & Windus.
Mookerjee, A. and Khanna, M. (1977) *The Tantric Way: Art Science Ritual*, London, Thames and Hudson.
Radhakrishnan, S. (1971) *The Hindu View of Life* (16th edn), London, Unwin Books.
Rawson, P. (1988) *The Art of Tantra*, London, Thames and Hudson.
Sen, K.M. (1973) *Hinduism* (8th edn), London, Penguin.
Swami Swarupananda (1982) *Srimad-Bhagavad-Gita*, Calcutta, Advaita Ashrama.
Swami Vivekananda (1963) *Hinduism*, Madras, Sri Ramakrishna Math.
Zaehner, R.C. (1972) *Hinduism* (3rd edn), London, Oxford University Press.

4. Islam

Martin Forward

The sources of devotional life

What is worship? It is a controversial word, difficult to define. I understand it to indicate two basic attitudes in a religious believer: prayerfulness; and the acknowledgement that its focus, which for a Muslim is Allāh, the one God, is worthy of deepest commitment.

Individual Muslims derive their sense of worship from many sources, which might include: the regular life of devotion at home or in the mosque; a person whose example has led him or her to turn to God; a sense of God's close and abiding presence. However, all Muslims acknowledge two major sources from their religion which encourage them to worship God: Qur'ān and *Ḥadīth*. The Qur'ān is God's word, revealed piecemeal to Muhammad, the last and greatest of the prophets, by the angel Gabriel (in Arabic, *Jibrā'īl*) from 610 to 632 CE.[1] Its influence is all-pervasive in a Muslim's life. Specifically, on the theme of worship, it commends and commands a life of prayer (e.g., 11: 114), and its teaching, especially about the unity of God, and the future judgement of human beings so that some will go to heaven and others to hell, is the focus of the believer's deepest commitment. *Ḥadīth* has the important specialist sense in Arabic of being the 'Traditions' of the Prophet Muhammad, a record of his and his closest companions' sayings and doings. As such, *ḥadīth* is held by Muslims to be second only in importance to the Qur'ān as a source of Islamic law, dogma and ritual. The two most famous and respected compilations of *ḥadīth* are by al-Bukhari (810–870) and Muslim b. al-Hajjaj (817–875). It is believed that they recorded authentic traditions, worthy of a Muslim's trust and commitment. South Asian Muslims also regularly use the *Mishkāt al-Māṣabiḥ*, 'niche for lamps', which in its popular form dates from the fourteenth century and is a less reliable work than either Bukhari's or Muslim's. However, its popularity and relative accessibility in English translations make it a useful source-book. Stories about the Prophet's life of prayer and commitment to God and his will abound in the traditions, which have shaped the form and content of devotional life.

On the basis of Qur'ān and *ḥadīth*, the scholars of Muslim law (*'ulamā'* or religious jurists) codified details of spiritual life in Islam, establishing times and places as well as content of prayer, and the state in which each worshipper must approach God. Manuals of devotion, some local and of limited range, some classics spanning time and place, have also influenced the spiritual life of Muslims.

Formal prayer: a pillar of Islam

Formal prayer (*ṣalāt*) is, in Islam, the second of the *arkān al-dīn*. The word *arkān* means 'support' or 'basic element', and the phrase is usually translated 'pillars of Islam'. So ritual prayer underpins Islam, which is built upon it and the four other supports. First is the *shahādah*, the 'profession of faith' made in Arabic, which in English is 'I bear witness that God alone is God, and Muhammad is his prophet'. Then comes *ṣalāt*, which is followed by *ṣawm*, 'fasting' from dawn to dusk during the month of *Ramaḍān*. The fourth pillar is *zakāt*, a religious tax of one-fortieth of a Muslim's property, to aid the poor and needy. The last pillar is *ḥajj*, 'pilgrimage' to Makkah.

These observances mark out who is a Muslim. Although most scholars do not place them in order of importance, there is a certain appropriateness in the sequence in which they are usually listed. Muslims move from an explicit affirmation of their faith, which devotional manuals and the *ḥadīth* encourage them to make frequently, to daily ritual prayer during which the *shahādah* is uttered. The last three pillars are occasional events in the sense that, important as they are, they are not regular daily events.

Formal daily prayer locates worship as one of the basic elements of Islam, a pillar which supports the religion and its devotees. It is important to emphasise that worship is also pervasive in the other pillars. The *shahādah* functions as a kind of prayer. During *Ramaḍān* and *ḥajj*, many prayers are said, which we shall describe later. *Zakāt* has not attracted to itself special prayers and devotions, but giving money or property to others is an expression of believers' commitment.

Even though observance of the five pillars is required of all believers, not all practise them. There are 'secular' Muslims, not only in the West but also in the heartlands of Islam, for whom religion is at most a matter of cultural identity, deciding matters of language, marriage, inheritance and so forth. There are also many Muslims who pray and fast occasionally, give charity from time to time, who sit lightly to rituals and maybe even beliefs. Many of their co-religionists condemn them, but their integrity and importance should not be underestimated; it is not only the orthodox who shape a religion.

The conditions of *ṣalāt*

Formal prayer is obligatory upon every Muslim who is sane, responsible and healthy. Many children begin formal prayer by the age of seven and should certainly have started by ten. Women cannot pray during menstruation or during childbirth and nursing. They are permitted up to ten days' freedom from prayer in the first circumstance, and forty days in the latter.

Prayer is not valid unless certain requirements are met. These requirements emphasise the worshippers' desire to be pure. To this end they dress modestly. A man must cover his body, at least from the navel to the knees. A woman must show only her face, hands and feet. Neither sex must wear transparent clothes. The worshipper must declare the intention that the act is for the purpose of worship and purity. The word *niyyah*, 'intention', is very important in Islam. A well-known *ḥadīth* states that actions are judged by the intentions associated with them and that doers will receive what they intended. So formal prayer is not just a formality if the prayer is to be effective.

Moreover, the 'minor ablutions' (*wuḍū'*) must be performed, as follows. The pray-er declares a sincere intention, and then, usually squatting on haunches and next to a tap or other source of water, washes the hands up to the wrists three times, then rinses out the mouth with water three times, and preferably with a brush. Then the nostrils are cleansed by sniffing water into them three times, and expelling it. Then the face must be washed three times, from the top of the forehead to the bottom of the chin, and from ear to ear; and the right arm, followed by the left, also three times, up to the far end of the elbow. The whole head or any part of it is wiped with a wet hand and the inner sides of the ears with wet forefingers and their outer sides with wet thumbs. The neck is wiped all around with wet hands and the two feet up to the ankles, three times, the right foot first. The *wuḍū'* is then complete. Although it is best done in the order described, it is not forbidden to proceed differently, though the actions recounted must be done.

Sometimes, earth, sand, stone or snow can be substituted for plain water. This is usually allowed for reasons of health and availability. Substitution (*tayammum*) is performed in this manner: the worshipper strikes both hands lightly on the medium of purity, then shakes the hands and wipes the face with them. Then the hands are again placed in the sand (or whatever) and shaken, and the right arm is wiped to the elbow by the left hand, and vice versa. *Tayammum* is therefore less complete than *wuḍū'*, but performs the important task of symbolising the worshipper's intention to be pure in preparation for prayer.

Wuḍū' can be nullified by a number of occurrences. A bodily discharge, such as faeces, urine, flatulence, vomit, the flow of blood or pus voids it. So does falling asleep or taking any intoxicating drug or drink. After such an event, the worshipper must perform *wuḍū'* again.

Wuḍū' is the minor purification. After a major impurity (*janāba*), caused by orgasm, copulation without ejaculation, a wet dream, menstruation, or puerperal discharge after childbirth, and at the end of a nursing mother's confinement period estimated at a maximum of forty days, the major purification (*ghusl*) is obligatory. Many Muslims believe that it is also required on Fridays and on the two festivals of *'Īd al-Fiṭr* and *'Īd al-Aḍḥā*, at the end of the months of fasting and pilgrimage. The worshipper begins by cleansing the body from sexual fluid, blood or any other impure matter. Then *wuḍū'* is done. Thereafter, a bath is taken, and the body is thoroughly cleansed with water. As with *wuḍū', tayammum* can be performed when no water is available. Many manuals of devotion urge the worshipper to combine such acts of purification with utterances praising God and asking him for guidance.

The times, places and content of *ṣalāt*

Until the *hijrah*, or 'emigration', by Muhammad and his followers, from Makkah to Medina in 622, there seem to have been only two daily prayers: sunrise and sunset (20: 130; 17: 78). After the *hijrah*, the Qur'ān mentions intermediate time or times: 'Glorify God in the evening hour and the morning hour . . . and in the late afternoon, and when the sun begins to go down' (30: 17f.).

Many *ḥadīth* stress the importance of prayer: 'Abu Huraira reported God's messenger as saying, "The five [daily] prayers, Friday to Friday and *Ramaḍān* to *Ramaḍān* make atonement for what has happened since the previous one when major sins have been avoided"' (Robson, vol. 1 1970: 114). The *ḥadīth* also fix the number of prayers as five. The Prophet was heard to say:

> 'Gabriel came down and acted as my *imam* [prayer leader], and I prayed along with him, then I prayed along with him, the I prayed along with him, then I prayed along with him, then I prayed along with him', reckoning with his [Muhammad's] fingers five times of prayer.
>
> (Robson, vol. 1 1970: 120)

Ḥadīth also establish the times of the five prayers, which are regulated by the position of the sun. They are called *ṣalāt al-fajr* (or *ṣalāt al-ṣubḥ*), at dawn before sunrise; *ṣalāt al-ẓuhr*, after the sun passes its zenith; *ṣalāt al-'aṣr*, in the late afternoon; *ṣalāt al-maghrib*, immediately after sunset; and *ṣalāt al-'ishā*, between sunset and midnight. The noon (*ẓuhr*) and afternoon (*'aṣr*) prayers can be said together, as can sunset (*maghrib*) and evening (*'ishā*) prayers, if a person is travelling or sick.

There are accounts of Muhammad settling prayer times, but important *ḥadīth* also stress how significant his companions believed prayers and their timings to be:

> It is told of 'Umar b. al-Khaṭṭāb [the second *khalīfah*, 'successor' to the Prophet as political head of the Muslim community, who ruled from 634 to 644] that he wrote to his governors, "The most important matter which concerns you in my opinion is prayer; whoever observes it and is attentive to it will guard his religion, but whoever neglects it will be more neglectful of other things." Thereafter he wrote telling them to observe the noon prayer in the period when the shade was a cubit long up to the time when a man's shadow was as long as himself; the

> afternoon prayer when the sun was high, white and clear, when there was still time for a rider to go two or three leagues before sunset; the sunset prayer after the sun had set; the night prayer between the ending of the twilight and the passing of a third of the night (adding three times "if one lies down to sleep may his eye not sleep"); and the morning prayer when the stars were still visible and out in abundance.
>
> (Robson, vol. 1 1970: 120)

Some jurists and scholars think it important that Islam has set the times of prayer in such a way that spiritual refreshment coincides with times of physical nourishment: so, breakfast, lunch, afternoon tea or coffee, dinner and supper, match the times of the five daily prayers. However, it is important to note that these times vary depending on where a Muslim lives. In Saudi Arabia, where Islam began, the time of dawn and dusk varies only slightly throughout the year. In Britain the sun can rise from about 4.30am to 8am, and set from 3pm to 9pm, depending on the month of the year. This controls the times of prayer considerably.

There are certain times when prayers must not be said: when the sun is rising; when it is at its height; when it is setting; when a woman is menstruating, is in childbirth or is a nursing mother; or when a Muslim is in a state of impurity. Some scholars have argued that the ban on *ṣālāt* at sunrise and sunset is related to Hindu worship of the sun. Since Islam believes strongly in *tawḥīd* (the oneness of God), South Asian Muslims refused to pray during the sun's nadir and zenith lest their prayer should be mistaken for Hindu 'idolatry'.

All prayers should be offered at their due time unless there are compelling reasons otherwise. Muslims are commanded to make up for delayed prayers, except women who are menstruating, are in childbirth or are nursing mothers, and Muslims who are insane or unconscious for some time. Delayed prayers must be said in their original form. For example, if the *fajr* prayers are missed and performed later, their content must be followed, whatever time they are done.

There is no special place where prayers must be said, though some sites are considered unclean and therefore inappropriate, for example, graveyards and lavatories. The mosque, or *masjid*, 'place of bowing down', is a desirable location, where the company of other believers is a stimulus to prayer. In South Asia custom has determined that women say their prayers at home, not in the mosque, even the Friday congregational prayers, and that habit has transferred to the United Kingdom where most Muslims have their roots in India, Pakistan or Bangladesh. But some Muslims are challenging this habit as un-Islamic. In other parts of the Muslim world, women pray in mosques, but in different sections from the men.

When they pray, Muslims face the *qiblah*, the direction of prayer towards the *ka'bah*, the cube-shaped building within the precincts of the Great Mosque of Makkah, built originally by Adam and then rebuilt by Ibrāhīm ('Abraham') and Ismā'īl ('Ishmael'). More precisely, the *qiblah* points to the place between the waterspout and the western corner of the *ka'bah*. Believers pray on the *sajjādah*, a prayer-mat, which symbolises space between the believer and the humdrum physical world. A stick or some other object pointing towards Makkah is placed in front. Nobody may pass in between or disturb the devotee.

Among other distractions, Muslims specifically forbid music and dancing and pictures imaging God, especially but not only in the mosque. However, the visual arts are represented there in the form of calligraphy. The *qiblah* is indicated by the *mihrab* or niche in the wall of the mosque. The *mihrab* is often beautifully decorated with calligraphy, tiles and mosaics. Here, craftsmen are encouraged to give full expression to artistic expression in the service of religious fervour. Although music is banned, it has been argued that the *adhān*, 'call to prayer', which is chanted, is a most musical event.

Before each time of prayer, the *adhān* is made by the *mu'adhdhin* (anglicised as 'muezzin') from the minaret, one of the towers of a mosque. In Britain and many western countries, where not all mosques are purpose-built but may be erstwhile shops, factories or private homes, the *adhān* is done from wherever seems appropriate, or, indeed, usually not at all because of legislation banning noise during certain hours of the day and night. (Many Muslims resent this ban when church bells can often be rung without any hindrance.) The first *mu'adhdhin* was a black African from Ethiopia called Bilal, appointed by Muhammad himself. Muslims often remind themselves of this story to stress the equality of all people before God, which is a central tenet of Islam. The *mu'adhdhin*, always a man, faces towards Makkah, and begins just before the set time for prayer, except in the case of the morning prayer, when it is usually said in the last sixth of the night so as to give people time to rise and prepare themselves. Nowadays, in many large cities of the Muslim world, and some smaller ones, the *mu'adhdhin* has been replaced by a recorded tape played through a loudspeaker. Not all Muslims approve of this development.

The *adhān* is in Arabic, which translates into English as follows. First the *mu'adhdhin* says, 'God is greater' four times. Then, 'I testify that there is no other god than God' twice. After this, 'I testify that Muhammad is God's messenger' twice. Then, 'Come to prayer' twice. Thereafter, 'Come to prosperity' twice. Then, 'God is greater' twice. Finally, 'There is no other god than God' once. Just before the dawn prayers, after saying 'Come to prosperity', he adds, 'Prayer is better than sleep' twice. After the utterance 'Come to prosperity', Shi'ah Muslims (who nowadays form about ten per cent of Muslims)[2] interject, 'Come to the best work' at all prayers.

Whether or not the *adhān* is made, the worshippers inaugurate prayer with the *iqāmah*. It is the same as the *adhān* except that the only phrase said twice is, 'God is greater', and it ends after the statement, 'Come to prosperity'. Then, each devotee says, 'Prayer has begun!' twice.

All five daily prayers consist of a number of *rak'āt* (singular, *rak'ah*), which means 'bowings'. Each *rak'ah* is a 'unit of prayer' consisting of a number of ritual prayers and invocations, all of them in Arabic, while standing, bowing, prostrating and sitting.

The following account of the practices, positions and utterances of the formal prayers is the basic pattern. Different schools of Muslim law lay down slightly divergent practices. For instance, some require no *witr* prayers (which are explained below), while others require them in the *fajr* as well as *'ishā* prayers. If prayers are in the mosque, the *imām*, or prayer leader, may appropriately perform some specified spoken parts of the prayer on behalf of all, but these and other differences are relatively slight and not of momentous import.

In the *ṣalāt al-fajr*, two *rak'āt* may be offered first as supererogatory (*sunnah*) units. Then there are two obligatory (*farḍ*) units. Both proceed in the same manner except when stating the intention (*niyyah*). The worshipper stands facing the *qiblah*, raises the hands up to the ears, and says, 'I declare my intention to offer the supererogatory [or obligatory, as the case may be] prayer of the morning.

God is the greater'. Then the arms are lowered and the right hand is placed over the left one just below the navel. (This is the *waqūf* position). Then, in a low voice, the devotee says:

> Glory be to you, O God. Yours is the praise, and blessed is your name, and exalted is your majesty. There is no god apart from you. I take refuge in God from the accursed devil. In the name of God, most gracious, most merciful.

Then, silently or out loud, the opening chapter of the Qur'ān is recited, followed by any other passage from scripture. The opening chapter, *Fātiḥah*, runs:

> In the name of God, most gracious, most merciful. Praise belongs to God, the Lord of the Worlds, most gracious, most merciful, master of the day of judgement. We worship you; to you only we pray for help. Show us the straight path, the path of those whom you have favoured, not of those with whom you are angry or who wander away.

Thereafter, the worshipper utters, 'God is greater', bowing the head and placing both palms of the hands on the knees (this position is called *rukū'*) and saying three times, 'Glory to my Lord the great'. Afterwards the *waqūf* position is resumed and, hands remaining at each side, this is said, 'God accepts all who are thankful; our Lord, praise be to you'. Then, the *sujūd* position is taken; the believers prostrate themselves, touching the ground with the toes of both feet, both knees and hands, and forehead saying, 'God is greater' and, three times, 'Glory to my Lord, the most high'. As they say, 'God is greater' again, they move to the *jalsah* position, sitting so that the outer side of the left foot and the toes of the right one touch the ground, with both hands placed on the knees. After this, a second prostration is repeated in the same way and with the same formulae as the first. This completes one *rak'ah*. After it, the faithful rise, saying, 'God is the greater', and assume a standing position for the second unit. Before beginning it, they recite the *Fātiḥah* and a qur'anic passage. After the second *rak'ah*, they assume the *jalsah* position and recite the *tashahhud*, which runs:

> All reverence, all worship, all sanctity are due to God. Peace be to you, O Prophet, and the mercy of God and all his blessings. Peace be on us all

> and on all the righteous servants of God. I bear witness that there is no god but God and I bear witness that Muhammad is his servant and apostle.

During this prayer the fingers of the right hand are clenched except for the index finger which is raised and extended. Worshippers may, if they wish, add the *darūd*:

> O God, shower your blessings on Muhammad and on his descendants as you did on Abraham and his descendants. In truth, you are the praiseworthy, the glorious. O God, bless Muhammad and his descendants as you blessed Abraham and his descendants. In truth, you are the praiseworthy, the glorious.

They may also say *du'ā*, a private prayer, such as: 'O Lord, make me and my offspring faithful in prayer. Our Lord, grant our prayers. Our Lord, forgive me and my parents and all the believers on the day when the reckoning will be held'. Finally, worshippers turn their faces to the right, saying, 'Peace be on you, and the mercy of God'. Then they move their faces to the left, saying the same.

The *ṣalāt al-ẓuhr*, or noon-prayer, has four *farḍ* units which must be spoken silently or softly, and may be preceded by four units of *sunnah* and followed by two more *sunnah* units. The first two obligatory *rak'āt* are performed as for the dawn prayers. When worshippers recite the *tashahhud* after the second unit, they stop before the *darūd* to resume a standing position. In the third and fourth units, no qur'anic passages are spoken after the *Fātiḥah*. *Darūd* is said after the final *rak'ah*, and then the greetings of peace, right and left.

The *ṣalāt al-'aṣr* has four *farḍ* units, preceded by four supererogatory ones. They are said in the same way as the noon prayers, also in a low voice. The *ṣalāt al-maghrib* has three *farḍ* units followed by two *sunnah*. They are performed in the same way as the noon or mid-afternoon prayers except that two are said out loud and one silently. The *ṣalāt al-'ishā* consist of four *farḍ*, then two *sunnah* and three *witr* units. The *farḍ* units are two silent, two aloud. *Witr* means 'odd' or 'uneven', and they are performed as the sunset prayer except that in the third *rak'ah* the *Fātiḥah* is followed by a portion of the Qur'ān and, while standing after bowing but before prostration, the worshipper says:

> O God! We beseech you for help and guidance, and seek your protection and believe in you and rely on you, and extol you and are thankful to you and are not ungrateful to you, and we separate ourselves from and forsake whoever disobeys you. O God! We pray to you and prostrate ourselves, and to you we come, and are quick to obey you, and we hope for your mercy and fear your punishment, for your punishment overtakes the unbeliever. O God! Exalt our master Muhammad, and his people, and his true followers.

Witr prayers are voluntary but regarded as more important than *sunnah*. A *ḥadīth* describes God as being, and loving, *witr*.

Congregational prayers

All prayers except for one can be done privately, although Islam encourages congregational prayer. In congregational prayer there is a prayer leader (*imām*). The *imām* is chosen from among the worshippers. He is a man, respected for his religious learning and piety. In some mosques he is paid to lead prayers and sometimes to teach Arabic and Islam, especially to the children. He stands in front by himself while the congregation line up in straight lines behind him, all facing the *qiblah*. A congregation can be any number, even the *imām* and just one other. After declaring the intention of prayer, the *imām* recites out loud the *Fātiḥah*, the short opening chapter of the Qur'ān, and a passage from the Qur'ān in the *fajr* and the first two *rak'āt* of the *'ishā* prayers. He is listened to respectfully by the congregation who respond 'Ameen' (which has a longer vowel sound than the Christian 'Amen') after the *Fātiḥah*. When the *imām* stands after the bowing position, he says in Arabic, 'God accepts any who are thankful to him', and the congregation responds, 'Our Lord, praise be to you'. The congregation follows the *imām* in the actions of prayer.

The midday prayers on Friday (*ṣalāt al-jumu'ah*) must be said by all Muslim men in a mosque, or some other suitable gathering place such as a home or park. It takes the place of the *ẓuhr* prayers and falls at the same time as they would. It is important because God has ordained it. In the Qur'ān (62: 9) the believers are commanded, when they hear the call to prayer on Friday, to hurry to the remembrance of God and to cease trading. It is an opportunity to show solidarity with fellow-Muslims and to demonstrate that the call of God takes precedence over material and other considerations. No Muslim can offer this prayer by himself. If he cannot meet with others, he must say the *ẓuhr* prayers instead.

When the time for prayer arrives, the *adhān* is said wherever possible. The four units of *sunnah* prayer are offered silently. Then the *imām* faces the congregation who sit while he stands on the *minbar* ('pulpit'), and preaches the *khuṭbah* or 'sermon'. It is in two parts, both beginning with words of praise of God and blessings on Muhammad. At the end of the first part the *imām* sits. He stands for the second part, which contains prayers for the good of all Muslims. After this, the *iqāmah* is made, followed by the two *farḍ* units. The prayer is then completed. The two *sunnah* units may follow, said silently, individually and not following the *imām*.

After these prayers Muslims can return to work, just as they can come from employment to them. There is no Muslim equivalent to the Jewish Sabbath or Christian Sunday, although many Muslim countries take Friday and Saturday as days of rest instead of the Saturday and Sunday common in the West.

The meaning of *ṣalāt*

Prayer is a basic element of religion, a foundation pillar. God does not need prayers since he is free of all needs, but human beings need to pray since prayer is a great teacher. The content of the formal prayers, performed regularly, reminds people of the greatness of God, and of the importance of Muhammad and the message that God gave through him. By punctuating the day with prayer, people withdraw from other concerns, however important they may seem, and so assent to God's supreme importance.

There are no sacraments in Islam. But the Qur'ān itself makes much of the signs of God, things which reveal God's presence to the eyes of faith: moon, sun and stars, wind and rain, the creation of people from human semen, and so on (e.g., 30: 20–7). So it is not surprising that some scholars have argued that the prayer postures of bowing and prostration are a vivid sign of *Allāhu akbar*: 'God is greater' even than humans, his *khalīfah*, 'vicegerents' on earth (2: 30–9), who, despite their status, must worship and obey him.

Prayer stresses God's will, which Muslim theologians believe is his greatest attribute. Extempore prayers are not a central part of *ṣalāt*, which concentrates on God's words, commands, and human responses to them, rather than human requests to God.

Prayer, especially performed in the mosque with others, stresses the solidarity of all Muslims. Some Muslim women and men believe that South Asian cultural practice, which excludes women from mosques in Britain, ironically weakens the universality which Muslims claim prayers demonstrate. This debate continues.

Prayer focuses on the purity which God demands. The ritual washings of *wuḍū'* and *ghusl* symbolise the desire of Muslims to be ethical beings, choosing the good and spurning the evil. Muslims say that when they pray they experience inner peace and stability, patience and hope, courage and strength to resist wrongdoing.

'Īd prayers

'Īd means festival and there are two main festivals in the Muslim year. The first is *'Īd al-Fiṭr*, breaking the fast at the end of the month of *Ramaḍān*. The second is *'Īd al-Aḍḥā*, the festival of sacrifice, celebrated on the tenth day of *Dhū'l Ḥijjah*, the month of pilgrimage. The significance of *'Īd* prayers is great. They have all the benefits of daily prayers, plus a particular sense of joy, comradeship and solidarity. Presents are often given and exchanged. There is also a feeling of victory: in *Ramaḍān*, worshippers who have kept the fast from dawn to dusk, which in a British summer can be from about 4.30am to 9pm, celebrate their achievement: and, during *Dhū'l Hijjah*, believers associate themselves with Abraham, his obedient willingness to slay his son, and his uncompromising monotheism.

'Īd prayers are congregational. They can take place any time between dawn and dusk. Usually, they take place in the morning so that the rest of the day can be given over to rejoicing with family members and friends. In some countries, they are done in parks or on common ground rather than in the mosque. No *adhān* or *iqāmah* is required. The prayer has two *rak'āt*, with the *imām* reciting out loud in each the *Fātiḥah* and another qur'anic passage. The *imām* says 'God is greater' three times, raising his cupped hands to his ears each time, and then lowering them to his sides. Then he places his right hand over the left one under the navel. The congregation follows the *imām* in all these sayings and actions.

At the end of the first *rak'ah* the *imām* rises, saying, 'God is greater' and then proceeds as in the first unit. After the two *rak'āt* are completed, the *imām* gives his *khuṭbah* in two parts. The first part begins with 'God is greater' nine times, and the second likewise but seven times. In *'Īd al-Fiṭr*, the sermon mentions the *ṣadaqah al-fiṭr*, the charity of breaking the fast, a voluntary tax, whereby Muslims are urged to give one full meal or its value to the poor. If a Muslim has any dependents, then he gives one meal or its equivalent for each of them, also to the poor or needy. At *'Īd al-Aḍḥā*, the *imām* must emphasise the duty of sacrifice. Each household must slaughter a goat or sheep, preferably after the prayers, and share it with the poor. This is not possible in countries like the United Kingdom, where the slaughter of animals has to be done in particular places by designated people.

The *'Īd* prayers are in addition to the five daily prayers. Before both *'Īd* prayers a special prayer is said, called the *takbīr al-tashrīq*:

> God is greater [three times]. There is no god but God. God is greater [twice]. His is the praise. Truly, God is greater. His is the abundant praise. Glory to him, night and day. There is no god but God, truly. He fulfilled his promise, supported his servant [Muhammad], granted his soldiers a manifest victory, and inflicted complete defeat on the united enemies. There is no god but God, and we worship none but him, with sincere devotion, though unbelievers resent it. O God! Exalt and shower blessings on our master Muhammad, and on the people of our master Muhammad, and on the companions of our master Muhammad, and on the supporters of our master Muhammad, and on the wives of our master Muhammad, and on the descendants of our master Muhammad, and salute all of them with great peace.

Especially during *Ramaḍān*, there are other special prayers that can be said. Some say the *ṣalāt al-tarāwīḥ*, a prayer of twenty *rak'āt*, recited every evening after *'ishā* prayers. Another voluntary (*sunnah*) prayer is the *tahajjud* or night vigil, which the Prophet is said to have observed regularly. The prayer is made between midnight and dawn, consisting of two to eight *rak'āt* which must be performed two at a time. It is considered a means of purification and spiritual renewal, and particularly meritorious during *Ramaḍān* and just before the two great feasts.

Additional formal prayers

Muslims follow traditions of the Prophet, which prescribe prayer at certain times. For example, it is incumbent to pray during an eclipse of the sun:

> There was an eclipse of the sun and the Prophet got up in trepidation fearing that the last hour had come. He then went to the mosque and prayed, standing, bowing and prostrating himself longer than I [the Prophet's companion, Abu Musa] had ever seen him do. He then said, 'These signs which God sends do not come on account of anyone's death or on account of his birth, but God produces dread in his servants by means of them. So when you see anything of that nature, apply yourselves to making mention of Him, supplication of Him and asking pardon of Him.'
>
> (Robson, vol. 1 1970: 310)

Similarly, there are prayers for specific occasions which are more common than solar eclipses. Among such times are: after childbirth; when going to bed, or getting up from it; entering and leaving the lavatory; starting a journey; visiting a graveyard; and at times of distress. All these prayers are in Arabic. Here are some examples. Before eating or drinking, a Muslim utters: 'In the name of God and with blessings from God'. When visiting the sick, Muslims say, 'Take away the sickness, O Lord of all people! And restore to health, for you are the healer; there is no healing except the healing you give. Grant recovery which leaves no malady behind'. When a person sneezes, bystanders declare, 'Praise be to God'.

These are examples of a formalised piety which touches all Muslims' lives every day. Many British Muslims comment on how religious statements in the West have become swearwords: 'Jesus', 'Christ', even 'God Almighty' have become casual curses rather than pious ejaculations. Analogous Muslim utterances, on the other hand, show how deeply devotional and prayerful statements and intentions are rooted in Islam. Perhaps the most common pious expression a Muslim says is, 'if God wills' (*in shā'a-Llāh*) after a purposive statement. The ways this expression is used can also illustrate the dangers of this utterance: formal piety can become formalised. Anyone who has travelled on an aeroplane of a Muslim country might be taken aback to hear the words, just before landing: 'In a few minutes, *in shā'a-Llāh*, we shall arrive safely in Karachi (or wherever) airport'. And there are Muslims who say of a besetting sin, 'I shall give it up tomorrow, *in shā'a-Llāh*'.

Many Muslims have been quick to recognise how formal prayers can ossify into rigidity, going through the motions, encouraging a joyless obedience. Such has always been the case. Hence the attraction of mystical and popular Islam.

Mystical Islam

The derivation of the word Ṣūfī is uncertain. The most likely solution is that it comes from the Arabic word ṣūf, meaning wool. A very early revelation describes the Prophet as 'enmantled' (74: 1), a state of dress associated with mystics. Other qur'anic passages can be interpreted to portray the Prophet as a mystic. At the beginning of some qur'anic chapters are a series of letters: for example, chapters 10 to 15 begin with *alif, lām* and *rā* (in English, a, l and r), and 13 has *mīm* (m) as well. One suggestion is that these represent the effort made by the Prophet as he began to speak the revelation Gabriel gave him from God. This is a fascinating though unproveable hypothesis. What is certain is that the very theory of revelation in Islam, that God gave his actual word to Muhammad through Gabriel when the Prophet was in a trance-like state, indicates some kind of mystical experience.

The Qur'ān (17: 1) describes a night-journey by the Prophet. *Ḥadīth* amplify this to describe his rapture from Makkah to a mosque in Jerusalem. Other *ḥadīth* interpret events described in sūrah 53 as a mystical experience:

> When God's messenger was taken up to heaven he was brought to the lote-tree of the boundary which is in the sixth heaven, to which what is taken up from the earth reaches and of which what is sent down from above reaches and of which something is grasped. He said that 'Behold, there overshadows the lote-tree what overshadows' [53: 16] meaning a covering of gold. He said God's messenger was then given three things: he was given the five times of prayer, he was given the last verses of *Sūra al-Baqara* [chapter 2], and forgiveness of sins was granted to those of his people who did not associate anything with God.
>
> (Robson, vol. 2 1970: 1270)

The important point is that Sufism, or mystical Islam, is grounded in the Qur'ān by its Muslim practitioners. Nowadays, various groups, influenced by New Age language or by a desire for esoteric experiences, call themselves Ṣūfīs. But this is a spurious claim. Sufism is not rootless recondite beliefs and practices. Sufism is soaked in the language of the Qur'ān and devotion to the Prophet.

The Arabic word for Sufism is *taṣawwuf*. It has been called 'the Science of the Heart'. The history of Sufism is a complicated and contentious subject, and beyond the scope of this chapter. We shall look briefly at four important figures in Islamic mysticism to illustrate the spiritual needs that were met by *taṣawwuf*.

The most famous woman Ṣūfī, and one of the earliest, was Rābi'a al-'Adawiyya (713 or 714 or 717–801), who passed all her life in Basra, a major city now in southern Iraq. She was enslaved as a child and became an ascetic when released. She emphasised the love of God, refusing marriage and preferring rather to be beloved of God. When asked what was the basis of her faith, she replied:

> I have not served God from fear of Hell, for I should be like a wretched hireling, if I did it from fear; nor from love of Paradise, for I should be a bad servant if I loved for the sake of what was given, but I have served Him only for the Love of Him and the Desire of Him.[3]

Some contemporaries ascribed to her these words:

> I have loved Thee with two loves, a selfish love and a love that is worthy
> As for the love which is selfish, I occupy myself therein with remembrance of Thee to the exclusion of all others.
> As for that which is worthy of Thee, therein Thou raisest the veil that I may see Thee.
> Yet there is no praise to me in this or that.
> But the praise is to Thee, whether in that or this.[4]

Such an outpouring of devotion has been given different explanations. Some scholars emphasise the fact that when Islam spread from Arabia into a wider empire it was taken over by corrupt and cynical leaders who manipulated the religion to their own ends. Furthermore, city life encouraged enthusiasm for material rather than spiritual improvement. So, someone like Rābi'a was, to some extent, acting in response to these irreligious trends. Others stress

Rābiʿa's commitment to God's love and suggest that orthodox ritual prayers cannot contain such fervour. There may be some truth in these analyses, but they are often simplistically expressed. The desert or oasis life is not always a spiritual paradise compared with the temptations of urbanisation! Moreover, ritual prayer can provide space for fervent praise of God and the Prophet, even if it is formally expressed: it is not uncommon to see a Muslim at *ṣalāt*, with tears of joy and thankfulness welling up in his or her eyes.

In that devotional outpouring of Rābiʿa, a significant word is remembrance. 'Remembrance (*dhikr*) of God' is an important qur'anic theme. Human beings are not regarded as corrupt or fallen so much as forgetful of the signs and mercies of God: 'Believers! Do not let your possessions or children turn you from the worship of God. Any who do so are losers' (63: 9). As Sufism developed, *dhikr* acquired the technical sense of 'litany', in which the name of God, *Allāh*, or a phrase like 'God is greater' (*Allāhu akbar*) is constantly repeated, and often linked to physical movement or techniques of breathing. When the *dhikr* is recited communally, often on a Friday, it is called *ḥaḍrah*, 'presence'. Ṣūfī groups still follow such practices.

Rābiʿa was doubtless a remarkable person. It may be significant that although every religious person could aspire to observing a discipline such as daily prayers in his or her tradition of faith, the achievements of someone like her are rare and not required of everyone. It is certainly significant that she did not live as a hermit, but gathered many disciples around her. Throughout Islamic history, Ṣūfī leaders have lived in communities or at least encouraged their followers to do so, and these have not been celibate groups but married people with families. It is also important that although Rābiʿa did not condemn the daily prayers, she is not remembered for her dedication to them but for her celebration of the love of God. Many Muslims have frowned upon Ṣūfīs for despising the rituals of Islam, including daily prayer, and some Western scholars have applauded them for seeing through them to something more profound. The truth may lie elsewhere. Many Ṣūfīs, being enthusiasts, might have scorned rituals, but many more have performed them yet looked for something extra.

Another figure in the early history of Islam and Sufism who has caused orthodox Muslims to frown upon *taṣawwuf*, and some Westerners and Christians to romanticise and Christianise it, was al-Husayn b. Mansur al-Hallaj (857–922). His sayings, actual and imputed, provoked much controversy in his lifetime and later. He was crucified for seeming to claim that he was identical with God. The unforgivable sin in Islam is *shirk*, 'sharing' God's godness with someone or something else. al-Hallaj was probably killed for political as much as religious reasons, but is notorious for his alleged claim, 'I am [religious] Truth' (*anā 'l-Ḥaqq*). When anyone uses religious language, it is not always clear how such language functions, what it means, whether it is literal, poetic, metaphorical or whatever. When a mystic uses it, it becomes even more uncertain. It is not necessarily the case that mystics are mystifying because they are notably imprecise. Indeed, many mystics are abnormally exact in their use of religious terminology, but the meaning they discern is known only to themselves and, sometimes, their more astute followers. Moreover, in the case of al-Hallaj and other mystics from the distant past, it is difficult, if not impossible, to recover what they meant, filtered as it is to us through the prejudices of enemies or even friends. al-Hallaj may have been claiming deity, in which case he is justly condemned as one who used Islamic teaching and concepts to gravely un-Islamic ends. It is quite possible, however, that like many mystics, he was claiming not an identity of being, but an identity of vision: he was, as it were, so caught up in his desire for God as to see things through God's eyes and desire only God's purposes. Certainly, there have been Muslim mystics who have, or seem to have, abandoned religious orthodoxy by claiming an identity with God that denies the central Muslim concept of *tawḥīd*, God's unity. But many more have had an experience or experiences which are beyond the power of language to describe, and which, being recounted, mislead more pedantic minds into condemnation.

As Sufism developed, it acquired technical expressions for some of these inexpressible experiences. It offered a series of stages through which initiates passed in their deepening experience with God. The final two stages are *fanā'* and *baqā'*. In *fanā'* ('extinction', 'annihilation', 'passing away'), the mystics' imperfections and earthly ties are annihilated, and they are absorbed into God, freed from contemplating self. This does not, however, mean that they lose all individuality, since *baqā'* ('remaining', 'abiding') is used to indicate a further stage in which the mystic 'abides' in God. Many mystics explained this in parables, realising that the concept was difficult if not impossible to convey in straightforward language.

It is no wonder that many have been perplexed by, and suspicious of, Ṣūfīs and what they were trying to say, claim and achieve. The figure who did much to make *taṣawwuf* respectable to orthodox Muslims was Abu Hamid Muhammad al-Ghazali (1058–1111). He was a teacher of Islamic theology and philosophy in Baghdad, when he was struck silent before his class one day in 1095. Nowadays, we might call it a psychosomatic illness, but this explains nothing. Six months earlier he had written *Tahāfut al-falāsafah* (*The Refutation of the Philosophers*), in which he exposed what he saw as the pretensions of metaphysical philosophy and theology. It is not surprising that he found it literally impossible to teach to his class what he despised. His was, also literally, a crisis of integrity. He wrote, 'My feet were standing on a sand-bank which was slipping beneath me, and I saw that I was in danger of hellfire if I did not do something to change my ways'.[5] He went on pilgrimage to Makkah and then retired to Tus in Khurasan (his birthplace) where he lived as a Ṣūfī. He returned to writing and (briefly) teaching. He spent his last years integrating the spiritual, ascetic and academic. He came to believe that he would be the Renewer of Islam for the new Islamic century.

Certainly, his was as much a reaffirmation of Muhammad's message as a reconstruction: he became a conservative, perhaps reactionary, writer. So he is the villain of many Muslim modernists. For example, the Indian author and judge, Syed Ameer Ali (1849–1928), believed him guilty of *taqlīd* ('imitation'; reliance on irrelevant past precedent and law), and dismissed him as 'quietist' and 'naive'.[6] Some contemporary scholars dismiss his importance: one of them argues that his brother Ahmad was a far more important figure in the history of Sufism.[7] That may be so, and it is certainly true that Christian scholars have admired al-Ghazali greatly and perhaps overestimated his importance in Islamic history. Nevertheless, at the very least, he stands as an example of an eminent figure who combined, in his later years, a Ṣūfī way with a commitment to orthodox Islamic teaching. He gives the lie to those who affirm that *taṣawwuf* is inevitably prone to *bid'ah* 'innovation', which is the opposite of *sunnah*, the 'trodden path' or 'customary practice' of those who follow the teachings of the Prophet.

The period after al-Ghazali's death saw the rise of many Ṣūfī orders. The inspiration behind one of these orders – some argue the founder of it – was Jalal al-Din Rumi (1207–73), a Persian mystic and poet. This particular order, which originated in Turkey, was the *mawlawiyyah*, the 'whirling dervishes'. Their dance is performed with music during their *dhikr*. According to one interpretation, it attempted to symbolise the motion of the spheres. Rumi wrote a lengthy poem, the *Mathnawī*, which celebrates the Divine Beloved. He had found its image in a wandering dervish called Shams al-Din, whom he met in 1244. Rumi took him into his house where, for a year or two, they were inseparable. Rumi's son, Sultan Walad, likened his father's relationship with this 'hidden saint' to the journey of Moses with Khadir, described in the Qur'ān (18: 65–82). Later, Rumi found inspiration in a disciple, Husam al-Din Hasan ibn Muhammad, whose name he mystically associated with the *Mathnawī*[8]

The *Mathnawī* begins with 'The Song of the Reed':

> Hearken to this Reed forlorn,
> Breathing ever since 'twas torn
> From its rushy bed, a strain
> Of impassioned love and pain.
>
> "The secret of my song, though near,
> None can see and none can hear.
> Oh, for a friend to know the sign
> And mingle all his soul with mine!
>
> 'Tis the flame of Love that fired me,
> 'Tis the wine of Love inspired me.
> Wouldst thou learn how lovers bleed,
> Hearken, hearken to the Reed!"

Such poetry largely speaks for itself. It is, however, necessary to point out that the Persian reed-flute has always been associated with the *mawlawiyyah* order, in which music and dancing are prominent features: 'Rumi uses it as a symbol for the soul emptied of self and filled with the Divine spirit'.[9]

This seems hostile to Islamic orthodoxy, which forbids or frowns upon music and dance. Moreover, the passage's erotic, arguably homo-erotic, analogy of divine and human all-embracing love is anathema to many Muslims. But much of Rumi's thought is grounded in Islamic orthodoxy: he condemns asceticism as practised by Christian hermits (the Qur'ān disapproves of monasticism, 57:

27); and defends the orthodox Muslim belief in *jabr* ('compulsion', 'determination'). He is careful to portray Ṣūfī leaders as the 'light of the Prophet' – a large claim to be sure, but not exactly *bid'ah*, 'innovation', since it does not take away Muhammad's status as the last and seal of the prophets (33: 40). Indeed, comparing himself with al-Hallaj, the poet wrote: 'Rumi hath not spoken and will not speak words of infidelity: do not disbelieve him!'.[10]

The point is not to over-emphasise either the closeness or distance of *taṣawwuf*, or at least some of its most distinguished practitioners, from Sunni Islam (the majority branch of Islam, which adheres to the *sunnah*, 'customary practice' of the Prophet), though, to be sure, the worship of Ṣūfīs has at times antagonised their more cautious co-religionists, and caused them and others to wonder how Islamic *taṣawwuf* is. Rather, it is to underline that whatever twists and turns Sufism has given to Islam, however shocking some of its beliefs and practices may seem or actually be, it has usually remained rooted in Qur'ān, *ḥadīth*, and even developed Muslim law. Its achievement has been to broaden the possibilities of how communion with God might be effected and what such intercourse might be.

Popular Islam

Although it may be an exaggeration to describe Ṣūfīs as 'spiritual athletes', it is certainly the case that many display a level of commitment which is not possible for, or desired by, ordinary Muslims for whom a less overwhelming yet sincere response is more germane. These Muslims may practise the daily prayers, required by the religion, fully or to some extent. They may also add certain, often controversial, practices. One such practice is the use of prayer-beads (*subḥah*). A full Islamic rosary consists of ninety-nine beads, a series of three times thirty-three beads, each indicating one of the ninety-nine beautiful names of God. These 'most beautiful names' (*al-Asmā' al-Ḥusnā*), an Arabic phrase found in the Qur'ān (e.g., 7: 180), are mostly found in the Qur'ān, though some come from the *ḥadīth*. Some of the most important are: the two titles, *al-raḥmān, al-raḥīm*, 'most gracious, most merciful': two more, *al-awwāl, al-ākhir*, 'the first, the last'; *al-qaiyūm*, 'the self-subsisting'; and so on. It is characteristic of Islam that God is described epigrammatically and elusively; he is rarely the subject of detailed theological scrutiny. The number, ninety-nine, hints at our incomplete knowledge of God:

it is an artificial number in that there are enough descriptions of God in Scripture and traditions to increase that number, but no Muslim ever names the hundredth name. That incompleteness witnesses to a God who is beyond our reach: 'He reveals nothing of himself save what he wills' (2: 255). There is an Arabic proverb that the superior smile on the face of a camel is because he knows the hundredth name! At any rate, Muslims learn to recite the names and so learn about God's nature through their use of the rosary.

Another popular practice throughout much of the Muslim world is devotion to, and intercession at, saints' shrines. This is very common in South Asian Islam. Throughout that subcontinent, shrines can be found to *walī 'ullāh*, a 'friend of God', someone (most often a Ṣūfī 'saint') who has become so close to God as to be able to bestow blessings on those who turn to him for aid. Muslims flock to the tombs of saints. There they perform *ṣalāt* and *du'ā* (private, petitionary prayers). They listen to *qawwalī*, religious songs, performed by musicians or, increasingly these days, on tapes or even compact discs over loudspeakers. They may tie ribbons to overhanging trees, and ask for health, prosperity, the gift of children, any of the things the human heart most desires. They may go individually, or in large numbers, for some important festival such as the anniversary of the saint's birth or death. A 'friend of God' is often known by the Persian word, *pīr*. A *pīr* may be dead and buried many generations or a few years, or he may be alive and well, with a group of disciples who dedicate themselves to his teaching. Muslims tend to talk about their *pīr* as if he were alive, even when he died long ago. In South Asia, these practices may be coloured by the influences of Hinduism.

Such devotional practices can easily verge on the superstitious. Ja'far Sharif, whose reminiscences were first published in 1832, wrote about the festival of one saint, Zinda Shah Madar, said to be an eleventh century converted Jew, who died near Kanpur (Cawnpore) in North India. He is called Zinda, which means 'the living one' in Urdu, the local Muslim language. He is supposed to be still alive, the Prophet having given him the ability to live without breathing. Both Hindus and Muslims visit his shrine. Women are forbidden, since it is believed that, if one were to enter, she would suffer pain, as if her whole body were aflame. People make vows to Zinda and put belts of gold around the necks of their children. On the date of his physical death, some people make special food. Fire-walking is done in his name. A large fire is kindled, upon which sandal-wood is thrown, then some fakirs, devotees of the saint, recite the *Fātiḥah* (first chapter of the Qur'ān), and jump into it, calling out words which protect them from being burned. On the saint's birthday, a black cow is killed in ritual fashion, but in the name of the saint, and meat is distributed to the fakirs (Sharif, Herklots and Crooke, 1921: 195f.). These and similar practices are still not uncommon in parts of South Asia. Even in Britain, many Muslims have a *pīr*, living or dead, whose guidance they seek.

Dedication to saints, or even to the use of the rosary, is condemned by many Muslims. In particular, the *Wahhabis*, followers of the strict teachings of Ibn 'Abd al-Wahhab (1703–92) of the Hanbalī school of Muslim law, the most rigorous of the four main schools, are very opposed to such practices. In South Asia and the United Kingdom, their views are expressed through the *Jamā'at-i Islāmī*. These 'puritanical' views have a certain economic and political importance, since Wahhabism is influential in Saudi Arabia, and has been promoted by the government there at home and abroad through financial grants. But popular Islam is deeply integrated into local structures of belief, and into social and religious practices in much of the Islamic world. It involves Muslims' prayerfulness and deepest commitments. Even at its most debased, it contains elements of the influence of Qur'ān and *ḥadīth*.

NOTES

1. Muslims follow a lunar calendar which is different from the solar Gregorian calendar used in the West. The Muslim year is shorter. I have followed the Gregorian dating in the text, which has become widely accepted as the 'Common Era' or 'Christian Era'. When Muslims write about Muhammad, they follow his name with an honorific formula, usually either 'PBUH', shorthand for 'Peace be upon him', or (S), for an Arabic expression meaning 'May God bless him and grant him salvation'. There is no wholly adequate translation of the Qur'ān into English, so I have provided my own rendering of the text. The best version is: Khatib, M.M. (1986) *The Bounteous Koran*, London, Macmillan.
2. Shi'ah Muslims belong to the 'party' of 'Ali, believing that this son-in-law of the Prophet should have succeeded him as political and religious leader of the Muslim community.

3. Smith, M. (1928) *Rabi'a the Mystic*, Cambridge, Cambridge University Press, p. 102.
4. Smith, M. (1928) *Rabi'a the Mystic*, Cambridge, Cambridge University Press, p. 102f.
5. Bowker, J. (1978) *The Religious Imagination and the Sense of God*, Oxford, Oxford University Press, pp. 192ff.
6. Ali, S.A. (1922 edn) *The Spirit of Islam*, London, Chatto & Windus, pp. 448–69.
7. Baldick, J. (1989) *Mystical Islam*, London, I.B. Tauris, pp. 65–7.
8. Nicholson, R.A. (1950) *Rumi: Poet and Mystic*, London, George Allen & Unwin, pp. 19–21.
9. Nicholson, *Rumi: Poet and Mystic*, p. 31.
10. Nicholson, *Rumi: Poet and Mystic*, pp. 70, 77, 143, 155.

FURTHER READING

Nasr, S.H. (ed.) (1991) *Islamic Spirituality: Manifestations*, London, SCM Press.

Robson, J. (1970) *Mishkāt al-Maṣabīh*, vol. 1, Lahore, Muhammad Ashraf.

Schimmel, A. (1975) *Mystical Dimensions of Islam*, Chapel Hill, University of North Carolina Press.

Sharif, J. with Herklots, G.A. (1921 revised edn by Crooke, W.) *Islam in India: The Customs of The Musulmans of India*, Oxford, Oxford University Press.

5. Judaism

Dan Cohn-Sherbok

In the Jewish faith worship is of fundamental importance. In addition to spontaneous prayer, the tradition prescribes both private and public worship. Private worship normally takes place in the home and is related to various formal occasions; public prayer is similarly fixed by time and takes place within the synagogue sanctuary where the Torah Scroll is contained within a sacred Ark. This chapter provides an introduction to these two basic patterns of prayer: the first section provides a survey of the development and nature of Jewish worship; this is followed by an outline of observances on the Sabbath, pilgrim festivals, High Holy Days, and Days of Joy.

For the Jewish people prayer has served as the vehicle by which they have expressed their joys, sorrows and hopes; it has played a major role in the religious life of the Jewish nation, especially in view of the successive crises and calamities in which they were involved throughout their history. In such situations Jews continually turned to God for assistance. Thus, in the Torah the patriarchs frequently addressed God through personal prayer. Abraham, for example, begged God to spare Sodom since he knew that by destroying the entire population he would destroy the righteous as well as the guilty (Gen. 18: 23–33). At Beth-el, Jacob vowed, 'if God will be with me, and will keep me in this way that I go, and will give me bread to eat, and raiment to put on . . . then shall the Lord be my God' (Gen. 28: 20–1).

Later Moses too prayed to God. After Israel had made a golden calf to worship, Moses begged God to forgive them for this sin (Exod. 32: 31–2). Joshua also turned to God for help. When the Israelites went to conquer the city of Ai, their attack was repulsed. In desperation Joshua prayed to God for help in defeating Israel's enemies (Josh. 7: 7). Later in the prophetic books, the prophets also offered personal prayers to God, as did the psalmist and others. This tradition of prayer continued after the canonisation of Scripture and, as a consequence, prayer has constantly animated the Jewish spirit – through personal encounter with the Divine, Jews have been consoled, sustained and uplifted. In addition to personal prayer, throughout history Jews have turned to God through communal worship.

In ancient times Jewish communal worship centred on the Temple in Jerusalem. Twice daily – in the morning and afternoon – the priests offered prescribed sacrifices while the Levites chanted psalms. On Sabbaths and festivals additional services were added to this daily ritual. At some stage it became customary to include other prayers along with the recitation of the Ten Commandments and the *Shema* (Deut. 6: 4–9, 11: 13–21; Num. 15: 37–41) in the Temple service. With the destruction of the Second Temple in 70 CE sacrificial offerings were replaced by the prayer service in the synagogue, referred to by the *rabbis* as *avodah she-ba-lev* (service of the heart). To enhance uniformity, they introduced fixed periods for daily prayer which corresponded with the times sacrifices had been offered in the Temple: the morning prayer (*shaharit*) and afternoon prayer (*minhah*) correspond with the daily and afternoon sacrifice; evening prayer (*maariv*) corresponds with the nightly burning of fats and limbs. By the completion of the Babylonian Talmud in the sixth century, the essential features of the synagogue service were established, but it was only in the eighth century that the first prayer book was composed, by Rav Amram, Gaon of Sura.

In the order of service, the first central feature is the *Shema*. In accordance with the commandment, 'You shall talk of them when you lie down and when you rise' (Deut. 6: 7), Jews are commanded to recite this prayer during the morning and evening service. The first section (Deut. 6: 4–9) begins with the phrase *Shema Yisrael* (Hear, O Israel: The Lord our God is one Lord). This verse teaches the unity of God, and the paragraph emphasises the duty to love God, meditate on his commandments and impress them on one's children. In addition, it contains laws regarding the *tefillin* and the *mezuzah*. *Tefillin* consist of two black leather boxes containing scriptural passages which are bound by black leather straps on the arm and forehead in accordance with the commandment requiring that 'you shall bind them as a sign upon your hand, and they shall be as frontlets between your eyes' (Deut. 6: 8). They are worn during morning prayer except on the Sabbath and festivals. The *mezuzah* consists of a piece of parchment, containing two paragraphs of the *Shema*, which is placed into a case and affixed to the right-hand side of an entrance. In accordance with the same decree, male Jews wear an undergarment with fringes (the smaller *tallit*) and a larger *tallit* (prayer shawl) for morning services. The prayer shawl is made of silk or wool with black or blue stripes with fringes (*tzitzit*) at each of the four corners.

The second major feature of the synagogue service is the *Shemoneh Esreh* (Eighteen Benedictions or *Amidah*). These prayers were composed over a long period of time and received their full form in the second century. They consist of eighteen separate prayers, plus an additional benediction dealing with heretics, which was composed by the sage Samuel the Younger at the request of Rabban Gamaliel in the second century. The first and last three benedictions are recited at every service; the thirteen other prayers are recited only on weekdays. On Sabbaths and festivals they are replaced by one prayer dealing with the Holy Day. They consist of the following benedictions:

1. Praise for God who remembers the deeds of the patriarchs on behalf of the community.
2. Acknowledgement of God's power in sustaining the living and his ability to revive the dead.
3. Praise of God's holiness.
4. Request for understanding and knowledge.
5. Plea for God's assistance to return to him in perfect repentance.
6. Supplication for forgiveness for sin.
7. Request for deliverance from affliction and persecution.
8. Petition for bodily health.
9. Request for God to bless agricultural produce so as to relieve want.
10. Supplication for the ingathering of the exiles.
11. Plea for the rule of justice under righteous leaders.
12. Request for the reward of the righteous and the pious.
13. Plea for the rebuilding of Jerusalem.

14. Supplication for the restoration of the dynasty of David.
15. Plea for God to accept prayer in mercy and favour.
16. Supplication for the restoration of the divine service in the Temple.
17. Thanksgiving for God's mercies.
18. Request for granting the blessing of peace to Israel.

On special occasions a number of special prayers are added to these benedictions.

From earliest times the Torah was read in public gatherings; subsequently, regular readings of the Torah on Sabbaths and festivals were instituted. In Babylonia the entire Torah was read during a yearly cycle; in Palestine it was completed once every three years. The Torah itself is divided into fifty-four sections, each of which is known as the 'order' or 'section' (*sidrah*). Each section is sub-divided into portions (each of which is called a *parashah*). Before the reading of the Torah in the synagogue, the Ark is opened and one or more Torah Scrolls are taken out.

The number of men called up to the reading varies: on Sabbaths there are seven; on *Yom Kippur*, six; on *Rosh Ha-Shanah* and the Pilgrim festivals (*Pesach, Sukkot*, and *Shavuot*), five; on *Rosh Hodesh* and *Hol Hamoed*, four; on *Purim, Hanukkah* and fast days, three; and on Sabbath afternoons and Monday and Thursday mornings (when the first *parashah* of the forthcoming *sidrah* is read), three. In former times those who were called up to the Torah read a section of the weekly *sidrah*; subsequently an expert in Torah reading was appointed to recite the entire *sidrah* and those called up recited blessings instead. The first three people to be called up are, in order: *Cohen* (priest), *Levi* (levite), and *Yisrael* (member of the congregation).

After the reading of the Torah, a section from the prophetic books (*Haftarah*) is recited. The person who is called up for the last *parashah* of the *sidrah* reads the *Haftarah* – he is known as the *maftir*. The section from the prophets parallels the content of the *sidrah*. Once the Torah Scroll is replaced in the Ark, a sermon is usually delivered based on the *sidrah* of the week.

Another central feature of the synagogue service is the *Kaddish* prayer. Written in Aramaic, it takes several forms in the prayer book and expresses the hope for universal peace under the Kingdom of God. There are five main forms:

1. Half *Kaddish*, recited by the reader between sections of the service.
2. Full *Kaddish*, recited by the reader at the end of a major section of the service.
3. Mourners' *Kaddish*, recited by mourners after the service.
4. Scholars' *Kaddish*, recited after the reading of talmudic midrashic passages in the presence of a *minyan* (quorum of ten men).
5. Expanded form of the Mourners' *Kaddish* which is recited at the cemetery after a burial.

A further feature of the service is the *Hallel*, consisting of Psalms 113–18. In the talmudic period it was known as the 'Egyptian *Hallel*' because the second Psalm (114) begins with the words: 'When Israel went forth from Egypt'. (This designation was used to distinguish this group of Psalms from another Psalm (136) – the Great *Hallel* – which is recited on the Sabbath and festivals during the morning service.) The complete *Hallel* is recited on the first two days of *Pesach*, on both days of *Shavuot*, on the nine days of *Sukkot*, and the eight days of *Hanukkah*. Part of the *Hallel* is recited on the intermediate days (*Hol Hamoed*), and the last two days of *Pesach*.

Since the thirteenth century the three daily services have concluded with the recitation of the *Alenu* prayer which proclaims God as king over humanity. In all likelihood it was introduced by Rav in the third century as an introduction to the *Malhuyot*, the section recited as part of the *Musaf* service for *Rosh Ha-Shanah*. In the middle ages this prayer was the death-song of Jewish martyrs. The first part of the prayer proclaims God as king of Israel; the second anticipates the time when idolatry will disappear and all human beings will acknowledge God as King of the Universe.

The traditional liturgy remained essentially the same until the Enlightenment in the nineteenth century. At this time reformers in Central Europe altered the worship service and introduced new prayers into the liturgy in conformity with current cultural and spiritual developments. Influenced by Protestant Christianity, these innovators decreed that the service should be shortened and conducted in the vernacular as well as in Hebrew. In addition, they introduced western melodies to the accompaniment of a choir and organ, and replaced the chanting of the Torah with a recitation of the *sidrah*. Prayers viewed as anachronistic were abandoned (such as the priestly blessing given by *cohanim*, the *Kol Nidre* prayer on the Day of Atonement, and prayers for the restoration of the Temple and the reinstitution of sacrifice). Further, prayers of a particularistic character were amended so that they became more universalistic in scope.

The Conservative movement also produced prayer books in line with its ideology. In general the Conservative liturgy followed the traditional *siddur* except for several differences:

1. Prayers for the restoration of sacrifice were changed.
2. The early morning benediction thanking God that the worshipper was not made a woman was altered.
3. Prayers for peace were altered to include all of humanity.
4. In general the *Yekum Purkah* prayer for schools and sages in Babylonia was omitted.
5. *Cohanim* (priests) usually did not recite the priestly benediction.
6. The *Amidah* was not usually repeated except on the High Holy Days.

In recent times all groups across the Jewish spectrum have produced new liturgies (such as those that commemorate Holocaust Remembrance Day, Israel Independence Day and Jerusalem Reunification Day). Moreover, a wide range of occasional liturgies exist for camps, youth groups and *havurot* (informal prayer groups). Among non-Orthodox denominations there is a growing emphasis on more egalitarian liturgies, with gender-free language and an increasingly democratic sense of responsibility. Thus prayer and worship continue to be of vital importance to the Jewish people, yet there have occurred a variety of alterations to its nature within all branches of the Jewish faith.

Sabbath

Genesis 2: 1–3 declares:

> The heaven and the earth were finished, and all the host of them. And on the seventh day God finished his work which he had done, and he rested on the seventh day from all his work which he had done. So God blessed

> the seventh day and hallowed it, because on it God rested from all his work which he had done in creation.

This passage serves as the basis for the decree that no work should be done on the Sabbath. During their sojourn in the Wilderness of Zin, the Israelites were first commanded to observe the Sabbath. They were told to work on five days of the week when they should collect a single portion of *manna*; on the sixth day they were instructed to collect a double portion for the following day was to be 'a day of solemn rest, a holy sabbath of the Lord' (Exod. 16: 23). On the seventh day, when several individuals made a search for *manna*, the Lord stated: 'How long do you refuse to keep my commandments and my laws? See! The Lord has given you the sabbath, therefore on the sixth day he gives you bread for two days; remain every man of you in his place, let no man go out of his place on the seventh day' (Exod. 16: 28–9).

Several weeks later God revealed the Ten Commandments, including prescriptions concerning the Sabbath day:

> Remember the sabbath day, to keep it holy. Six days you shall labour, and do all your work, but the seventh day is a sabbath to the Lord your God; in it you shall not do any work, you, or your son, or your daughter, your manservant, or your maidservant, or your cattle, or the sojourner who is within your gates; for in six days the Lord made heaven and earth, the sea, and all that is in them, and rested the seventh day; therefore the Lord blessed the sabbath day and hallowed it.
>
> (Exod. 20: 8–11)

The Book of Deuteronomy contains a different version, emphasising the Exodus from Egypt:

> Observe the sabbath day, to keep it holy, as the Lord your God commanded you. Six days you shall labour, and do all your work; but the seventh day is a sabbath to the Lord your God; in it you shall not do any work. . . . You shall remember that you were a servant in the land of Egypt, and the Lord your God brought you out thence with a mighty hand and an outstretched arm; therefore the Lord your God commanded you to keep the sabbath day.
>
> (Deut. 5: 12–15)

According to the Book of Exodus the Sabbath is a covenant between Israel and God:

> Say to the people of Israel, 'You shall keep my sabbaths, for this is a sign between me and you throughout your generations, that you may know that I, the Lord, sanctify you' . . . Therefore the people of Israel shall keep the sabbath, observing the sabbath throughout their generations as a perpetual covenant.
>
> (Exod. 31: 12, 16)

By the time the Sanhedrin began to function in Hasmonean times the observance of the Sabbath was regulated by Jewish law. Following the injunction in Exodus 20: 10, the primary aim was to refrain from work. In the Five Books of Moses only a few provisions are delineated: kindling a fire (Exod. 35: 3); ploughing and harvesting (Exod. 23: 12); carrying from one place to another (Exod. 16: 29). Such regulations were expanded by the *rabbis* who listed thirty-nine categories of work (which were involved in the building of the Tabernacle). According to the Mishnah they are:

> 1. sowing; 2. ploughing; 3. reaping; 4. binding sheaves; 5. threshing; 6. winnowing; 7. sorting; 8. grinding; 9. sifting; 10. kneading; 11. baking; 12. shearing sheep; 13. washing wool; 14. beating wool; 15. dyeing wool; 16. spinning; 17. sewing; 18. making two loops; 19. weaving two threads; 20. separating two threads; 21. tying; 22. loosening; 23. sewing two stitches; 24. tearing in order to sew two stitches; 25. hunting a deer; 26. slaughtering; 27. flaying; 28. salting; 29. curing a skin; 30. scraping the hide; 31. cutting; 32. writing two letters; 33. erasing in order to write two letters; 34. building; 35. pulling down a structure; 36. extinguishing a fire; 37. lighting a fire; 38. striking with a hammer; 39. moving something.

In the Talmud these categories were discussed and expanded to include within each category a range of activities. In order to ensure that individuals did not transgress these prescriptions, the *rabbis* enacted further legislation which served as a fence around the law. Yet despite such ordinances, there are certain situations which take precedence over Sabbath prohibitions. Witnesses of the New Moon, for example, who were to inform the Sanhedrin or *Bet Din* of this occurrence, were permitted to do so on the Sabbath. Other instances include: circumcision can be performed on the Sabbath; dangerous animals may be killed; persons are permitted to fight in self-defence; anything may be done to save a life or assist a woman in childbirth.

The Sabbath itself commences on Friday at sunset. About twenty minutes before sunset, candles are traditionally lit by the woman of the house who recites the blessing: 'Blessed are You, O Lord our God, King of the universe, who has hallowed us by your commandments and commanded us to kindle the Sabbath light'. In the synagogue, the service preceding Friday *maariv* takes place at twilight. Known as *Kabbalat Shabbat*, it is a late addition dating back to the sixteenth century when kabbalists in Safed went out to the fields on Friday afternoon to greet the Sabbath queen. In kabbalistic lore the Sabbath represents the *Shekhinah* (divine presence). This ritual is rooted in the custom of Haninah (first century) who, after preparing himself for the Sabbath, stood at sunset and said: 'Come let us go forth to welcome the Sabbath', and that of Yannai (third century) who said: 'Come Bride! Come bride!' On the basis of such sentiments Solomon Alkabets composed the Sabbath hymn, *Lekhah Dodi*, which has become a major feature of the liturgy. In the Sephardi rite, Psalm 29 and *Lekhah Dodi* are recited, whereas the Ashkenazi rite comprises Psalms 95–9, *Lekhah Dodi* and Psalms 92–3. The Reform prayer book offers a variety of alternative services, including abridged versions of these psalms and the entire *Lekhah Dodi*. The Reconstructionist service commences with biblical passages, continues with an invocation and meditation on the Sabbath, and proceeds to a reading of psalms and *Lekhah Dodi*.

Traditionally, when the father returns home from the synagogue, he blesses his children. With both hands placed on the head of a boy, he says: 'May God make you like Ephraim and Manasseh'; for a girl: 'May God make you like Sarah, Rebekah, Rachel and Leah'. In addition, he recites the priestly blessing. Those assembled then sing *Shalom Aleikhem* which welcomes the Sabbath angels. At the Sabbath table the father recites the *Kiddush* prayer over a cup of wine:

> Blessed are you, O Lord our God, King of the universe, who has sanctified us by your commandments and has taken pleasure in us, and in love and favour has given us your holy Sabbath as an inheritance, a memorial of the creation, that day being the first of the holy

> convocations, in remembrance of the Exodus from Egypt. For you have chosen us and hallowed us above all nations, and in love and favour have given us your holy Sabbath as an inheritance. Blessed are you O Lord, who sanctifies the Sabbath.

This is followed by the washing of the hands and blessing over bread (*Ha-Motzi*). The meal is followed by the singing of table hymns (*zemirot*) and concludes with the Grace after Meals. This, which Jews are obligated to recite after every meal, originally consisted of three paragraphs in which worshippers thank God for sustenance, the land and the Torah, and pray for the restoration of the Temple. Later a fourth paragraph was added, which contains the words: 'Who is good and does good'. Subsequently, short prayers beginning with 'the All Merciful' were added. On the Sabbath an additional prayer is included, dealing with the Sabbath day.

On Sabbath morning the liturgy consists of a morning service, a reading of the Torah and the *Haftarah*, and the additional service. In the service itself, introductory prayers prior to the *Shema* differ from those of weekdays, and the *Amidah* is also different. Seven individuals are called to the Reading of the Law, and an eighth for a reading from the Prophets. In the Reform movement the worship is abridged and has no additional service. On returning home, the morning *Kiddush* and *Ha-Motzi* are recited, followed by the Sabbath meal and then the Grace after Meals. In the afternoon service the Torah is read prior to the *Amidah*; three persons are called to the Torah, and the first portion of the reading of the law for the following week is recited. Customarily, three meals are to be eaten on the Sabbath day; the third meal is known as the *Seduah Shelishit*. It should take place just in time for the evening service. At the end of the Sabbath, the evening service takes place and is followed by the *Havdalah* service.

The *Havdalah* ceremony marks the conclusion of the Sabbath period; it is divided into four blessings. Three are recited over wine, spices and lights, and the service concludes with the *Havdalah* blessing. In the Sephardi, Ashkenazi and Yemenite rites, the blessings are similar, but the introductory sentences are different. The Ashkenazi rite contains biblical phrases with the term 'salvation'; the Sephardi requests the granting of bountifulness and success; the Yemenite prays for a successful week. The final blessing opens with the phrase, 'Blessed are you, O Lord our God, King of the universe, who distinguishes . . .', followed by a series of comparisons: between the holy and the profane, light and darkness, Israel and the nations, between the seventh day and the six days of the week. The hymn, *Ha-Mavdil*, follows the *Havdalah* ceremony and asks for forgiveness of sins and for the granting of a large number of children. A number of customs, including filling a cup and extinguishing the *Havdalah* candle in wine poured from it, are associated with the *Havdalah* ceremony. Within Reform Judaism an alternative *Havdalah* service incorporates additional readings with traditional blessings.

Pilgrim festivals

According to the Book of Deuteronomy Jews are to celebrate three pilgrim festivals each year:

> Three times each year all your males shall appear before the Lord your God at the place which he will choose, at the feast of unleavened bread, at the feast of weeks, and at the feast of booths.
>
> (Deut. 16: 16)

On the basis of this commandment large numbers of pilgrims went to Jerusalem during the First and Second Temple periods from throughout the Holy Land, Babylonia and the Mediterranean lands. There they assembled in the Temple area to offer sacrifice and pray to God.

The first of these festivals is *Pesach*, which is celebrated for eight days (seven in Israel) from 15 to 22 *Nisan*. The various names for this festival illustrate its different dimensions.

Pesach (Passover). This term is derived from the account of the tenth plague in Egypt when first-born Egyptians were killed whereas God 'passed over' the houses of the Israelites (whose door-posts and lintels were sprinkled with the blood of the *paschal* lamb). This term is also applied to the Passover sacrifice which took place on 14 *Nisan*; its flesh was roasted and eaten together with unleavened bread and bitter herbs.

Hag ha-Matzot (The Festival of Unleavened Bread). This term refers to the unleavened bread baked by the Israelites on their departure from Egypt. In accordance with God's command to Moses and Aaron while the people were in Egypt, no leaven was to be eaten during future Passover celebrations, nor was it to be kept in the house. All vessels used for leavening must be put away, and their place taken by a complete set used only for Passover. Although no leaven may be eaten during this period, the obligation to eat *matzah* applies only to the first two nights during the *seder* service.

Zeman Herutenu (The Season of Our Freedom). This term designates the deliverance from Egyptian slavery and the emergence of the Jewish people as a separate nation.

Hag ha-Aviv (The Festival of Spring). This name is used because the month of *Nisan* is described in Scripture as the month of *Aviv*, when ears of barley begin to ripen. In accordance with the biblical command, a measure of barley (*omer*) was brought to the Temple on the second day of Passover. Only when this was done could bread be made from the new barley harvest.

In preparation for Passover, Jewish law stipulates that all leaven must be removed from the house. On 14 *Nisan* a formal search is made for any remains of leaven. This is then put aside and burned on the following morning. The first night of Passover is celebrated in a home ceremony referred to as the *seder*. This is done to fulfil the biblical commandment to relate the story of the Exodus to one's son: 'And you shall tell your son on the day, saying: It is because of what the Lord did for me when I came out of Egypt' (Exod. 13: 8). The order of the service dates back to Temple times. During the ceremony celebrants traditionally lean on their left sides – this was the custom of freemen in ancient times.

The symbols placed on the *seder* table serve to remind those present of Egyptian bondage, God's redemption, and the celebration in Temple times. They consist of the following:

Three ***matzot***. These three pieces of unleavened bread are placed on top of one another usually in a special cover. The upper and lower *matzot* symbolise the double portion of *manna* provided for the Israelites in the wilderness. The middle *matzah* (which is broken in two at the beginning of the *seder*) represents the 'bread of affliction'.

The smaller part is eaten to comply with the commandment to eat *matzah*. The larger part is set aside for the *Afikoman* which recalls Temple times when the meal was completed with the eating of the *paschal* lamb. These three *matzot* also symbolise the three divisions of the Jewish people: *Cohen, Levi* and *Yisrael*.

Four Cups of Wine. According to tradition, each Jew must drink four cups of wine at the *seder*. The first is linked to the recital of *Kiddush*, the second with the account of the Exodus and the Blessing for Redemption, the third with the Grace after Meals, and the fourth with the *Hallel* and prayers for thanksgiving. These cups also symbolise four expressions of redemption in Exodus 6: 6–7.

The Cup of Elijah. This cup symbolises the hospitality awaiting the passerby and wayfarer. According to tradition, the Messiah will reveal himself at the Passover, and Malachi declared that he will be preceded by Elijah. The Cup of Elijah was also introduced because of the doubt as to whether five cups of wine should be drunk rather than four.

Bitter Herbs. These symbolise the bitterness of Egyptian slavery.

Parsley. This is dipped in salt water and eaten after the *Kiddush*. It is associated with Spring.

Haroset. This is a mixture of apples, nuts, cinnamon and wine. It is a reminder of the bricks and mortar that Jews were forced to use in Egypt.

Roasted Shankbone. This symbolises the *paschal* offering.

Roasted Egg. This commemorates the festival sacrifice in the Temple.

Salt Water. This recalls the salt that was offered with all sacrifices. It also symbolises the salt water of the tears of the ancient Israelites.

At the *seder*, the *Haggadah* details the order of service. It is as follows:

1. The *Kiddush* is recited.
2. The celebrant washes his hands.
3. The parsley is dipped in salt water.
4. The celebrant divides the middle *matzah* and sets aside the *Afikoman*.
5. The celebrant recites the *Haggadah* narration.
6. The participants wash their hands.
7. The blessing over bread is recited.
8. The blessing over *matzah* is recited.
9. Bitter herbs are eaten.
10. The *matzah* and *maror* are combined.
11. The meal is eaten.
12. The *Afikoman* is eaten.
13. Grace after Meals is recited.
14. The *Hallel* is recited.
15. The service is concluded.
16. Hymns and songs are sung.

The second pilgrim festival – *Shavuot* – is celebrated for two days (or one day in Israel) on the 6th and 7th of *Sivan*. The word *shavuot* means 'weeks'; seven weeks are counted from the bringing of the *omer* on the second day of *Pesach* (Lev. 23: 15). The festival is also referred to as *Pentecost*, a Greek word meaning fiftieth, since it was celebrated on the fiftieth day. Symbolically the day commemorates the culmination of the process of emancipation which began with the Exodus at Passover and was concluded with the proclamation of the Law at Mount Sinai. Liturgically, the festival is also called *Zeman Mattan Toratenu* (the Season of the Giving of our Torah). This name relates to events depicted in Exodus 19–20.

During the Temple period farmers set out for Jerusalem to offer a selection of first ripe fruits as a thank-offering. In post-Temple times, the emphasis shifted to the festival's identification as the anniversary of the giving of the law on Mount Sinai. In some communities it is a practice to remain awake during *Shavuot* night. In the sixteenth century Solomon Alkabets and other kabbalists began the custom of *tikkun*, in which an anthology of biblical and rabbinic material was recited. Today, in those communities where this custom is observed, this lectionary has been replaced by a passage of the Talmud or other rabbinic literature. Some congregations in the diaspora read a book of Psalms on the second night. Synagogues themselves are decorated with flowers or plants, and dairy food is consumed during the festival. The liturgical readings for the festival include the Ten Commandments preceded by the liturgical poem, *Akdamut Millin*, on the first day, and *Yetsiv Pitgam* before the *Haftarah* on the second day. The Book of Ruth is also recited. In many communities this festival marks the graduation of young people from formal synagogue education (or confirmation in Reform Temples). In Israel, agricultural settlements hold a First Fruits celebration on *Shavuot*.

The third pilgrim festival – *Sukkot* – is also prescribed in the Bible: 'On the fifteenth day of this seventh month and for seven days is the feast of Tabernacles to the Lord' (Lev. 23: 34). Beginning on the 15th of *Tishri*, it commemorates God's protection of the Israelites during their sojourn in the desert. Leviticus commands that Jews are to construct booths during this period as a reminder that the people of Israel dwelt in booths when they fled from Egypt (Lev. 23: 42–3).

During this festival a *sukkah* (booth) is constructed; its roof is covered with branches of trees and plants. During the festival meals are to be eaten inside the *sukkah*. Leviticus also declares that various agricultural species should play a part in the observance of this festival: 'And you shall take on the first day the fruit of goodly trees, branches of palm trees, and boughs of leafy trees, and willows of the brook; and you shall rejoice before the Lord your God seven days' (Lev. 23: 40). In compliance with this prescription the four species are used in the liturgy: palm, myrtle, willow and citron. On each day of the festival the *lulav* (palm branch) is waved in every direction before and during the *Hallel* – this symbolises God's presence throughout the world. Holding the four species, Jews make one circuit around the Torah which is carried on the *bimah* (platform) on each of the first six days. During this circuit *Hoshana* prayers are recited. On the seventh day of *Sukkot* (*Hoshana Rabba*) seven circuits are made around the Torah while reciting *Hoshana* prayers. During the service the reader wears a white *kittel* (robe).

The New Year and the Day of Atonement

In ancient times the Jewish New Year (*Rosh Ha-Shanah*) took place on one day; it is presently observed for two days, in both Israel and the diaspora, on 1 and 2 *Tishri*, marking the beginning of the Ten Days of Penitence which conclude on the Day of Atonement (*Yom*

Kippur). The term *Rosh Ha-Shanah* occurs only once in Scripture (Ezek. 40: 1). None the less, this festival has three other biblical designations:

1. *Shabbaton* – a day of solemn rest to be observed on the first day of the seventh month.
2. *Zikhron Teruah* – a memorial proclaimed with the blast of a horn (Lev. 23: 24).
3. *Yom Teruah* – 'a day of blowing the horn' (Num. 29: 1).

Later the *rabbis* referred to the New Year as *Yom Ha-Din* (the Day of Judgment) and *Yom Ha-Zikkaron* (the Day of Remembrance).

According to the Mishnah, all human beings will pass before God on the New Year; the Talmud expands this ideal by stressing the need for self-examination. In rabbinic literature each person stands before the Throne of God, and judgement on every person is entered on the New Year and sealed on the Day of Atonement. The tractate *Rosh Ha-Shanah* in the Talmud declares that 'there are three ledgers opened in heaven: one for the completely righteous who are immediately inscribed and sealed in the Book of Life; another for the thoroughly wicked who are recorded in the Book of Death; and a third for the intermediate, ordinary type of person, whose fate hangs in the balance and is suspended until the Day of Atonement'. In this light, *Rosh Ha-Shanah* and *Yom Kippur* are also called *Yamim Noraim* (Days of Awe).

On *Rosh Ha-Shanah* the Ark curtain, reading desk and Torah Scroll mantles are decked in white, and the *rabbi*, cantor and person who blows the *shofar* (ram's horn) all wear a white *kittel* (robe). In the synagogue service the *Amidah* of the *Musaf* service contains three sections relating to God's sovereignty, providence and revelation: *Malkhuyyot* (introduced by the *Alenu* prayer) deals with God's rule; *Zikhronot* portrays God's remembrance of the ancestors of the Jewish people when he judges each generation; *Shofarot* contains verses relating to the *shofar* (ram's horn) and deals with the revelation on Mount Sinai and the messianic age. Each introductory section is followed by three verses from the Torah, three from the Writings, three from the Prophets, and one from the Torah. On the first and second day of *Rosh Ha-Shanah* the Torah readings concern the birth of Isaac (Gen. 21: 1–34) and the binding of Isaac, or *Akedah* (Gen. 22: 1–24). The *Haftarah* for the first day is 1 Sam. 1:

19–2: 10, which depicts the birth of Samuel who subsequently dedicated his life to God's service; on the second day the *Haftarah* deals with Jeremiah's prophecy (Jer. 31: 2–20) concerning the restoration of Israel.

On both days of *Rosh Ha-Shanah* (except when the first is on the Sabbath) the *shofar* is blown at three points during the service: thirty times after the reading of the Law; thirty times during *Musaf* (ten at the end of each of the three main sections); thirty times after *Musaf*, and ten before *Alenu*. In the liturgy there are three variants of the blowing of the *shofar*: *tekiah* (a long note); *shevarim* (three tremulous notes), and *teruot* (nine short notes). According to Maimonides, the *shofar* is blown to call sinners to repent. As he explains in the *Mishneh Torah*: 'Awake you sinners, and ponder your deeds; remember your creator, forsake your evil ways, and return to God'. In the Ashkenazi rite the *U-Netanneh Tokef* prayer concludes the service on a hopeful note as congregants declare that 'Repentance, Prayer and Charity can avert the evil decree'.

Traditionally it was a custom to go to the seaside or the banks of a river on the afternoon of the first day (or on the second day if the first falls on a Sabbath). The ceremony of *Tashlikh* symbolises the casting of one's sins into a body of water. The prayers for *Tashlikh* and three verses from the book of Micah (Mic. 7: 18–20) express confidence in divine forgiveness. In the home after *Kiddush* a piece of bread is dipped in honey followed by a piece of apple, and a prayer is recited that the year ahead may be good and sweet. It is also a custom to eat the new season's fruit on the second night of *Rosh Ha-Shanah* to justify reciting the *Sheheheyanu* benediction on enjoying new things. The *hallah* loaves baked for this festival are usually round or have a plaited crust shaped like a ladder to represent hopes for a good round year or the effort to direct one's life upward to God.

The Ten Days of Penitence begin with the New Year and last until the Day of Atonement. This is considered the most solemn time of the year, when all are judged and their fate determined for the coming year. During the Ten Days a number of additions are made to the liturgy, especially in the morning service. *Selihot* (penitential prayers) are recited during the morning service, and various additions are made to the *Amidah* and the reader's repetition of the *Amidah*. The reader's repetition is followed by the *Avinu Malkenu* prayer. In some synagogues it is customary to recite Psalm 130: 1 in the morning service. It is also traditional to visit the graves of close relatives at this time. The Sabbath between the New Year and the Day of Atonement is *Shabbat Shuvah*.

The holiest day of the Jewish calendar is *Yom Kippur* which takes place on 10 *Tishri*. Like other major festivals, its observance is prescribed in Scripture: 'On the tenth day of this seventh month is the Day of Atonement; and you shall afflict yourselves . . . It shall be to you a sabbath of solemn rest, and you shall afflict yourselves; on the ninth day of the month beginning at evening, from evening to evening' (Lev. 23: 27, 32). According to the sages, afflicting one's soul involved abstaining from food and drink. Thus every male over the age of thirteen and every female over twelve is obliged to fast from sunset until nightfall the next evening. Sick people, however, may take medicine and small amounts of food and drink; similarly, those who are ill may be forbidden to fast.

During the day normal Sabbath prohibitions apply, but worshippers are to abstain from food and drink, marital relations, wearing leather shoes, using cosmetics and lotions, and washing the body except for fingers and eyes. The *rabbis* stress that the Day of Atonement enables human beings to atone for sins against God; however, regarding transgressions committed against others, pardon cannot be obtained unless forgiveness has been sought from the persons injured; as a consequence, it is customary for Jews to seek reconciliation with anyone they might have offended during the year. Previously, lashes (*malkot*) were administered in the synagogue to impart a feeling of repentance, but this custom has largely disappeared. The *kapparot* ritual still takes place before the Day of Atonement among Sephardi and eastern communities as well as among some Ashkenazim. During this ceremony a fowl is slaughtered and either eaten before the fast or sold for money which is given to charity – its death symbolises the transfer of guilt from the person to the bird that has been killed. In many congregations Jews substitute coins for the fowl, and charity boxes are available at the morning and afternoon services before *Yom Kippur*.

Customarily Jews were able to absolve vows on the eve of *Yom Kippur*. In addition, afternoon prayers are recited earlier than normal, and the *Amidah* is extended by two formulae of confession (*Ashamnu* and *Al Het*). Some pious Jews immerse themselves in a *mikveh* (ritual bath) in order to undergo purification before the fast. In the home, a final meal (*seudah mafseket*) is eaten and, prior to lighting the festival candles, a memorial candle is kindled to burn throughout the day. Further, leather shoes are replaced by non-leather shoes or slippers. The prayer shawl (*tallit*) is worn throughout all the services, and a white curtain (*parokhet*) adorns the synagogue Ark and the Scrolls of the Law. The reader's desk and other furnishings are also covered in white. Among Ashkenazim, *rabbi*s, cantors and other officiants also wear a white *kittel*.

On *Yom Kippur* five services take place. The first, *Kol Nidre* (named after its introductory declarations) ends with the concluding service (*Neilah*). Except for the extended *Amidah*, each service has its own characteristic liturgy. In all of them, however, the confession of sins (*viddui*) is pronounced; shorter confessions as well as longer ones are in the first person plural to emphasise collective responsibility. In some liturgies there are also confessions of personal transgressions. Of special importance in the liturgy is the *Avinu Malkenu* prayer, in which individuals confess their sins and pray for forgiveness.

In most congregations the *Kol Nidre* (declaration of annulment of vows) is recited on the eve of *Yom Kippur*. Among the Orthodox it was a custom to spend the night in the synagogue reciting the entire book of Psalms as well as other readings. Among Sephardim and Reform Jews the memorial prayer is recited on *Kol Nidre*. In addition to *selihot* and other hymns, the morning service includes a Torah reading (Lev. 16), describing the Day of Atonement ritual in the Sanctuary, and a *maftir* (additional) reading (Num. 29: 7–11), concerning the festival sacrifices. The *Haftarah* (Isa. 57: 14–58, 14) describes the fast that is required. Ashkenazim (excluding Reform Jews) then recite memorial prayers (*Yizkor*). Among Sephardi Jewry and eastern communities, the *Hashkavah* service is repeated.

Before the *Musaf* service a special prayer (*Hineni He-Ani Mi-Maas*) is recited. A number of liturgical hymns are also included in the reader's repetition of the *Amidah*, including the *U-Netanneh Tokef* passage. Interpolated in among the *selihot* and confessions toward the end of *Musaf* is the *Elleh Ezkerah* martyrology. Based on a medieval *midrash*, this martyrology describes the plight of the Ten Martyrs who were persecuted for defying Hadrian's ban on the study of Torah. In some rites this part of the service has been expanded to include readings from Holocaust sources. In the afternoon service Leviticus 18 is read, dealing with prohibited marriages and sexual offences; the *Haftarah* is the book of Jonah.

Before the concluding service (*Neilah*), the hymn, *El Nora Alilah*, is chanted among Sephardim. This part of the liturgy is recited as twilight approaches. During this time hymns such as *Petah Lanu Shaar* serve to remind congregants that the period for repentance is nearly over. In many congregations the Ark remains open and worshippers stand throughout the service. Worshippers ask God to inscribe each person for a good life and to seal them for a favourable fate. *Neilah* concludes with the chanting of *Avinu Malkenu*. This is followed by the *Shema*, the threefold recital of *Barukh Shem Kevod Malkhuto*, and a sevenfold acknowledgment that the Lord is God. The *shofar* is then blown, and the congregants recite *La-Shanah ha-Baah Bi-Yerushalayim* (Next Year in Jerusalem). After the service concludes it is customary to begin the construction of the *sukkah*.

Days of Joy

In the Jewish calendar there are a number of joyous festivals on which Jews are permitted to follow their daily tasks:

HANUKKAH

This festival (meaning 'dedication') is celebrated for eight days beginning on 25 *Kislev*: it commemorates the victory of the Maccabees over the Seleucids in the second century BCE. At this time the Maccabees engaged in a military struggle with the Seleucids, who had desecrated the Temple in Jerusalem. After a three year struggle (165–163 BCE), the Maccabees under Judah Maccabee conquered Jerusalem and rebuilt the altar. According to tradition, a small amount of oil for use in the *menorah* miraculously lasted for eight days. *Hanukkah* commemorates this miracle.

The central observance of this festival is the kindling of the festive lamp on each of the eight nights. This practice gave the holiday the additional name of *Hag Ha-Urim* (Festival of Lights). In ancient times this lamp was placed in the doorway or in the street outside to publicise the miracle; subsequently the lamp was placed inside the house. The lighting occurs after dark (except on Friday evenings when it must be done before the kindling of the Sabbath lights). The procedure for lighting the *Hanukkah* candles is to light one candle (or oil lamp) on the first night, and an additional candle each night until the last night when all eight candles are lit. The kindling should go from left to right. An alternative tradition prescribes that the eight candles are lit on the first night, seven on the second night, and so forth. These candles are lit by an additional candle called the *shammash* (serving light). In addition to this home ceremony, candles are lit in the synagogue.

In the synagogue liturgy this festival is commemorated by the recitation of the *Al ha-Nissim* prayer in the *Amidah* and Grace after Meals. In the morning service the *Hallel* is recited, and a special reading of the Law takes place on each day of the holiday. In both the home and the synagogue the hymn *Maoz Tsur* is sung in Ashkenazi communities; the Sephardim read Psalm 30 instead. During *Hanukkah* it is customary to hold parties which include games and singing. The most well-known game involves a *dreydel* (spinning top). The *dreydel* is inscribed with four Hebrew letters (*nun, gimmel, he, shin*) on its side – this is an acrostic for the phrase *nes gadol hayah sham* (a great miracle happened here). During *Hanukkah* it is customary to eat *latkes* (potato pancakes) and *sufganiyyot* (doughnuts). In modern Israel the festival is associated with national heroism, and a torch is carried from the traditional burial site of the Maccabees at Modiin to various parts of the country.

PURIM

Another festival of joy is *Purim*, celebrated on 14 *Adar* to commemorate the deliverance of Persian Jewry from the plans of Haman, the chief minister of King Ahasuerus. The name of this holiday is derived from the Accadian word '*pur*' (lots), which refers to Haman's casting of lots to determine a date (13 *Adar*) to destroy the Jewish people (Esther 3: 7–14). In remembrance of this date the Fast of Esther is observed on 13 *Adar* – on this day Queen Esther proclaimed a fast before she interceded with the king. On the next day, *Purim* is celebrated as the Feast of Lots which Mordecai, Esther's cousin, inaugurated to remember the deliverance of the Jewish people (Esther 9: 20ff). The 15th of *Adar* is *Purim Shasan*, since the conflict between the Jews and Haman's supporters in ancient Susa did not cease until the 14th and Ahasuerus allowed the Jews an extra day to overcome their foes. This means that the deliverance could only be celebrated a day later (Esther 9: 13–18).

The laws regarding the observance of *Purim* are specified in the tractate *Megillah* in the Talmud. In the evening and morning services the Esther-Scroll is chanted to a traditional melody. In most congregations *Purim* resembles a carnival – children frequently attend the reading from the Scroll in fancy dress and, whenever Haman's name is mentioned, worshippers stamp their feet and whirl noisemakers (*greggers*). In the *Amidah* and Grace after Meals, a prayer of thanksgiving is included; however, the *Hallel* psalms are excluded. During *Purim* it is customary to exchange gifts and donate to charity. During the afternoon a special festive meal takes place, including such traditional dishes as *Hamentashen* (Haman's pockets) – triangular buns or pastries filled with poppyseed, prunes, dates, etc. It is usual for parents and relatives to give children money (*Purim gelt*). On *Purim* it is customary to stage plays, and in *yeshivot*, students imitate their teachers. In modern Israel parades take place with revellers dressed in *Purim* costumes.

ROSH HODESH

Rosh Hodesh is another festival of joy. It occurs with the New Moon each month. Since the Jewish calendar is lunar, each month lasts a little more than twenty-nine days. Because it was not possible to arrange the calendar with months of alternative length, the Sanhedrin declared whether a month had twenty-nine or thirty days. If the outgoing month had twenty-nine days, the next day was *Rosh Hodesh*. When a month had thirty days, the last day of the outgoing month and the first day of the new month constituted *Rosh Hodesh*. In early rabbinic times, the Sanhedrin was responsible for determining the day of the New Moon on the basis of eye witnesses who had claimed to see the new moon. Only in the fourth century was a permanent calendar fixed by Hillel II.

During the period of the First Temple, *Rosh Hodesh* was observed with the offering of special sacrifices, the blowing of *shofars*, feasting and a rest from work. By the end of the sixth century BCE, *Rosh Hodesh* became a semi-holiday. Eventually even this status disappeared, and *Rosh Hodesh* became a normal working day except for various liturgical changes. The liturgy for *Rosh Hodesh* includes the *Yaaleh Ve-Yavo* prayer, read in the *Amidah* and in Grace after Meals, which asks God to remember his people for good, for blessing and for life. In the morning service the *Hallel* psalms of praise are recited. The Bible reading is from Numbers 28, which describes the Temple service for the New Moon. An additional service is also included, corresponding to the additional sacrifice which was offered on the New Moon.

TU BI-SHEVAT

A further joyous festival is the New Year for Trees (*Tu Bi-Shevat*) which takes place on 15 *Shevat*. Although this festival is not referred to in the Bible, it appeared in the Second Temple period as a fixed cut-off date for determining the tithe levied on the produce of fruit trees. Once the Temple was destroyed, the laws of tithing were no longer applicable; as a result, this festival took on a new character. Wherever Jews resided, it reminded them of their connection with the Holy Land. During the fifteenth century a number of new ceremonies and rituals were instituted by the mystics of Safed. Due to the influence of Isaac Luria, it became customary to celebrate the festival with gatherings where special fruits were eaten and hymns were sung and readings from Scripture were recited. Among the fruits eaten on *Tu Bi-Shevat* were those of the Holy Land. In modern Israel new trees are planted during this festival.

15 *AV*

Another joyous occasion is 15 *Av*, which was a folk festival in the Second Temple period. At this time bachelors selected their wives from unmarried maidens. According to the Mishnah, on both this day and the Day of Atonement young girls in Jerusalem dressed in white garments and danced in the vineyards where young men selected their brides. In modern times this festival is marked only by a ban on eulogies or fasting. In the liturgy the *Tahanun* prayer is not recited after the *Amidah*.

INDEPENDENCE DAY

The final festival is Independence Day – this is Israel's national day which commemorates the proclamation of its independence on 5 *Iyyar* 1948. The Chief Rabbinate of Israel declared it a religious holiday and established a special order of service for the evening and morning worship. This service includes the *Hallel*, and a reading from Isaiah (Is. 10: 32–11: 12). The rabbinate also suspended any fast which occurs on the day, the recital of the *Tahanun* prayer, and mourning restrictions of the *Omer* period. In Israel the preceding day is set aside as a day of remembrance for soldiers who died in battle. *Yizkor* prayers (including the *Kaddish*) are recited then and next-of-kin visit the military cemeteries. At home, memorial candles are lit and Psalm 9 is recited in many synagogues.

For the Jew, God is the creator and sustainer of the universe who has chosen the Jewish people from all nations. Out of covenantal loyalty the Jewish people have turned to their God in times of both joy and sorrow; through prayer and worship the nation has expressed its deepest spiritual longings and hope for the dawn of a new age when God will rule over all creatures. Both private and public prayer have thus played a central role in the Jewish tradition.

FURTHER READING

De Lange, N. (1986) *Judaism* Oxford, Oxford University Press.

Jacobs, L. (1987) *The Book of Jewish Practice*, New York, Behrman House.

Neusner, J. (1974) *The Way of Torah: An Introduction to Judaism*, Florence, Kentucky, Dickenson.

Pilkington, C.M. (1991) *Judaism*, London, Hodder and Stoughton.

Siegal, R., Strassfield, M. and Strassfield, S. (eds) (1973) *The Jewish Catalogue*, Philadelphia, Jewish Publication Society.

Steinberg, M. (1947) *Basic Judaism*, London, Harcourt Brace Jovanovich.
Strassfield, S. and Strassfield, M. (eds) (1966) *Encyclopedia of the Jewish Religion*, London, Holt, Rinehart & Winston.
Strassfield, S. and Strassfield, M. (eds) (1976) *The Second Jewish Catalogue*, Philadelphia, Jewish Publication Society.
Werblowsky, R.J. and Wigoder, G. (eds) (1966) *Encyclopedia of the Jewish Religion*, London, Holt, Rinehart & Winston.
Wouk, H. (1968) *This is My God*, New York, Doubleday.

This chapter is based on Dan Cohn-Sherbok, *The Jewish Faith*, London, Society for Promoting Christian Knowledge.

6. Sikhism

Beryl Dhanjal

In the indices of a collection of scholarly works on Sikhism, the word worship did not merit a single entry. Definitions in English to Panjābi dictionaries were also significant; the most common word used was *pūjā*, which indeed means honour or worship, but many people would associate the word more with the ritual associated with reverencing the image of a Hindu deity than with Sikhism.

Rather than such acts, the pre-eminent activity in Sikhism is *pāṭh karna* (reading from the Gurū Granth Sāhib). There are Sikh rites and congregational assemblies, and for most ordinary people these would be seen as the major public acts of worship, though their private daily acts are paramount. They rise before dawn, bathe and meditate on the *Nām*, the Name, the one beyond time. One elderly friend, speaking about his early morning devotions, said, 'I sit in the silence and I try to hear that divine music'. And throughout the day, he, and others like him, do not forget the *Nām*.

Guru Nanak and the *sant*s never ceased from stressing the importance of interior religion. There was no importance at all placed on traditional practices and modes of worship, like pilgrimages, complicated rituals, and severe austerities. In fact, all the usual institutions and activities were seen by Guru Nanak as liable to get in the way of a person becoming rightly attuned by meditating on the name of God and hearing his word in the heart. From his *bānī* (poetry) we know that Guru Nanak was well-informed about the religious practices of his day. He mentions Hindu religious writings, philosophies and epics, and deities. He knew of the different sects, and all sorts of holy men, renouncers, pandits and *jogīs*, and Jain monks (of whom he didn't approve at all). He knew of Islam and Muslims, the Qur'ān, sharī'āt, the '*ulamā*' (the educated élite, scholars) and the leaders and assorted holy men – *pīrs*, *walīs*, *qalandar*s and *darveśe*s.

His understanding of the scene seems comprehensive. His attitude is subtle. Since the main point for him is liberation through hearing the word of God in the depth of the heart, most of these things are a hindrance rather than a help. He does not deny the existence of Hindu deities. They are the creations of God too, but in *Japjī Sāhib* he puts them in the plural: no end of Śivas, Kṛṣṇas and Brahmās all praising the one. It conjures up a splendid picture.

All of the traditional approaches of the religious life are rejected in a forthright way. There is no sense in making pilgrimages. Nanak says, 'I would bathe at a place of pilgrimage if that would please him, but without his blessing nothing is gained' (Gurū Granth Sāhib, *Japjī*, *pauṛi* 6). The wanderings and immersings in water are of no help when the true pilgrimage is within the heart. The only temple that matters is inside oneself (Gurū Granth Sāhib: 152).

> Listening to the word one finds truth, contentment, spiritual perception.
> Listening to the word secures all that pilgrimage can achieve by bathing at every sacred site.
>
> (Gurū Granth Sāhib, *Japjī*, *pauṛi* 12)

There is no sense in worshipping deities in the form of *murtīs* (images).

> What can they give you? If you wash them in water and let go of them, they sink. How can they take you across the ocean of existence?
>
> (Gurū Granth Sāhib: 637)

Grewal (1969: 209) says that ritualistic reading or recitation has as little effect on a person as perfume has on a dog. This relates to a passage in the Gurū Granth Sāhib (143).

True rituals are ones within, which rid the heart of pride, low passions, and sensual appetites. Ritual specialists are fools unless they know God and set themselves on the path towards him. Without the true name all ritual and rites are meaningless. When Guru Nanak mentions the plethora of religious figures, he usually tells them to translate their religious impedimenta and trappings into something more worthwhile: translate the *jogī* ear-rings into contentment, the begging bowl into honest work, and meditate on God instead of smearing ash all over the body. While Nanak appears to favour the Ṣūfī (devotional) path of Islam, he advises Muslims to live their faith, accept God's order, believe in him and efface themselves, receiving God's grace. They are advised to translate their mosques into kindness and make truth their *pīr* (spiritual preceptor). God's grace is the *kalimah* (Islamic profession of faith) and *namāz* (prayer). (Gurū Granth Sāhib: 140). A real *darveś* abandons everything to meet the creator. But Nanak was a practical man; he talks in the same way of craft occupations – of minting the divine word, with continence as the forge, tranquillity the goldsmith, intelligence the anvil and knowledge the tools. Again, he mentions fear as the bellows, austerities the fire, and love the crucible with which to cast the divine word (Gurū Granth Sāhib, *Japjī*, *pauṛi* 38). For every person, true religion was all that mattered; superficialities, *panth*s (paths, groupings), were to be discarded, as they only impeded the way.

Yet if Nanak seems negative in rejecting traditional practices of worship, he was not simply negative. If he rejected contemporary practice, the reference was immediately followed up by a positive suggestion. To put it bluntly: Why waste your time on these diversions when you can have the real thing? God alone is the proper object of devotion. A sentence often used is, 'There is no other' (Gurū Granth Sāhib: 223, 357, 433, 660, 225, for example, and many similar sentiments elsewhere). Only devotion to the one leads anywhere: 'I serve only the one, I know no other' (Gurū Granth Sāhib: 225). To whom else can worship be directed? There is no other.

Knowing it, one has to follow the discipline of *Nām simaraṇ* or *Nām japnā*. *Nām simaraṇ* is a discipline, and those who can sustain it pass into a state of *sahaj* (bliss). One no longer returns and transmigrates. But the state of *sahaj* (blissful union), becoming at one with God and thus achieving liberation in life, is more important than transmigration. Blissful union with God is therefore attained through worship – worship understood as meditation on the attributes and qualities of God, and following the discipline. This kind of worship is the central plank of the teaching. But it is a difficult path, not easily understood and hard to practise.

Popular religion

Obviously a sophisticated concept of this nature is too difficult for many. For many people *Nām japnā* means uttering a word or syllable over and over, repeating a *mantra*. Often with Sikhs the word may be *Vāhigurū*, or *Satnām* (God). Some people use rosaries and say the word over and over. Another method is singing the *kīrtan*, the hymns of the Gurūs. These are sung in assemblies in gurdwaras. Many people also follow a daily routine of prayers, the *Nit Nem* (regular daily readings at set times).

Many of those who attend *kīrtan* do not actually join in the singing. They seem to prefer to sit and listen. Nowadays, many listen to recordings. There are plenty of tapes and records available. People in Britain can also listen to *śabad*s (hymns from the Gurū Granth Sāhib, as well as Hindu *bhajan*s and Muslim *qwalli*s) on Sunrise Radio. Radio is probably one of the most significant sources nowadays for transmitting *gurbāṇī*, and Asian religious music in general. In fact, the modern media are having a profound effect by making teaching and preaching more accessible than ever before. The majority of Sikhs have not been well-informed about the content of the Gurū Granth Sāhib and about the deep philosophy. There are not, and never have been, many sources of public education. There are no equivalents of seminaries, priests, and evangelism, and not many sources of instruction.

Proverbial summaries of popular religion

Many ordinary folk in Britain might say that 'Love your neighbour' or 'Do as you would be done by', would sum up the golden rule. Likewise, there are some popular, proverb-like sayings summing up Sikhism. An old three-word one is *Nām dān iśnān*, meaning the Name, charity and bathing. Nowadays, people often interpret the bathing part as pure living, though it seems likely that it did mean ablution. Nowadays some add other words – *sevā* meaning service, and *simaraṇ*, remembrance. *Sevā* is service of the *saṅgat* and gurdwara. It means serving or preparing food in the *laṅgar*, and sweeping up, or looking after the place. It may mean taking care of visitors' shoes, but nowadays some modern, educated Sikhs interpret it as wider community service.

There is another saying, *Nām japo, kirt kaṛo, vaṇḍ chhako*, which means meditating on the Name, doing honest work and giving a share of what you have honestly earned to others in charity. These are basic, sensible principles for living a decent life. The way life is led is worship, a discipline. Each person has to do it on his or her own level.

Are these things – the difficult discipline, the repetition of words, and the singing – worship? It seems reasonable to classify them as such, for they are acts of deep devotion and a discipline of interior religion. Internal discipline is the central point. This discipline can be practised anywhere at any time. A person can do it on the bus or at home. Sikhs ought to read a hymn from the Gurū Granth Sāhib in the morning, before breakfast. But *Rahit Maryādā* makes it clear that this is not a superstitious ritual. If they cannot manage it in the morning for any reason, they could do it later. And if there are times of difficulty, or if people are travelling and it is not possible, then they should not have superstitious fears about being unable to do the reading. They should do the best they can and be sensible about it. It is sometimes claimed that Sikhs could pray anywhere, and that in times past they used to pray often enough on horseback.

The development of rites and services

Meeting together is an important part of Sikhism. The *Rahit Maryādā* says that Sikhs should visit the gurdwara as often as possible. The Gurū is, after all, considered to be manifest in the *saṅgat*, the assembly, as well as in the Gurū Granth Sāhib. Apart from studying and living by the teachings, a person should be active in the community and perform *sevā* (service). It is held to be important to meet with holy people.

People meet at the gurdwara for congregational reading of the Gurū Granth Sāhib, and for rites of passage (which, given the extended Panjabi family, entails meeting rather frequently), and there are several festivals which are a time for coming together.

Guru Nanak's community

We cannot be very clear about what Guru Nanak's small community was like. In his later years he lived at a place called Kartarpur. Writers suggest that there was a community which gathered round him, and that people came to hear his preaching. Bhai Gurdas gives an account of the daily routine of the Sikhs, rising early to bathe and remember the Name. He records their service to the *saṅgat*, which he sees as the abode of God. Macauliffe (1909: 181) says *Sodar* and *Sohila* were chanted in the evening, and the *Japjī* repeated at the ambrosial hour of the morning. He mentions here the evening and morning prayers. Certainly there must have been some organisation. Before he died, Guru Nanak had appointed a successor to take over. This was not unusual, for holy men in India usually do so.

The same message, the same discipline, emerges through the rest of the succession of Gurūs, and although the sixth, seventh and eighth did not write poetry, the message was unaltered in the writings of the ninth and tenth. Guru Nanak's companion, Mardana, had a family, and his descendants in Pakistan have continued singing until the present. These things were set down in the scriptures, which have been accurately transmitted from that day to this.

Evolution of the community

While doctrine has been transmitted unchanged, the community has evolved. The belief developed that Guru Nanak and his successors had a special mission. Many authors have commented that the attitude towards the Gurū changed over time (Grewal 1969: 293; Hans 1988: 180; McLeod 1980: 242). The Gurū became *Satgurū* (True Gurū), and eventually *Saccā Pātśāh* (True Emperor). The Gurūs were seen as Prophets of God or even, in some extreme cases, as God himself. In the works of Bhai Gurdas, the scholar who lived between the times of the third and seventh Gurūs, and who emerged as an orthodox spokesman for the Gurūs' line against their opponents, Nanak's 'True Gurū' appears to become transposed to Nanak himself. However, when Gurdas writes of the Gurū, is it Nanak he means or Nanak's unseen Gurū? W.H. McLeod (1980: 240, 1989: 52) thinks it is both simultaneously, since the living Gurū embodies the spirit of the eternal Gurū, and is to be identified with God.

But because of this transposition, a *darśan* of the Gurū is a means to liberation. So powerful is the *darśan* of Nanak that the *darśan* obtained even at second-hand by reading the *janam sākhī*s is sufficient, and books end with the saying, 'He who reads this is assured of liberation'. Yet the message of the Name remained unchanged. Bhai Gurdas observed:

> If bathing at places of pilgrimage brings liberation, frogs must certainly be saved.
> If growing long hair sets one free, the banyan tree with dangling tresses is saved.
> If going about naked serves a purpose, then the deer in the forest must be pious.
> And the ass which rolls in the dirt must too, if smearing ashes on the body can gain salvation.
> The cows in the field are saved, if silence gains deliverance.
> Only the Guru can give us salvation.
> Only the Guru can set a man free.
>
> (*Vār* 36: 14)

The early institutions developed by the Gurūs and community were an interpretation or extension of the Gurū's mission. According to the *janam sākhīs*, whenever Guru Nanak overcame an opponent in argument (which is the outcome of just about every *sākhī*), the opponent would fall at the Gurū's feet and would open a *dharamsālā*. The first to open such a place was Sajjan Thag, a nasty character who was sitting beside the road offering succour to passing travellers. He had built a temple and a mosque there – to lure travellers into his house. Once he had them inside he robbed them and threw them down the well. He was going to rob Guru Nanak and Mardana but before he had a chance to do so, Nanak had sung a poem which convinced Sajjan Thag of the error of his ways. Sajjan begged forgiveness and opened a *dharamsālā*.

Unfortunately, there is not much indication of what a *dharamsālā* might have been like. But from early times, clearly *saṅgat* (communities) did meet. There was always a stress on meeting together and singing *kīrtan*. There is a picture of how the community met together during the *janam sākhī* period. In the *janam sākhī* (kept at the India Office Library, which is known as Manuscript B40, and which W.H. McLeod (1980) has translated and dated at 1733) there is a description of a *dharamsālā* beneath a Rājā's palace where the Sikhs sang hymns. Perhaps *dharamsālā*, which seems to have been the meeting place of the early *Paṅth*, was replaced by gurdwara once the printing press had arrived and made copies of the Gurū Granth Sāhib more generally available.

The B40 *janam sākhī* also refers to the selection of hymns suitable for last thing at night, called *Ārатī Sohila*, and to Guru Nanak telling the Sikhs to go to sleep after it had been sung. Macauliffe (1909, vol. 2: 264) says that Guru Ram Das 'composed the following for the instruction of his Sikhs in the practice of their religion':

> Let him who calleth himself a Sikh of the true Guru, rise early and meditate on God.
> Let him exert himself in the early morning, bathe in the tank of nectar,
> Repeat God's name under the Guru's instruction, and all his sins and transgressions shall be erased.
> Let him at sunrise sing the Guru's hymns, and whether sitting or standing meditate on God's name.
> The disciple who at every breath meditateth on God, will please the Guru's heart.

This suggests that from early times there was an emphasis on the discipline of an early morning order.

Gurbāṇī used for daily services

It is also clear, from the organisation of the Gurū Granth Sāhib, that some pieces are selected and placed at the front of the volume and repeated again in their logical place in the strict order of that volume. They are the pieces in daily use.

These pieces are intended for specific times of day. Sikhs should rise early, bathe and meditate. They should repeat Guru Nanak's *Japjī Sāhib*. It is the single most important piece of *gurbāṇī*, which comes at the beginning, uniquely has no musical mode ascribed to it, and so may be intended for deeper meditation. It starts with Guru Nanak's description of God, and considers what a human being's response should be – to meditate on his Name. There are thirty-eight stanzas, so it is quite long, but it does have some built-in aids to memory. And it is pithy, condensed, full of observation, and imagery. Some lines are absolutely unforgettable. In *Japjī Sāhib*, Guru Nanak denounces ritual; one must walk according to God's path, leading a righteous life and seeking to arrive at the realm of righteousness. Altogether there are five realms. After righteousness there are realms of knowledge, surrender, grace and truth. One passes through them to be united with God.

The second poem in the daily routine should be Guru Govind Singh's *Jap*, a lengthy collection of attributes pertaining to God. Finally, the Ten *Savaiyye* should be recited. These are invocations, in which the Gurū points out the uselessness of conventional ritual and practice, and of earthly pomp and might: 'only they who love God can find Him' (McLeod 1984: 95).

The next selection of pieces is intended for the end of the working day. This would be at sunset in India. These are verses by Gurus Nanak, Ram Das and Arjan. They can be said individually or in a congregation. The joyful *Ānand*, 'joyful bliss is mine when the Guru comes', is usually sung.

Late in the evening, the final readings of the day are *Kīrtan Sohila*, a short passage said before sleep. It is intended to calm the mind and free it from the distractions of the daily round, focusing it on God.

There are several other pieces of *gurbāṇī* which are frequently read or recited. In the morning, people in gurdwaras sing, and many individuals turn to *Asā dī Vār*. *Asā* is a *rāga*, a musical mode, suitable for morning. A *Vār* is a poetic form used for heroic deeds. The hero in this *Vār* is the Lord. There are twenty-four stanzas by Guru Nanak concerning the role of the *satgurū*, the voice heard within the heart.

There is one other piece of *gurbāṇī* which is enormously popular and frequently read, although it is not actually part of the regular daily prayers. It is a very long piece by Guru Arjan, called *Sukhmanī Sāhib*. The name is a pun, meaning either 'the Pearl of Peace' or 'the Peace of Mind'. It is a hymn about the beauty of the Name of God, and the efficacy of the name in the quest for liberation. It is popular with both Sikhs and Hindus. *Sukhmanī Sāhib* is often read in the morning.

These works are not intended for mere ritual reading. At each hour of the passing day, appropriate passages are assigned to focus the mind on the Name.

Ardās

One other prayer ought to be noted. It is unique in that it is the solitary piece which is recited regularly in gurdwaras and which does not have its source in the Gurū Granth Sāhib. It is known as *Ardās*, which means petition. It concludes Sikh ceremonies. There is not one single authorised version, though there is a version in *Rahit Maryādā* (1978), the code of conduct.

In the first part of the *Ardās*, the words quoted are from *Caṅḍī dī Vār* in the *Dasam Granth*. They recall the Sikh Gurūs, the Gurū Granth Sāhib and various events in history. Specific prayer requests can be added. People can pray for others, the sick, suffering or bereaved. God's blessing on all humanity is requested. While the *Ardās* is said, people stand, facing the Gurū Granth Sāhib, with hands together.

On the first day of each month of the Indian calendar some people read a special poem, which describes the yearning of the wife (the devotee) for her Lord as the months of the year pass by. This form of verse is a popular one in India, and Gurus Nanak and Arjan both produced fine examples. People have tended to bathe and observe the first day and the darkest night of the Indian lunar months, but these are traditional observances, not holy days as such.

Communal worship

In the *Mahimā Parkāś*, a *janam sākhī* dating from the eighteenth century, it is written that Guru Arjan laid down routines and ceremonies: for bathing, having the Granth read, holding *Darbār* and receiving people, *kīrtan*, and *laṅgar* at the Darbār Sāhib (Golden Temple), and these routines were adhered to elsewhere. But there were periods when the Gurūs lost control of the temple and it is said that other practices were introduced at that time.

Later, Guru Govind Singh appointed one of his companions, Bhai Mani Singh, to conduct the proper rites and Granth reading at the Darbār Sāhib.

The service of large temples was complicated and involved a lot of work. Arrangements had to be made for the collection of tithes, revenues, taxes and *octroi* (a duty levied on goods entering a town, a system encountered also in continental Europe). Arrangements were required for the management of village lands attached to the gurdwara. The Mahārājā and others in power used to donate the revenue due from villages and areas towards the support of religious institutions.

There had to be many officials and servants of the temples: a treasurer, a man to say *Ardās*, a man to wave the *chauri* (fly-whisk), mace-bearers, people to spread sheets, people to wash sheets, musicians, artisans, *granthīs* (who sat in attendance on the Gurū Granth Sāhib), and *pūjārīs* (who accepted and invoked blessings on *praśād*). During the eighteenth century, *sardārs* (chieftains, warlords) gave monies and had improvements made and buildings erected. Ranjit Singh, who was Emperor from 1799 to 1839, gave generously to the Darbār Sāhib and paid to have walls inlaid with gold. He would visit the Darbār Sāhib often, especially on *amāvas* and *sankrānti* days. These are the first day and the dark night of the Indian lunar months.

Ranjit Singh was not a good-looking man. He was pock-marked and blind in one eye. He was illiterate but clever and was noted for his generosity to all religious traditions. He would give generously to religious institutions of all kinds, including Muslim and Hindu institutions. He would listen to the Gurū Granth Sāhib in the afternoon, would worship at Hindu *mandīrs* and is said to have paid an enormous amount for a Qur'ān which a calligrapher had spent a lifetime on preparing. When he was praised for being so positive in his attitude to all faiths, he said, 'God wanted me to look upon all religions with one eye, that is why he took away the light from the other'.

Many people, looking back on the rituals of those days, condemn Ranjit Singh and his contemporaries for their espousal of 'Hindu' forms. But Sikh ceremonies and worship in their present form are a modern tradition. Aside from people writing specifically about religion, people with a purely practical interest in these matters, e.g., army recruitment staff, give a fairly conventional account of the ceremonies of the life-cycle of Sikhs of their day – the late nineteenth century – describing ceremonies which would nowadays be regarded with horror and branded as Hindu. Prakash Tandon (1988: 16) refers to intermarriage between Hindus and Sikhs of the same caste who had the same customs – not surprisingly, as this was their primary identity. Intermarriage still happens.

What has changed is that a reform movement has renewed Sikh ceremonies. The Singh Sabha felt that the once pristine faith had been sullied, ceremonies and forms hallowed by the Gurūs in the golden age had been displaced by creeping Hinduism.

What they in fact did was to displace older forms of Sikhism, and replace them with one orthodox model. They were demarcating Sikh space by throwing out *murtīs* (deities) from shrines, whitewashing frescoes, using the Panjābi language, replacing rituals (life-cycle, daily and festival), trying to remove the observance of the usual Hindu ones and replace them with those which are more specifically Sikh. In this process of demarcation, the life-cycle rituals, marking important phases in a person's life, were of paramount importance. There were a very large number of publications around the turn of the century on the correct way to perform rites of passage. After a campaign, the *ānand* form of marriage was legally recognised in 1909. Instructions for the rites of passage are laid down in *Rahit Maryādā*. There are also instructions for reading the Gurū Granth Sāhib.

Festivals

Festivals are not mentioned in the *Rahit* and no observances are prescribed. There are not many festivals which are universally observed. Many events are celebrated at the places where they actually happened – commemorated might be a better word; one doesn't really celebrate deaths and martyrdoms. There were shrines all over Panjab, both Indian and Pakistani Panjab, where events in the lives of Gurūs and other holy people were recalled in local festivals. Nowadays, a few *gurpurb*s are remembered more or less universally, the birthdays of Gurus Nanak and Govind Singh, for example. The central feature of the commemoration of these is an *akhaṇḍ pāṭh*.

The most important festival is *Baisākhī*, usually 13 April. Until recently, *Baisākhī* was regarded as a secular festival. Tandon (1988: 57) describes *Baisākhī*s of his own childhood as a bacchanalian thanksgiving celebrated in town and country by Hindus, Muslims and Sikhs. It is still regarded as a *melā* (fair), and is different from a strictly religious festival like a *gurpurb*, the birth or death anniversary of a Gurū. *Baisākhī*, however, has become most important as a celebration of the founding of the *Khālsā*, which traditionally dates from the first day of the Indian month of *Baisākh* 1699, when Guru Govind Singh initiated the first members. Initiations are common at this time, therefore. An *akhaṇḍ pāṭh* is held. There is also a ceremony centred on the flagpole which is to be found outside any gurdwara. The flagpole is lowered, the old cloths in which it is wrapped are removed. The pole is washed with yoghurt and re-wrapped in new cloths, and a new *niśān sāhib*, the

Sikh symbol on an orange pennant, is attached to the top. The whole community assembles for this important occasion. Sikhs are not tradition-bound however. One local gurdwara in London makes it a point to have something new and different for *Baisākhī* every year. There are policemen playing bagpipes, a procession of the children singing English translations of *gurbāṇī*, a new chandelier, five *akhaṇḍ pāṭh*s being read simultaneously. People come from afar to see, wondering whatever they will do next! Often a *nagar kīrtan*, procession around town, may be held at this time. The Gurū Granth Sāhib, mounted on a decorated lorry, is taken around the town.

Dīvālī comes in October/November time. It is a time of fun, with fireworks at night, and people exchange gifts and give sweets to friends. Traditionally, it marks the release of Guru Hargovind from prison. Gurdwaras are illuminated with lights and lamps.

These festivals are important because they are all times when there is a big assembly. Sikhs make a special effort to attend the gurdwara and participate in community acts of worship. An enormous number of people attend on *Baisākhī* to perform the ritual with the new *niśān sāhib*. In addition, many people attend as their relatives and friends take their initiation into the *Khālsā* on that day. (This is one ritual which is not open to non-members of the *Khālsā*.) There is always an *akhaṇḍ pāṭh*. The assembly of people sit together to listen to *kīrtan*, and everyone eats in the *laṅgar*.

Everyday rituals

The main rituals of Sikhism are the rites of passage, and the everyday routine of the ordinary gurdwara. All rites require that the Gurū Granth Sāhib is installed under its canopy, upon its throne. It will be placed there in the morning with due reverence. Certainly the daily routine at the large historic shrines is more complex than at a village gurdwara. A large historic gurdwara has many volunteers and officials to carry out functions. A small village may not have a gurdwara at all, or only a very small one, where a *granthī* opens the Gurū Granth Sāhib and people come for a *darśan* whenever they can. People are expected to do their best in their own circumstances but not to make a binding ritual out of their observance.

If the Gurū Granth Sāhib is being read, a *chaur* (whisk, symbol of royalty) will be waved over it. If it is closed, it will be covered with some beautiful cloths called *rumālās*.

The Gurū Granth Sāhib will be opened to take the orders for the day, and the daily routine of *gurbāṇī* will be read. When people come to the gurdwara, some of them touch the threshold with their hand and put the hand to their forehead, applying the dust which has fallen from holy feet.

People remove their shoes and cover their heads. Men who wear turbans are already covered. For bareheaded men, any hat would serve – or a handkerchief. Women cover their heads with a *chuṅnī* or *dupattā*, a gauzy veil or scarf. Many gurdwaras keep a basket full of suitable pieces of cloth at the entrance so that they can be borrowed by visitors. Everyone bows, kneeling and then touching the forehead to the floor – this is called *mathā tekṇā*. It is a way of showing respect to God; they are not worshipping the book.

If people have brought an offering in kind, they leave it at the side of the *maṅjī*, the throne in which the Gurū Granth Sāhib is installed. It might be a bottle of milk (crates are often left ready to receive bottles). It might be some rice or flour, sugar or lentils. Sweets, flowers or fruit can be offered. Or a person might just offer some money in the collection box placed there for the purpose. Everyone offers something. The person should then move back, but without turning his or her back to the Gurū Granth Sāhib.

Then, if *kīrtan* is actually in progress, the person should cause no disturbance and inconvenience but go and find a place to sit. Men and women sit on separate sides, as is customary. There is no deep theological reason for this. Modern Sikh women are not considered inferior. They can read the Gurū Granth Sāhib and can take part in running gurdwaras. (See the chapter on Sikhism in *Women in Religion* in this series.)

The assembly always sits on the floor. The women often have children with them and the children sometimes play at the back. Of recent years in the United Kingdom there has been a tendency for children to invade the men's side and visit Dad more than they perhaps did in the past. Nowadays, there tends to be a lot more 'shhsh-ing' than formerly!

The fact that the Gurū Granth Sāhib consists of hymns set to musical modes means that music and poetry are the centre of ritual and are clearly important. Anyone who is capable (and who has the courage to do so publicly) is allowed to read, but in practice nowadays at most congregational occasions a *bhāī*, *granthī* or *giānī* (various grades of officiants) leads the ceremony, and the singing is led by a group of *rāgīs* (musicians).

Officiants

It is often stated that there is no priesthood in Sikhism. Throughout history, there were traditional practitioners and office-bearers. There were several orders of religious teachers, providing *mahaṅts* and *udāsīs* who ran the shrines. These positions, like almost everything else in India, tended to become hereditary. When the Singh Sabha embarked on the reform movement, the *mahaṅts* were unhappy. Their positions were challenged and under threat.

They were the descendants of families or successors of holy men who had been running shrines for several hundred years. The descendants of the Gurūs, the *mahaṅts*, brahmans, *purohits* and others were dispossessed of their shrines. They were characterised in Singh Sabha writings as wicked and depraved. Some of them probably were. Some came to terms with the changes; others responded to the challenges of the reform movement with violence. There were some unfortunate events, and people were killed. The traditional religious leaders were removed. *Mahaṅts*, *purohits* and brahmans went, and *bhāīs*, *rāgīs*, *giānīs* and *granthīs* and others emerged to take their places. Brahman verse went out, Gurū Granth verse came in.

There are some *ṭaksāls* (literally mints, as in places where coins are minted), traditional schools which instruct students, but there is no formal recognition and no equivalent of ordination. Mostly, people seem to prefer their *granthīs* to be steady, married middle-aged or elderly men. It has always been a male occupation, perhaps because it would not be possible for a female *granthaṅ* to take care of a building and be alone in some remote place. The *granthī*'s job is attending the Gurū Granth Sāhib, reading aloud, and looking after the gurdwara. Good *granthīs* steer clear of all temptations and of gurdwara politics. Traditionally, *granthīs* have never had any kind of pastoral role; people have normally relied on the extended family to cope with their troubles. Nowadays in the United Kingdom, though, gurdwaras play an increasing role in helping people with their problems and troubles, filling in forms and doing social work. However, a *granthī* has no special authority. He is not given any special position or respect. All Sikhs are equal.

Sadly, of recent years, there has been trouble in Panjab. The western press often refer to the 'High Priests' and their involvement in the political situation. They are actually referring to the Chief *Granthīs* from Amritsar (Darbār Sāhib and the *Akāl Takhat*), and the *jathedārs* (commanders, group leaders) of the *Takhats* (thrones, five historic sites associated with Sikh Gurūs). They are not priests and, as modern Sikhism is emphatic in its espousal of egalitarianism, neither can they be called 'high'. They have, however, been used in political manoeuvres.

There are also many *sants*, pious men (but not saints) revered and looked up to for their teaching. Some of them have lineages, with one teacher succeeding another. Some of them have personal authority and attract many devotees who attend to hear their teaching.

Congregational assemblies

Congregational assemblies are called *dīwān* (court). They usually last for several hours – two or three hours at least. *Dīwān* is usually held on Sundays or other holidays because people are able to attend then. At *dīwān*, the Gurū Granth Sāhib is opened, and there is singing of the hymns (*kīrtan*). There is usually a lecture, an explanation of a hymn. The speaker might explain it line by line and might use various stories from history, anecdotes, sayings. In some gurdwaras the speaker may also talk of current affairs, what is happening locally, politically even. Other gurdwaras steer clear of politics. Speakers may refer to other religions and their books but must do so in a respectful manner. Some gurdwaras in the United Kingdom invite people of other faiths to address the *saṅgat*, and they make positive efforts towards interfaith understanding. At the end of *dīwān* the final prayers should be offered and *kaṛāh praśād* distributed.

Kaṛāh praśād

This is the special food distributed in gurdwaras. Anyone can prepare it, in the manner prescribed, and offer it at the gurdwara where it will be given to all who come. It is made of semolina or wheat flour, butter and sugar, and is prepared in clean conditions. Certain sections of *gurbāṇī* are repeated while it is being prepared.

Once it is in the gurdwara it is placed near the Gurū Granth Sāhib, and is touched with a sword before being distributed. It is accepted in cupped hands and is treated with respect. It is usually eaten immediately, though some people might take some home for a family member who could not attend.

Laṅgar

There are other ancient traditional institutions. The idea of the *laṅgar*, the Gurū's kitchen, is seen as going back to Guru Nanak, when those who came to him would eat together and tidy up afterwards. No one actually knows when compulsory inter-dining began. McLeod (1989: 12) mentions that Guru Amar Das possibly borrowed the practice from the Ṣūfīs.

Commensality is seen as important. People are equal, and caste bonds are broken if people eat together. People sit in one line, regardless of status. No one knows who brings the food, who prepares it, who serves it. *Kaṛāh praśād* and *laṅgar* therefore break social distinctions. This is part of worship. People are as one. It is sometimes said that people who have taken *amrit* have been initiated into the *Khālsā* and should eat apart from the others. This is said to be an encouragement for those who have not taken *amrit* to do so.

The provision of *laṅgar* is also charity. No one need ever go hungry for the *laṅgar* is open to all. Another aspect, the work of preparing food, is important. It is *sevā*, service to the gurdwara and the *saṅgat*. This is service to be performed selflessly and is also a form of worship.

FURTHER READING

Cole, W.O. and Sambhi, P.S. (1978) *The Sikhs: Their Religious Beliefs and Practices*, London, Routledge and Kegan Paul.

Grewal, J.S. (1969) *Guru Nanak in History*, Chandigarh, Panjab University Press.

Hans, Surjit (1988) *A Reconstruction of Sikh History From Sikh Literature*, Jalandhar, ABS Publications.

Loehlin, C.H. (1958) *The Sikhs and Their Scriptures*, Lucknow, Lucknow Publishing House.

Macauliffe, M.A. (1909) *The Sikh Religion*, Oxford, Clarendon Press. (Reprinted 1963, New Delhi, S. Chand).
McLeod, W.H. (1980) *Early Sikh Tradition: A Study of the Janam Sakhīs*, Oxford, Oxford University Press.
McLeod, W.H. (1984) *Textual Sources for the Study of Sikhism*, Manchester, Manchester University Press.
McLeod, W.H. (1989) *The Sikhs, History, Religion and Society*, New York, Columbia University Press.
Rehat Maryada (1978) Amritsar, Shiromani Gurdwara Parbandhak Committee.
Tandon, Prakash (1988) *Punjabi Saga: 1857–1987*, New Delhi, Viking.
Webster, John C.B. (1974) *Popular Religion in the Punjab Today*, Delhi, ISPCK for Batala, Christian Institute for Sikh Studies.

7. Chinese Religions

Xinzhong Yao

Whether or not we can use the word 'worship' to refer to such Chinese practices and rituals as are in relation to spiritual powers is a disputed question. Some people insist that these should not be called 'worship' unless the meaning of this word be extended to its widest possible use, while others argue that it is proper to call them 'worship'. For example, in the late seventeenth century and the beginning of the eighteenth century there was a bitter argument between the Jesuits and other Christian missionaries in China concerning the nature of the cult of Confucius and the veneration of ancestors. However, this chapter makes no attempt to confront this question but accepts all these performances of cults and veneration as worship.

Worship and worshippers

Chinese religions are a syncretism of Confucianism, Taoism, Buddhism, primitive practices and animistic beliefs. Thus, in worship the practices are extremely complicated. The objects of worship range from the highest god to the spirits of trees and stones, from the universal supernatural beings to the family deities. The ceremonies of worship vary from time to time and from place to place.

Concerning its nature, there are two prominent kinds of worship: 'official worship' and 'popular worship'. According to the *Book of Rites*, official worship should be given

> to those who gave laws to the people; to those who have laboured unto death in the discharge of their duties; to those who through their

> laborious toil have strengthened the state; to those who have warded off great evil. . . . As to the sun and moon, forests, streams, valleys and hills, these supply them with the materials for use which they require.
>
> (Quoted in Yang 1967: 146)

For these objects of veneration, proper sacrifices at the proper time were essential parts of the government's duties. Ignoring them would result in various punishments. Official worship appeared in the very beginning of Chinese civilisation, and from that time it dominated Chinese religious and political life until 1911, when the old empire was overthrown. Its most significant forms included 'worship of *T'ien* (Heaven)' which provided the divine connection between the dynasties and the highest god; 'worship of the Gods of Soil and Grains', which could set up a firm foundation for the empire; 'worship of the royal ancestors', which was regarded as the necessary guarantee for the continuity of the reign; and 'worship of Confucius', which was thought of as one of the most essential moral lessons for the whole nation. Popular worship refers to those acts of worship made in local areas, by popular religious organisations or non-official Buddhist or Taoist priests, and for the purposes of individuals or communities. Most acts of popular worship – for example, worship of Taoist immortals, of Buddhist *bodhisattva*s, and of many other human or natural deities – were concerned with evoking the spiritual power. This kind of worship was presented in many forms, such as the peasants' worship of the agricultural protective gods, and the worship of the numerous patron deities among economic groups.

There are various contrasts between these two kinds of worship. For official worship, the time was usually fixed, such as at the beginning of the spring and autumn, while for popular worship, there was no fixed time: it could be at the birthdays of the gods, or at the time of local festivals. For official worship, the place was usually chosen, the temple built, and the expense met by government, and the gods being worshipped usually bore some titles bestowed by the high official or even by the emperor; while for popular worship, individuals, communities or religious organisations played a central role.

Concerning the worshippers, there is group worship and individual worship. Group worship contains such practices as the veneration of the ancestors both in the family and in the clan; the family cult of the home gods or spirits; the cult of the gods of city, the gods of earth, and the King Dragon in the common festivals or on other special occasions. The worship of these gods or spirits is the responsibility of specific social units, of which the most common forms are family, clan or village. The performances are usually organised by these communities, or by the local government, or even by the Buddhist or Taoist temples. In contrast, individual worship refers to all those practices that are engaged in by individuals, and for the different purposes of individual persons. In history, such worship took many forms: a Confucian scholar who wanted to be successful in the civil examination would worship the patron god of literature and the Star of Literary Success; a devoted Taoist who hoped to prolong his life indefinitely would worship Lao Tzu and other Taoist immortals; a business man who hungered for big profit would worship the god of wealth; while a layman, to whom the *bodhisattva* Kuan Yin, the Goddess of Mercy, appealed so much, would request her help for any purpose, from saving life to giving birth to a healthy baby. Individual worship may be enacted in many ways, such as visiting a temple, burning incense, bowing down (or kow-tow), or praying privately to one's own patron god.

As Smart points out, 'To worship is to perform a piece of ritual' (Smart 1972: 5). Worship is usually connected with some kind of ritual. However, some of these rituals are overt and bodily actions, while others are not. In this sense, the former may be called 'ritualistic worship', while the latter 'informal worship'. Ritualistic worship in Chinese history was always made according to the special *Li* (propriety, ceremonies or rites), accompanied by sacrifices, prayers, and dances in conjunction with music. These forms of worship had to proceed in special places, such as on the top of the sacred mountains, in the ancestral temples, or in the Buddhist or Taoist temples, and were conducted by specialists, such as the ritual officials, or sorcerers or sorceresses, and Buddhist monks or Taoist priests. Informal worship, on the other hand, took place occasionally, without fixed places and programmes. The rituals, if any, were usually ignored, changed or created at the will of, or for the convenience of, the worshipper or worshippers. In most cases, kow-tow or presenting of a flower or even a branch of a tree was enough to fulfil a special act of worship. This kind of worship became popular when the individualistic aspects of Taoism and Buddhism was embraced and, due to its simplicity and individuality, it was especially favoured by poets and travellers or wanderers.

Once these classifications have been established, it becomes comparatively easy to grasp the nature and patterns of worship in Chinese society. These patterns provide us with a useful and convenient guide in exploring various practices of worship. However, they should not be used mechanically and absolutely. There are close relations not only between the pairs but also between the sets. The nature of a particular form of worship may be identified as 'group worship' on the one hand, and as an 'official' and a 'ritualistic' one on the other. Furthermore, a certain performance can be both official and popular worship, depending on where it is performed and who performs it. In this case, the most striking example is ancestor worship. Ancestor worship would be an official ritual if it was performed in the imperial Temple of Ancestors by the royal house, but it is also a kind of popular worship because every family venerates its ancestors.

Through these pairs and sets, we can find four practices of worship which have been of comparatively great significance for the Chinese, for Chinese culture and for Chinese history. They are 'Heaven worship', 'Ancestor worship', 'Sage or cultural hero worship', and 'Spirit worship'. What we aim to do in this chapter is to embroider a portrait of Chinese worship under these four headings.

Heaven worship

Scholars have not yet reached an agreement on whether or not there was any God worship in ancient China. Obviously, in Chinese religions, there was no such God as the Creator God of Christianity or of Islam. However, from this we should not conclude that in Chinese religions the concept or figure of a highest god who *governed* the whole world did not appear. There exist abundant records in China's history, which reveal to us a belief in, and worship of, the highest god. In the Shang dynasty (*c.* 1766–1123 BCE), it was *Shang Ti*, translated as Sovereign on High or High Lord; from the Chou dynasty (*c.* 1122–221 BCE) on, *Ti* of the Shang People was gradually merged into, or was replaced by, *T'ien* (Heaven) of the Chou people. And it was this *T'ien* (Heaven) which became the divine foundation of Chinese culture, and 'many of the religious influences in Chinese political life stemmed from the basic concept of Heaven and its subordinate system of deities as a supernatural force that predetermined the course of all events in the universe' (Yang 1967: 127). What Heaven was and what features Heaven was given are described in the chapter on Chinese religions in *Picturing God* in this series. Our present attention is on why, where and how the ancient Chinese offered their worship to Heaven.

The purposes of this worship are multiple, and can be put into three classes. The first purpose was, by the help of Heaven, to overcome such difficulties as those caused by drought, insects, or invasion by the enemy. The second was, by the blessing of Heaven, to obtain a peaceful reign, a good harvest or a successful campaign. The third was, by the good-will of Heaven, to strengthen harmonious relationships between the human world and the spiritual world.

Generally speaking, there were two places for this kind of worship. One was in the Altar of Heaven (see *Sacred Place* in this series); the other, called *Feng Shan* (or more accurately called *Feng; Shan* was the sacrifice to the Sovereign Earth), was on the sacred mountains, especially on the Eastern Peak, Mount Tai, which remains the most sacred mountain in China. The Altar of Heaven was built in the southern suburb of the capital as early as at the beginning of the Chou dynasty, and the worship of Heaven may be traced to an even earlier age. Every year at the winter solstice, the emperor – 'son of Heaven' – went to this altar to offer his great sacrifices to Heaven and to pray for the blessings from Heaven. While this worship was performed annually in the Altar of Heaven, *Feng Shan*, also with a long history, was carried out only occasionally.

It is true that the worship of Heaven was always an official matter, and especially a privilege of the emperor. However, by this we should not mean that it had nothing to do with the common people. In fact, we can find a strong belief in Heaven among the common people. One of the religious reasons for people's obeying an emperor came from their acceptance that the power of the royal house was endowed by Heaven – the emperor was a representative or son of Heaven – and from their belief that it was Heaven who controlled not only the fate of the dynasty but also the fate of any person's life. In its long history, this belief became religious common sense, so that 'following Heaven and accepting fate' became the basic religious principle of Chinese people.

However, one point has to be made about this. The Heaven in ordinary people's minds was quite different from that of the literati classes. Due to the dual influences of Taoism and Buddhism, Heaven in popular religion was imagined as a place where a supreme administration was located. The monarch of Heaven was the Jade Emperor, whose court consisted of a hierarchical system of all kinds of gods. Therefore, for the ordinary people who also appealed to Heaven when they met difficulties, their appeals were usually to the Jade Emperor or the heavenly gods, seldom to Heaven itself.

Ancestor worship

Herbert Spencer points out, 'Ancestral worship is the root of all religions' (Bredon and Mitrophanow 1966: 30). Family occupies a central position in Chinese culture, and glorifying one's ancestors is not only the greatest duty but also the greatest honour for a person. Correspondingly, the worship of ancestors is a basic practice in Chinese religious life.

The religious motives for ancestor worship were two-fold: one was concerned with the dead, hoping that the deceased continue to enjoy a life similar to that they used to live, and informing them that their contribution to the family-enterprise was remembered and carried on; the other was concerned with the living, hoping that the descendants would obtain blessings and help from their departed ancestors in overcoming difficulties or avoiding disasters.

Deriving from this motive, mortuary systems developed (see *Rites of Passage* in this series), and sacrifices were carried out in the home and in clan temples of ancestors. The traditional Chinese believed that ancestors were not only alive but also powerful in determining the destiny and welfare of the living community. If not provided with proper sacrifices, and if not informed periodically about the situation of the family's affairs, the ancestors return would be angry or anxious and therefore to punish their descendants who did not show their filial piety. In sacrifices, the dead were symbolised by the spirit tablets that were installed on the family altar or/and in the clan temple. The places for this worship varied according to the social position and economic situation of the family. The royal house had the splendid Temple of Ancestors, and the worship performed in the royal Temple of Ancestors was among the most important acts of official worship. A rich or an official family had its 'ancestral hall' to honour its great forefathers, while a poor family had only a shelf or a table dedicated to the tablets of their ancestors.

The Chinese believed that the life of human beings comes from the combination of two parts, one called *hun*, spirit from Heaven, and the other called *po*, soul from the earth. When a person was born, these two parts combined and the life began. When a person died, they departed and *hun* went to Heaven and *po* went to the earth. Therefore, to start the worship of ancestors, the descendant should first revoke separately these two parts of the spirit: the spirit from Heaven by music, and the soul from the underearth by the wine. When the music ascended to the palace of the heaven, and when the smell of wine descended to the Yellow Spring of the earth, the spirit and the soul of the ancestors would be recalled back from their spiritual world and would return to their 'home', residing in their tablets and receiving the sacrifices from their descendants.

Sacrifice to ancestors was a great offering. According to the provisions in the *Book of Rituals*, the main offering in the ceremony consisted of three domestic animals: a bull, a sheep and a pig. The animals were killed, their flesh was boiled, roasted or broiled, and then offered before the tablets of the ancestral spirits. In addition to the meat, vegetable products and crops of the fields were also widely used in the ceremonies. Among them, cooked millet was the main offering in the northern part and rice was the major offering in the southern part. Wine, music and dance were three of the most important things the descendants should offer to their ancestors during the sacrifice. While wine was present with each course of offerings, the music and dance was a more essential part of the ceremony. Every offering and every prayer must be accompanied by appropriate music and dance.

For the common people, daily offering to their ancestors was the most important duty of the family, which might consist of burning incense and bowing in front of the tablets or the portraits. More elaborate ceremonies were performed on such occasions as the anniversary of a death, festival days, and special events such as weddings or births. Worship at the ancestral temple of the clan or the family was offered on some special festivals, such as on New Year's Day, on the Festival of Ch'ing Ming and on the Feast of the Souls.

Confucianism was specially responsible for the popularity of ancestor worship, because it conserved and encouraged the old rites and developed them into a national belief and practice. Confucius, who believed the intimate relation between the ancestor and the descendant was the foundation of religion and politics, stressed that the descendants should give three years to mourning for their deceased parents and should treat their ancestors as if they were still alive. However, we should not attribute this worship only to Confucianism. In fact, it was rooted in Chinese civilisation and grew into an essential part of any form of Chinese religion. Even Buddhism, which in India called people to abandon their family, had to make some changes to reconcile itself to this tradition.

The worship of ancestors was important not only because it provided the descendant with some religious dependency, but also because it made for continuity in an endless chain relating the ancestors and the descendants. In this worship, each generation was treated as a necessary link of this chain, and every work was a contribution to the huge enterprise that was opened by the ancestors and developed by their successors. By this worship, the young obtained their sense of moral responsibility and the elderly gained respect. In this way, the family would become more and more prosperous, and the state would be in harmony and peace.

Sage or cultural hero worship

The Chinese are a people who pay great respect to the old and to the past, especially to those who made great contributions to the state and to the people. Confucianism developed this tendency into a political theory and into religious rituals, and the worship of the sage became another characteristic of Chinese culture and Chinese religious life.

In history, the names listed in the official worship canon are counted in hundreds and thousands. Among them, three classes are prominent. The first is that of the legendary or ancient sage-kings, such as Fu Hsi, Huang Ti, Yao, Shun, Yu the Great, Tang, King Wen, King Wu and the Duke of Chou, who either made great cultural contributions, or set up new dynasties, or had a profound influence on later political and moral development. Of these 'sages', Huang Ti, or the Yellow Emperor (2697–2598 BCE), as the common ancestor of the whole Chinese people, has enjoyed worship for several thousand years. At the Festival of *Ch'ing Ming* and at his so-called birthday, many people, even those living in remote areas, come to burn incense and kow-tow before his grave. The second class is concerned with the founders of the great schools of thought, such as Confucius in Confucianism, and Lao Tzu in Taoism. The worship of Confucius has special significance for the Chinese people in general and was the state cult for two thousand years. The third is of those who carried out the ancient sages' ideal (and their contributions were recognised by later generations), such as Kuan Yu, a hero of the period of the Three States (220–280 CE), later a universal god in the whole country.

Worship of these three classes of sages or cultural heroes was carried out at two levels. In the upper strata of society, especially among the Confucian officials and scholars, the sages were worshipped because they were regarded as the model for all people and for ten thousand generations. It was their teachings, writings, virtues, merits and the *Tao* of life, but not their supernatural power, that were appealed to and propagated. In the lower strata of society, under Taoist and Buddhist influence, the sages were deified and became the gods either of the whole nation, or of specific areas. The worship of Confucius is an example of the former, while the cult of Kuan Yu is an example of the latter.

Confucius (551–479 BCE) began to be worshipped soon after his death, in particular by his disciples who, following the ancient rituals, gave three years to mourning. It is traditionally believed that a temple was set up by the Prince of *Lu* (the home state of Confucius) in 478 BCE, but among modern scholars, there are some doubts as to whether this is so (Shryock 1966: 94). With the triumph of Confucianism in the Western Han dynasty, Confucius was promoted as the object of state worship. In the first year of the common era, the emperor repaired the Confucian temple in his home town and Confucius was given the title of 'Duke Ni'. In 59 CE, Emperor Ming of the Eastern Han dynasty, who also was responsible for the official introduction of Buddhism from India to China, ordered sacrifices to be made in all schools. In 657 he was styled 'the perfect Sage, the ancient Teacher', and from then on this title has remained to the beginning of this century. This title reveals the nature of the worship: Confucius was worshipped because he was the greatest teacher and perfect moral model for ten thousand generations. Since the morality of human beings was thought to be the same as the principle of heaven and earth, therefore it would be natural for the Chinese people to worship a man like Confucius who had exerted his moral sense to the utmost, and to make sacrifices to him in the same way as they did for heaven and earth. Indeed, in almost two thousand years, in every city or centre of education, Confucius had a temple which his followers, scholars, officers, and royal members visited at main festivals. In many of these temples there was an inscription: 'He forms a triad with Heaven and Earth'.

The worship of Kuan Yu followed another course. Yang points out: 'Among the contemporary national cults of deified men, none was more prominent than that of Kuan Yu, whose temple became an integral part of every major Chinese community' (Yang 1967: 159). Kuan Yu, originally a warrior and general of Liu Pei (the emperor of the state of Shu) during the period of the Three States, was deified soon after his death, and was given such titles as Kuan Kung (Duke Kuan) and Kuan Ti (God Kuan) because of his loyalty, heroism, righteousness and wisdom. His statue stood almost everywhere, and he was worshipped not only as god of war, but also as god of wealth, as a chief protective god, and even as a curer of disease. Naturally, his temple became the centre of local people's religious activities.

Spirit worship

Primitive beliefs and practices, encouraged by Taoism and influenced by Buddhism, developed a popular 'spirit worship' that became one of the dominant factors in the common people's religious life. Beside the gods of heroes and ancestors, any other being, such as animals, plants and trees, might also become spiritualised, and all natural phenomena, such as wind, rain, thunder, lightning and eclipses, were strongly believed to be caused by spiritual powers. The spiritual beings or powers could do good or harm to humans; at the same time human beings were able to turn the harm to good by offering them sacrifices.

These 'gods' or spirit beings that were objects of worship can be conveniently classified into four sub-systems according to their proper dwelling and official responsibilities.

GODS IN HEAVEN

These were 'noble' gods or an aristocracy of gods, some residing in the Celestial palace, some outside. In the palace, they behaved just like the high officials in the imperial capital and palace, and served the Jade Emperor as the latter served the emperor of the dynasty. Outside the palace, there were many gods whose functions were like those of the governors in the provinces, and on some special date, or at the call of the Jade Emperor, they went to the palace; otherwise they lived in their own residence and did their own work. All these gods or spiritual beings, with different functions and duties, were responsible to the Jade Emperor. According to their power and function, corresponding temples were set up for them in different areas. Of these temples, the temple of the King Dragon was of special importance. The King Dragon, living in the seas, was imagined as being in charge of rain. Too much or too little rain meant nothing but disaster for the agricultural people; therefore, how to get the proper amount of rain became an overwhelming purpose when this worship was carried out on the specific day (usually on their birthdays), and during drought or flood.

GODS ON EARTH

Some gods lived on the earth and were responsible for dealing with the affairs of people's lives. On ordinary days, they enjoyed the offerings, on special days they ascended to heaven to report on how they had carried out their duties. There are two kinds of these gods:

1. Gods in general, whose temples appeared everywhere, with multiple functions. Besides Kuan Yu, who has been discussed above, the most famous of them was Kuan Yin, the Goddess of Mercy, a Buddhist *bodhisattva*, who was believed to be able to bless the people and save the soul of people from sin.
2. Local gods, such as Cheng Huang (tutelary gods of the cities) and Tu Ti (local gods of rural areas).

Of these, Tu Ti was of special interest. Each plot of earth possessed a god of its own, and the earth was divided according to the human group that occupied it. A large village often had a more powerful god of earth than did a small village. This might be recognised by the size of their temples and the number of their worshippers.

FAMILY GODS

They were the protective gods for the home, such as gods of doors, of wells, of wealth, and of the hearth. Every year, the family gods, like all other gods, had to leave for Heaven to report what they heard or saw in the family to the Governor of Destiny who was in charge of the span of people's life, or to the Jade Emperor himself. Therefore, at the due time, sacrifices to these gods became an important affair in traditional families. The worship of family gods was of a pragmatic nature and the worshippers expected to be repaid with the protection or blessing for their offerings.

GODS UNDER EARTH

After Buddhism was introduced to China, the concept of hell became pervasive in Chinese religions. Underearth, the world of the ghosts, called the *yin* world, was contrary to the *yang* world, the world of living people. However, the officials who were in charge of this *yin* world should not be called ghosts, because they had the same responsibility as other gods. In this system, besides the Buddhist *bodhisattva*, Ti Tsang, the most popular worship was offered to Yan Wang (the Judges of Hell). Yan Wang had many servants, and sent forth mandates to collect the souls of people when their lives were due to end, according to the 'book of destiny'. Then in hell the souls were judged, chastised and reincarnated. In order to avoid premature death and torture in hell, the temples of Yan Wang were visited and sacrifices were offered on specific days.

Worship in Chinese religions, in its more than three thousand years' history, kept changing along with changes in the social and political background. Great differences arose from time to time, and even more have been seen in this century, and between the mainland and other Chinese communities, such as those in Hong Kong and Taiwan, where traditional worship is preserved much more than on the mainland. What has been discussed in this chapter focuses only on those rituals and practices that have left a deep impression on Chinese culture, and which can be identified in today's Chinese attitudes to the spiritual world, in their ways of thinking or in their everyday life.

FURTHER READING

Bredon, Juliet and Mitrophanow, Igor (1966) *The Moon Year – A Record of Chinese Customs and Festivals*, New York, Paragon Book Reprint Corp.

Eberhard, Wolfram (1952) *Chinese Festivals*, New York, Henry Schuman.

Goodrich, Anne Swann (1964) *The Peking Temple of the Eastern Peak*, Nagoya, Monumenta Serica.

Loewe, Michael (1987) 'The Cult of the Dragon and the Invocation for Rain', in Charles Le Blanc and Susan Blader (eds) *Chinese Ideas about Nature and Society – A Study in Honour of Bodde*, Hong Kong, Hong Kong University Press.

Maspero, Henri (1978) *China in Antiquity*, trans Frank A. Kierman, Jr, Folkestone, Dawson.

Parrinder, Geoffrey (1974) *Worship in the World's Religions*, London, Sheldon Press.

Shryock, John K. (1966) *The Origin and Development of the State Cult of Confucius*. New York, Paragon Book Reprint Corp.

Smart, Ninian (1972) *The Concept of Worship*, Basingstoke, Macmillan.

Wieger, L. (1969) *A History of the Religious Belief and Philosophical Opinions in China*, New York, Arno Press Inc.

Yang, C.K. (1967) *Religion in Chinese Society*, California, University of California Press.

8. Japanese Religions

Ian Reader

Introduction

Every year, especially in January and early February, Shinto shrines and Buddhist temples, especially those dedicated to the Shinto deity of learning, Tenjin, or to Monju, the *buddha* of wisdom, are visited by hordes of Japanese school children and university students who come to venerate the deities, pray earnestly to them and purchase various religious talismans and charms. The reason for this is to be found in the famed 'examination hell' of Japan's pressurised education system, in which the annual entrance examinations generally have major repercussions on the rest of the student's life: success means entrance into a prestigious school or college and opens up the door to a secure career in business or government, while failure can bring uncertainty and limit career choices. It is little wonder, then, that the period prior to these crucial examinations is a time of immense trial and tribulation for all concerned. The students heading to shrines at this time pray to the gods and *buddhas* for support in their time of stress, and ask them for help in attaining success.

A popular Japanese phrase, *kurushii toki no kamidanomi*, 'turning to the gods in times of distress', is used to describe this phenomenon, which is indicative of a common thread in Japanese religions, and symptomatic of many aspects of Japanese worship and of the ways in which Japanese people approach religious centres and deities, whether of the Buddhist or Shinto traditions. Praying – even on a casual basis – for personal help and amelioration, which often, as in the case of students, is primarily concerned with worldly success, is an important element in popular Japanese religiosity. The majority of Japanese people, even those who at other times eschew religious activities, visit shrines and temples to pray for help in such matters; according to the numerous surveys on popular religiosity carried out by Japanese researchers, some sixty per cent or more of Japanese people affirm the custom of praying to and venerating deities at religious centres in times of distress. Entering an unpropititious year in the life-cycle is one such occasion: for men the age of forty-two, and for women thirty-three, is considered especially unlucky and is known as the *yakudoshi* ('dangerous year') and many people visit shrines at this time to ask for special protection against misfortunes. At any point at which the fortunes of the individual may appear uncertain (as with examinations when the students, no matter how hard they have worked, find themselves at the mercy of the system), the processes of worship and prayer become viable avenues for Japanese people to express their worries and seek emotive solace. It is equally common to make periodic visits to shrines to pray for happiness and prosperity; over the first days of each year over seventy five per cent of the Japanese population visit shrines and temples to make offerings to the gods and pray for good luck and prosperity in the coming year.

The forms in which such approaches may be made vary according to the individual, ranging from a simple act of veneration, making a small offering (usually a coin or two), bowing, joining the hands in prayer and uttering a few words, to asking a shrine priest to perform a special ritual invoking the deity and blessing a special talisman which the supplicant will take home. Many supplicants acquire a tangible sign of the deity's benevolence, in the form of a talisman or amulet that will be carried on the person or placed in an appropriate place in the home or elsewhere. All of these practices necessitate an act of worship, and imply entering, even if only temporarily, into a relationship with one or more deities. What also strikes the observer is that such activities are generally participated in with a general degree of relaxed humour, enthusiasm, and even excited amusement. Veneration, especially at popular shrines and temples, is a joyous and, especially at festivals, exuberant rather than a sombre occasion.

Basic Japanese patterns of worship

The above brief description introduces many themes concerning worship in Japanese religious contexts and indicates that it may be extremely informal, casual, joyful and individual in nature. Many people who visit religious centres at socially festive occasions such as New Year may worship the deities, offer prayers and make requests just because it is customary to do so at such times, and because they just happen to have gone to the shrine along with their fellows for the occasion. This does not preclude more heartfelt prayers, of course, but merely shows that veneration and supplication can cover a wide spectrum.

Also, while religious centres may be crowded with visitors at such times, worship and prayer are largely personal and individual rather than congregational. Even in the midst of a New Year's crowd, people pray individually rather than collectively. They also do so sporadically, as and when the individual feels necessary, rather than on a regular basis. Such worship, being closely linked to the practice of seeking help, is thus contextual and situational, and based largely on personal needs. The students who visit shrines prior to their high school entrance examinations may well not visit them again, except perhaps at a major festival such as New Year, for a number of years until, for instance, the university entrance examinations come up.

This also indicates an underlying world- and life-view within Shinto, but found throughout the Japanese religious world, which sees human existence as something experienced, upheld and lived in co-operation with the spiritual world, of which the Shinto *kami* (deities) form a part. This view is ultimately human-centred and is in many respects one with a this-worldly orientation, a trait especially pronounced within Shinto, which tends to eschew eschatological considerations, but which also comes through in the perspectives of the new religions and to some extent, too, of Buddhism.

Worship in Japan thus may often have a pragmatic, functional and temporally limited dimension, in which deities are perceived as being there to be approached when humans require their help. Indeed, many Japanese who visit shrines and temples to pray to the gods may not cognitively believe in the existence of those deities. Survey responses indicate that a little over twenty per cent of the Japanese believe in the existence of *kami*, even though seventy to eighty per cent pray to them at festivals and the like. Need, or the social circumstances and customs of mass-participatory religious events, however, may change the person's perspective and bring them to a religious centre to perform acts of supplication and worship that, despite their apparently casual nature, reflect the inner understandings of the participants. In this, too, worship can be seen to have certain transactional dimensions, with requests being put to the deity as an intrinsic part of the process of worship.

It should be stressed that not all Japanese people approach the worship of deities in such a seemingly casual or occasional way. Communal services and rites of worship do occur, notably at local shrine festivals, at the heart of which is usually a religious ritual of some sort, led by priests and often participated in by community leaders and representatives. Many people also, on an individual basis, perform regular acts of worship at a particular shrine or temple, often forming a special relationship of gratitude and devotion to one deity or *buddha* figure. It is especially common for those who have previously asked favours of deities to return to give thanks for the help they feel they have received, to undertake various devotions in order to seek the deity's favour, or even to perform acts of asceticism as ways of showing their devotion to a *buddha* or *kami*, mirroring the expression of gratitude and the repayment of obligations (*ongaeshi*) incurred, which are intrinsic and vital aspects of Japanese socio-cultural behaviour and attitudes, in which the observation of reciprocity and the maintenance of harmonious relationships are considered essential to social existence. Indeed, these notions of returning and expressing gratitude, both to deities and to other human beings who have helped one, are important ethical duties and practices taught by just about all religious traditions in Japan, from Shinto and Buddhism through to the new religions. Such expressions of gratitude, underpinned as they are by ethical values and the upholding of religious relationships, should also be considered as acts of worship in themselves.

The above synopsis has highlighted many of the themes within worship in Japanese religious settings, while the aforementioned patterns of visiting religious centres to pray and to worship at times of festivity and need reflect the sense of accessibility that characterises the religious traditions of Japan, where neither formal belief nor membership are pre-conditions of religious participation, or hindrances to the availability of divine favour.[1]

Forms and meanings of worship: Shinto

The deep connections between festive behaviour and worship alluded to above are rooted in the basic meanings of the Japanese word *matsuri*, a word and concept most closely associated with Shinto. Although most commonly used to denote communal religious festivals, *matsuri* also has a further meaning of worship of and service to the Shinto *kami* (Ono 1962: 50; Ueda 1972: 42–5). Though the latter meaning is far less well known, especially in the contemporary age, it is nevertheless crucial to an understanding of the nature of worship, for it shows how this is closely related to notions of festivity. In such contexts the seemingly casual nature of veneration described above becomes more readily comprehensible.

In Shinto terms, while worship may be a simple individual act involving little more than a bow, clapping twice (to attract the attention of the deity) and a brief prayer, it generally is considered to contain four basic aspects: purification, offering, prayer and symbolic feast. These aspects are most specifically observed during formal rituals and communal worship led by priests during festivals and the like, but they may equally be followed in part or whole during individual visits to shrines. Purification seeks to remove all spiritual pollutions and evils and makes the worshipper spiritually pure enough to encounter and make entreaties to the *kami*. In communal ceremonies and shrine rituals this purification is usually performed through a symbolic blessing made by a priest or shrine maiden, but in private acts it may be done by such ablutions as rinsing the mouth out and washing the hands. Shrines usually have a small fountain or similar place near their entrance where water is available for this purpose. Sometimes, too, as at the major Shinto shrines at Ise, the visitor/worshipper crosses a bridge over a stream on the way into the shrine, thereby undergoing symbolic purification.

Offerings are then made to please the deity. In shrine rituals this may involve foodstuffs such as rice, *sake*, fruits, water and salt, while a small branch of *sakaki*, a sacred tree, is another common offering. Individuals may also offer a small coin or two. Larger denominations of banknotes may also be offered, wrapped in special paper. Offerings may involve material goods other than food, and may include entertainments put on for the benefit of the *kami* and designed to make them receptive to the entreaties that will subsequently be put to them. Among such common forms of devotional entertainment are performances of ritual shrine music and the ceremonial dances (*kagura*) done by shrine maidens.

Offerings are generally followed by prayers. In communal prayer rituals, priests may intone *norito*, ceremonial prayers written in classical Japanese. Individuals generally content themselves with a more simple supplication. At the end of formal rituals a ceremonial feast (*naorai*) takes place. For most worshippers, this will generally involve just receiving a sip or two of *sake* donated to the shrine and previously placed on the altar as an offering. Sometimes, though, a formal meal for special guests may take place, and on a number of occasions when I have been invited to attend special Shinto rituals I have taken part, with the priest and other guests, in such meals, when rice, fish, plentiful *sake* and other delicacies have been served.

In such respects, then, worship in Shinto terms takes the form of a ritual cycle, although individual worshippers may truncate or omit aspects of it depending on their own wishes. For the performers, especially for those seeking to make some entreaty to the deities, the third part (prayer, which generally involves making direct requests) is the most crucial, but the other parts of the cycle are also important in creating the required ambiance for the successful expression of the prayer.

The Shinto *kami* are regarded as the source of many benefits – especially of fertility and production – that enhance human life. In pre-modern Japan, farmers prayed to and venerated them when seeking good harvests or protection from misfortune, as did fishermen who, prior to putting out to sea, would pray for a safe return and a good haul. In contemporary times, such practices are still found in rural areas, while it is not uncommon in the cities as well for commercial concerns such as companies and manufacturers to have small company shrines at which a guardian *kami* of business is enshrined and venerated with offerings on a regular basis.[2] The gods thus underpin the processes of production and are concerned with the sustenance of everyday economic life, through which humans may live fruitfully and happily, and it is the continuation of these themes that also underpins much of Shinto worship. To some extent, too, the importance of worship in Shinto terms, and of carrying out the appropriate rituals of worship and of paying attention to the *kami*, express the underlying view that the gods are humanesque in nature and hence need attention, and need to be cared for and venerated periodically if they are not to be malevolent and antithetical to human needs.

Forms and meanings of worship: Buddhism

The *buddha*s of the Buddhist tradition are also widely venerated for their compassionate ability to intercede either in this world to ameliorate ills, or in other worlds to salve the sufferings of the dead. Their compassion makes them less capricious, and hence less in need of appeasing than the *kami*, and they are thus widely prayed to and venerated for their innate benevolence. As at Shinto shrines, people may perform some act of purification – often at Buddhist temples by wafting incense smoke over themselves, although usually purificatory water is also available – before bowing and making offerings. Here, too, food, drink and coins are common. The prayers that are made may, both individually and in Buddhist services, be led by a priest, and involve the recitation of Buddhist texts such as the *Hannya Shingyō*, the shorter *Heart Sūtra* that is widely used in popular prayer contexts in Japan,[3] and of short mantric spells specific to the particular *buddha* figure. Equally, individuals may just bow and mutter a silent prayer with their hands held together before them, palm against palm. It is not uncommon, also, for people to clap their hands before addressing a *buddha*. Though this is technically an action only to be performed when seeking to pray to a *kami*, many Japanese use the same form before the *buddha*s, largely because most Japanese people do not differentiate all that much between *kami* and *buddha*s but treat them as parts of one greater whole.

Unlike the *kami*, who normally remain formless, Buddhist figures of worship are personified through statues, and it is these that are a major focus of veneration and worship. Such statues provide a tangible and visible dimension to the *buddha*s and this has certainly enhanced and deepened the relationship that has grown up between the Japanese and popular Buddhist figures of worship. The most widely venerated of these are Kannon, the *bodhisattva* of compassion, Jizo (who particularly cares for the souls of dead children, but who also is a patron of travellers), Fudo, a fiery and powerful figure associated with power, the attainment of wishes, asceticism and mountain cults, and Amida, the Buddha of the Pure Land. All are widely represented by statues throughout Japan, both in temples and along wayside paths. Even in apparently remote areas, such statues may have a few offerings placed before them and be cared for.

Kannon is widely venerated because of her compassion and because of the belief that she will intercede to save anyone in distress. One prevalent phenomenon in Kannon worship in particular has been the erection of large statues of her (in some cases several hundred feet high) that operate simultaneously as symbols of devotion and as tourist attractions. Jizo, Fudo and Kannon are also the focus of pilgrimages that form another channel through which worship and devotion are expressed. Kannon pilgrimages are the most common of these, with numerous routes, each involving thirty-three temples dedicated to Kannon,[4] throughout Japan. The most popular of these, the Saikoku pilgrimage that circles the Kyoto-Nara region, has existed for at least eight centuries, and continues to attract several thousand pilgrims a year.[5]

The figure of Jizo also is central to many devotional practices that may be casual or intense depending on the participant. Much of the attention that statues of Jizo receive from worshippers demonstrates just how close and affectionate relationships can be between people and objects of worship, and hence how familiar and personalised acts of veneration may be. Bald-headed Jizo statues are often decked out with woollen hats knitted by devotees who do not wish him to become cold in winter. They may also be wrapped in bibs, which usually bear the name of a deceased infant or child on them. In doing this, the worshipper is asking Jizo to care for the child or perhaps rescue it from the Buddhist hells. People also relate to statues of Jizo – and also, though less commonly, to other *buddha* figures – in other physical ways, perhaps patting him on the head in a gesture which, for some, may symbolise the transference of pain from sufferer to reliever of suffering, or of merit from the object of worship to the worshipper. For others still it might simply be seen as a gesture of affection, for Jizo in particular is regarded in a warm and affectionate way.

Fudo is considered to be a more demanding figure of worship, requiring regular attention and, often, displays of devotion of an ascetic nature. Regular recitation of *mantra*s and offerings before his statues are common elements in Fudo worship, and his devotees may also participate in more explicit acts of asceticism such as standing under waterfalls while reciting Buddhist spells and texts, or even (as is done by the mountain ascetic sects of Shugendō) participating in fire-walking ceremonies. Fudo has numerous devotees in Japan, and many people will take entreaties to him from time to time because of his great power in acceding to wishes, but because of the ascetically demanding aspects required for regular devotion, he perhaps has less of an overall following than either Kannon or Jizo, and is perhaps less casually prayed to than the other two.

Amida, the Buddha of the Pure Land, is especially venerated in the Pure Land sects that preach complete faith in his powers to save people at death and lead them to rebirth in the Pure Land. In Pure Land devotionalism, homage and thanks are regularly given to Amida through the recitation of the *nembutsu*, a short invocation of his name. Amida is also widely invoked by those who are not normally devotees, in times of crisis. There are many other *buddha* figures as well who are either the focus of cults in their own right or who are prayed to from time to time. Devotion to one particular *buddha* does not preclude praying to another, nor does not being a devotee preclude one from worshipping and seeking aid from any of these figures when needed; as with the *kami*, worship can be based on need and situation. To a great degree, too, the patterns of worship follow similar lines and express similar meanings.

Forms and meanings of worship: the home

The home is a major area of religious activity, and hence is a further setting for acts of worship. Many Japanese homes have either a *kamidana*, or god shelf, in which guardian household deities are enshrined, or a *butsudan*, or family Buddhist altar in which the household ancestors are memorialised, or both. The spiritual entities, especially the ancestors, enshrined in these altars play a role in guarding over the continuing prosperity of the household, and are thus due worship. In particular the ancestors at the *butsudan*, represented by mortuary tablets with their posthumous names carved on them[6] are the focus of veneration within the home, usually in the form of regular or occasional prayers and offerings of food, water and flowers, in some households daily, in others more infrequently. Many people 'talk' to the ancestors at the *butsudan*, relaying items of family news and the like. Unlike the *kami* and *buddha*s, the ancestors are particular to their household and family lineage,[7] and exist in a special and unique relationship with their descendants.

At times, too, a Buddhist priest is called in to perform rites at the altar and to conduct services which venerate and memorialise the ancestral spirit. Periodic rites at the family grave and at the family Buddhist temple also may be held. These practices of devotion to and memorialisation of the ancestors are strongly emphasised as important duties and as vital religious and ethical actions by all Japanese Buddhist sects, and (a point alluded to earlier) as expressions of gratitude for the life that the ancestors have bequeathed to the living. The ancestors symbolically represent the values and idea of tradition and continuity; hence to worship them is to pay homage to, and affirm, a sense of Japanese tradition and cultural identity.

Concluding remarks: proximity, relationship and co-operation

Japanese patterns of worship demonstrate that the relationship between the Japanese people and their deities is based on closeness and proximity, rather than on separation and distance. Humans and deities are not distant from each other, but closely related; indeed, the *kami* of the Shinto tradition are, in myth, the progenitors of the Japanese people, and act as a source of life and beneficence for them. Their purpose, then, is to sustain life and hence, to co-operate with humans, just as humans are, in the Shinto view, expected to work and co-operate with the *kami*, by according them appropriate respect. It is here that the processes of worship cement the bond and continue the relationship that should exist. In Buddhist terms, too, there is a closeness and familiarity, not just in the ways in which people may relate to a statue of Jizo, but in the sense that *buddha*s were once (at least in theory and in legend) humans, and that their compassionate nature meant that their nature was attuned towards aiding the living. This proximity may be physical too, with family altars in the home itself acting as the settings for devotion.

The close relationship and proximity between the human and spiritual worlds signifies an underlying acceptance and belief that human existence is itself lived in company with, and hence with the support and co-operation of, the spiritual realms. This does not mean that Japanese religious views are fatalistic or that people consider their efforts subordinate to the whims of the gods. Rather, they believe that human endeavour is essential for the completion of tasks; one does not simply worship the gods and expect results. At the same time one needs to recognise that human endeavour and ambition alone, without an understanding that benefits and indeed life itself are gifts to be enjoyed and to be grateful for, are inadequate and cannot ultimately provide a satisfactory and happy life. Japanese religious values are closely tied in to the aim of a happy and fruitful life, and the spiritual entities that are venerated – whether *kami, buddhas* or ancestors – act as signs and symbols of support to these ends. Their worship, whether through communal festive rites, casual prayers and offerings, or through ethical expressions of gratitude, serves to bring about these ends and to provide messages about the nature of life and about human action in the world.

NOTES

1. I have discussed all the issues covered in this chapter, and more specifically those covered in these first two sections, at greater length and in more depth in Reader (1991).
2. I have dealt with these matters at length in Reader (1991), especially pp. 55–76.
3. See my chapter on Japanese religions in the volume *Sacred Writings* in this series.
4. 33 because, in the *Lotus Sūtra*, this is the number of manifestations and forms Kannon vows to take on in order to save humanity and intercede to stop suffering.
5. Further information on this, and other Japanese pilgrimages will be found in my chapter in the volume *Sacred Place* in this series.
6. See my chapter on Japanese religions in the volume *Rites of Passage* in this series for a fuller discussion of household rites concerning the ancestors.
7. This is a generalisation: very famous and well-known people may become more widely venerated, especially if they are founders in some way or other: for example, the founders of the various Buddhist sects in Japan are worshipped as ancestor-figures by members of those sects.

FURTHER READING

Ono, S. (1962) *Shinto: the Kami Way*, Rutland, Vt., and Tokyo, Charles Tuttle.

Reader, I. (1991) *Religion in Contemporary Japan*, Basingstoke, Macmillan.
Ueda, K. (1972) 'Shinto' in I. Hori, F. Ikado, T. Wakimoto and K. Yanagawa (eds) *Japanese Religions: A Survey by the Agency for Cultural Affairs*, Tokyo, Kodansha, pp. 29–45.

Index